STILL TIME TO LIVE
A Biography of Jack Belden

Gary G. Yerkey

GK Press
Washington, D.C.

To My Mother and Father
And Karin
For Life and Love

GK Press.
P.O. Box 11816
Washington, D.C. 20008

ISBN: 0615458882
ISBN-13: 9780615458885

CONTENTS

PREFACE

I first met Jack Belden in the late 1970s, toward the end of his life, in Paris, where he had lived for many years. He was broke and broken, but he survived, barely, as best he could holed up in a one-room flat in the Marais district of central Paris – living off modest royalties from his books and the generosity of friends.

He was bitter, cantankerous and deeply troubled (or so it seemed to me). But above all, he was lonely.

"I've been called everything from an idealist to a man of action," he told me one day. "I've also been called a 'friend of China'. I aspire to no such distinctions. I am quite satisfied to be myself."

Being Belden meant being without a job and restless at 23 and signing on as an able-bodied seaman on the SS President Johnson and jumping ship in Hong Kong on Armistice Day in 1933 with 10 cents to his name.

He begged enough money to buy a train ticket to Beijing, where he taught English and worked as a proofreader at the *Peiping Chronicle* – an English-language daily – until he was hired by United Press in 1937, when, in July of that year, he was the only reporter to witness outside Beijing the opening battle of what would become all-out war between China and Japan. His life as a war reporter, like it or not, had begun.

Years later, after covering war on three continents for more than a decade, he would say that his life, "more than anyone I know, has been spent in lonely wanderings among the dreary wastelands of war...simply putting one foot ahead of the other, while keeping my eyes peeled over my shoulder for the blood-seeking thing that was hissing on the trail behind. "

In China, he would make a name for himself turning out powerful, first-hand accounts of armed conflict from the front lines.

A report he wrote for *Time* in 1941 verifying claims by the Chinese that the Japanese had used nerve gas in the battle of Ichang prompted the magazine to call Belden the "ablest field correspondent assigned to cover the China war."

From 1942 to 1945, as a correspondent for TIME-LIFE, he covered fighting in Burma, North Africa, Italy and France, and in 1946 he returned to China to report on the Communist takeover, which provided the material for *China Shakes the World* (1949), his most well-known book, whose sales, however, would be dampened by McCarthyism.

The China expert Peter Rand has called the book, written from the perspective of the peasants who fought alongside the Communists, "a lasting contribution to the literature of war and revolution. He was a superb reporter."

He was also the author of *Retreat With Stilwell* (1943) and *Still Time to Die* (1944) – two other classic works of war reporting.

Barbara W. Tuchman, the Pulitzer-prize-winning historian, said that Belden was one of the "more venturesome" reporters who covered China in the 1930s and 1940s. He "roamed the country 'from the heart'," she wrote – "a great romantic and idealist...moody, driven, alternatively gay and despondent."

Theodore H. White, who met Belden shortly after he arrived in China in 1939 fresh out of Harvard University and who recruited him for TIME-LIFE, said that he was clearly at the top of his profession then among foreign correspondents covering events in that part of the world.

Another colleague – Owen Lattimore – called him a "legendary figure," saying that he was a man who knew the seamy side of China, "where the lice lurked...Most of the rest of us...were a prosaic lot....He was the man who knew where underemployed peasants, underpaid workers, and sullen soldiery did about sex and drink and drugs."

John P. Davies Jr., an American foreign service officer who was posted in China when Belden was "roaming" the country, called him a "sad, ragged, torn, incredible character...."

Israel Epstein, the journalist, author, and fellow war correspondent, said that he was a "man without caution or calculation, intense, passionate, a writer of major and burning talent...." And Edgar Snow, whose fame and public persona would far surpass Belden's (some say unfairly), called him "mad and gifted."

In writing this book, I have chosen to focus on his most productive years, beginning in 1933 when he jumped ship in Hong Kong and ending in 1949 with the publication of *China Shakes the World*.

Those were the years that brought him his greatest fame. But they were also the years that brought him so much pain – both mental and physical – and a major source of his deep and abiding personal sadness in later life.

In the time I spent with him, and in researching this book, I do not pretend to have gained any profound insights into Belden the man – what drove him, why he did what he did, or what demons may have plagued him throughout his life. I leave that task to others more qualified or interested than I.

What I have attempted to do – as a journalist, and not as a psychologist or sociologist, which I am not – is to craft a long-overdue tribute to a brilliant American war reporter whose honesty, courage, integrity and hard-headed professionalism I will always admire.

1

AN AMERICAN NURSE

Death for Jack Belden would not come easy. He was a reporter who had covered war for nearly two decades, and he had seen his share of it. Now it was his turn. It was June 1989, and he was dying of cancer in Paris. He was 79.

Belden had lived in Paris for a quarter-century – an American, he said, who had been abandoned by his own country.

A few months before he died, from his flat in Paris, as the pain from his rapidly spreading disease was becoming unbearable, he wrote to a friend in Switzerland saying he had received a phone call from a woman who had not immediately identified herself.

"The voice was half stammering half hesitant and she asked me to guess who it was," Belden wrote. "I made a wild mistaken guess and then in a flash thought back 46 years. 'Beatrice.'" [1]

Back then, he was 33 years old and in his professional prime. He had spent nearly a decade reporting for United Press and TIME-LIFE from China, Burma, and North Africa and was being called one of the finest reporters of his generation. Now, in the fall of 1943, he lay in the 7th Station Hospital in Oran, Algeria – his right leg shot up during the landing of the U.S. Fifth Army in Salerno, Italy.

"Cheer up," one U.S. soldier told him as he was being lowered from the transport ship that had brought him from Italy to Oran. "You'll have a pretty nurse."

As it turned out, in fact, his nurse would be very pretty. Her name was Beatrice Weber, a Wisconsin native who had enlisted in the Army Nurse Corps a few months earlier.

"I suppose many combat soldiers, when they think of being wounded, dream of the nurse they are going to get," Belden wrote in article in the March 20, 1944, issue of *LIFE* magazine, which recounted his hospital experience. "I know I used to dream this way. Sometimes it was an old sweetheart who would appear in a nurse's uniform to heal me. More often, though, I dreamed of some unknown vision of loveliness would come and bend over my stretcher with ineffable tenderness as it was carried from the battlefield. When I got to the hospital I fancied some nurse would tuck me in, smooth my brow and say: 'Is there anything I can do for you?' Later I hoped she would press her lips against mine and say: 'Hurry up and get well; I'm waiting for you.'"

Belden said that Weber, who was not identified by name in the article, had hair like "golden silk" and that "her eyes were like the Mediterranean outside, and her lips were always laughing. She was just over 20 and shone with good health and the joy of service."

One afternoon, after digging around under his bed among a pile of papers, musette bags and stray cigarettes, she stood up and said to Belden, "You're the messiest patient in this ward. 'He needs a wife,' a young naval ensign who was visiting me said. 'Oh, he'll get caught someday,' she said, turning toward me and laughing. 'I wouldn't consider it getting caught,' I said. When she started to go, I tried to think of something to hold her there. 'Would you marry me?' I blurted out. She looked me up and down in an appraising manner. 'Sure,' she said, smiling."

Later, Belden wondered what what had gotten into him and what had caused him to become a "sentimental fool" – "imagining that I was in love with a nurse."

"I knew that any patient in a hospital for a long time, shut off from friends, might possibly become interested in his nurse," he wrote. "Also I knew that any soldier, cut off from women for a long time and living amidst violence, might be doubly sensitive to a nurse. But I could not say that I was a typical soldier. I had been in a war area for seven continuous years, years of perpetual violence and little tenderness. So I told myself that I was merely breaking down before a woman's kindness."

One night, when Weber stopped by his bed, he asked her if patients always fall in love with their nurses. "'No,' she replied. 'That happens only in storybooks.' 'It's happened to this patient,' I said. 'You're kidding me,' she said, and I knew she was being generous. 'No,' I said. 'I may be kidding myself, but I'm not kidding you.'"

At night, Belden wrote, she was like a vision. "I was choking with the beauty and the nearness of her and I could not speak. I looked across a gulf of aching hope but could only glare."

" 'Are you lonely,' she said. It was not a question. It was a statement. She had not dragged it out of me; she had not forced me to say it; she had said it for me; and I silently thanked her for it. The wonder of her overcame me. I took her hand and pressed my lips into it. Then I laid my cheek against it and caressed it."

A few days later, after six weeks in the hospital in Oran, Belden was discharged for transfer back to the United States and further recovery.

"Then they picked me up —she did not say goodbye – and bore me down muted corridors and there was no pain. They carried me out under a palm tree and slid me in an ambulance and I thought of all the wrong things I'd said and all the right things I'd left unsaid; and there was no pain.

"As the driver drove with practiced gentleness through the streets of the port [of Oran], the man beside me sang in my ear his happiness at going to America. But I only lay there and thought: I am going away from her."

A half-century later, in the fall of 1988, Weber was 68 years old and living in the United States. One day, while rummaging through an antique store, she came across a copy of the March 20, 1944, issue of *LIFE* magazine. She read the article Belden had written about her and his time at the 7th Station Hospital in Oran, and she sensed, somehow, that he was not well.

Through his publisher – Monthly Review Press in New York City – she obtained his phone number in Paris and called him. According to Belden, "she just wanted to hear about me."

"As she was talking," Belden later wrote a friend, "she began to stammer and stutter. Start a sentence and stop. 'I want you, Jack, to know – I'm going to bat for you.' Stop. 'I love you.' " [2]

I met Weber a while back and I asked her about that call and her feelings about Belden. She said she remembers his fatherly voice and soft eyes – "it was very impressive to a young girl." But she had quickly forgotten about him, she said, except occasionally when she would think to herself that, wherever he was, he was probably not at peace with himself or with the world.

"I always thought of him as someone who would never find happiness," Weber told me.

In the fall of 1988 – a week or so after they had talked by telephone – she received a letter from him.

"Yes, dear ghost," he wrote. "I could think I'm going crazy. After we hung up I searched for your address and phone number and couldn't find anything. I then began to think I'd imagined the whole thing and that indeed you were a ghost of youth come back to torment with time lost – time gone."

"I'm sorry, Sweetness and Light," he continued. "I'm tired and haunted and positive thinking is not my style. But please please write or communicate with me. It was very brave of you to look me up and call me....I shall think of you. Hold my hand. Jack." [3]

Apparently touched, Weber immediately flew to Paris to be with him, insisting to me later, however, that it had nothing to do with love but only with someone responding to the call of another person in need.

For nearly a month, she spent long hours talking with Belden each day as his condition worsened and he was moved from one hospital to another.

On some mornings, she said, when he felt more alert, he would ask her to come by early, and she would stay with him until well into the night. In the afternoons, they would sit outside in the sunlight and talk. His mood would often brighten and they conversed freely and happily, Weber said. "I hated to see those few days end," she said. "We stretched them out as long as possible."

At the end of May, Weber returned to the United States, emotionally drained. Belden died a week later.

Weber told me that one evening, at the Army hospital in Oran, Belden had given her a note, which she took back to her room and read.

"Sweetness and Light," the note said. "You are my destiny, the center of my life, the girl I have been searching for all my life. Providence brought us together because of our appreciation and need for each other. Without our togetherness neither of us will ever find happiness and we'll live in loneliness for the rest of our days. No one will ever appreciate you as I do." [4]

Years later, Weber would say that the longings and feelings that Belden had expressed to her in Oran had simply overwhelmed her young, war-confused mind.

"His desperation paled me," she wrote in an unpublished account of Belden's life, as she knew it. "I knew he'd never be a happy man anywhere, anytime [and] possibly I needed him more than he needed me....As I looked at his face on the pillow, his dark hair and eyes, I saw the saddest, loneliest man in the world, so quiet, just looking at me from a depth in his eyes that had no bottom." [5]

2

"THIS IS GOODBYE"

Jack Belden was born in Brooklyn, N.Y., on February 3, 1910, to a father who was never home and to a mother who was the love of his life. On Sundays, his father, Alfred G. Belden Jr., would take his wife and children Jack and Kathleen to a restaurant where they were served by tall waiters in white coats. When they were finished, he would hand each child an envelope stuffed with dollar bills, and that would be the last time the family would see him until the following week.

When he was seven years old, his parents divorced, and his mother, Mabel Swezey, eventually remarried. But he and his stepfather, Joseph M. Howland, a businessman who moved the family to Summit, N.J., did not get along. He once told his mother he never felt welcome in his own home.

"I guess this has been partially my own fault," Belden wrote in a note to his mother when he was in his early twenties. "Brooding and petulant... without reason." [1]

He later said that not knowing a real father had haunted him for the rest of his life.

His uncle, Christopher Swezey, wrote to him from his home in Vermont when he was 21 years old expressing sympathy for his misfortune. "In all frankness, Jack, let me say that I appreciate the handicap you have had in not having been able to get the counsel of your father," he wrote.

"No doubt, Mr. Howland has tried to help you from time to time and in a sincere manner, but I know that that is not as well taken as when coming from one's own father." [2]

But it was his stepfather who would find him a job in the midst of the Great Depression after he had graduated with a B+ average from Colgate University in 1931, where he majored in geology and minored in English literature.

Years later, he would say that the job – working as an "ordinary" on the British freighter SS Steel Seafarer – had sparked his life-long yearning for adventure. "It was an education beyond worldly description," he told Beatrice Weber shortly before his death in 1989. "It enhanced my dreams and made a wanderer out of me. It surely wasn't the life I had been reared and educated for. It gave me a broader perspective of the real world....I'd never be content to settle for less than the whole world and all of life in it." [3]

But after several months at sea, when he passed the time reading Coleridge, Shakespeare and Milton's *Paradise Lost* and listening for hours to the ship's crew of tough old salts telling stories "in amusing dialects foreign to my ears," he returned home to Summit, N.J. [4]

The temptation to follow his stepfather's advise and enter the world of business was strong, particularly given the economic situation at the time, and his stepfather – a vice president at the Federal Composition and Paint Co. in New York City – offered to help. But he felt he had a more noble calling.

"I have been told that I have to do certain things in business," Belden said in another note to his mother. "But when those things – inconsequential as they may be – stoop below the truly decent, I refuse to do them, even to please the big vice presidents." [5]

So, at 23 years old, he made a decision that would set the course of his life: to return to sea. And he wrote a brief note to his mother informing her of his decision.

"This is goodbye," he wrote. "A sad word, isn't it? Yes and a sad thought too. But go – I must...." He said he had been mulling the decision for months. "I don't know where I am going or how, and not even why," he said. "There is something in me that says stay and something else that cries go."

"It would be far easier to hold onto my job and drift along with the tide," Belden wrote. "But I'm afraid that my later years would cry out to my youth, 'You never dared'."

He said he did not know how long he would be gone – maybe a week, maybe years. "Let's hope I return sometime," he said. "You and I have been far apart for many years. But when you remember me forget all these bleak years and call to mind that blushing youngster who walked up the aisle to receive a golden medal at a military academy commencement, or the tiny child who broke open his China pig bank in a Philadelphia boarding house and showered his mother with all his pennies because he loved her so." [6]

3

A NEW WAR, A NEW WAR CORRESPONDENT

By the summer of 1933, the SS President Johnson had been plying the world's oceans for some thirty years – as a troop carrier in World War I (as the USS Manchuria) and as a passenger liner making round-trip runs from New York to Hamburg and from New York to San Francisco, through the Panama Canal.

Now the 615-foot-long ship with leaky decks was easing out of New York harbor again at the start of a round-the-world cruise. On board were 250 passengers who could still afford such luxury at the height of the Great Depression.

Also on board, employed as an "able-bodied seaman" for $45 a month, was Jack Belden – a would-be poet seeking adventure and a means of escape from small-town life in New Jersey and rising pressure to enter the business world. He wrote later that the vessel, despite its pretension of luxury, was "an ancient hulk of a ship...with wooden decks that leaked." [1]

From Europe to Asia, meanwhile, the seeds of another world war were being sown. Adolf Hitler had been made chancellor of Germany (January). Japan had withdrawn from the League of Nations (February) and seized the north China province of Jehol, a precursor to its announcement a year later it intended to control all of China and act as "guardian of peace and order in East Asia." Construction of the first German concentration camp, at Dachau, had also been completed (March). And the Gestapo had been created (April).

But the United States had problems of its own, and some uniquely American concerns.

On March 4, Franklin Delano Roosevelt was sworn in as president, saying in his inaugural address, referring to the Great Depression, that the only thing to fear was fear itself. The next day, he announced that all banks were being closed and that all financial transactions were being frozen. But he had little to say about what Winston S. Churchill would call Hitler's widening "shadow" on the European continent. On March 9, Congress began enacting legislation to implement Roosevelt's New Deal – a week after the film "King Kong," with Fay Wray, had premiered in New York City to rave reviews.

From New York, the SS President Johnson headed east, stopping in Hamburg, where Belden had planned to jump ship but was advised against doing so by a prostitute who said he would not live long if he stayed there, so he re-boarded the ship after several days ashore.

As ship continued east, with Belden still unhappily on board, President Roosevelt began expressing concern over the Japanese government's actions and intentions with respect its Chinese neighbor.

The Japanese Army, in fact, had begun its occupation of Manchuria in 1931, and the following year the United States adopted as national policy the so-called Stimson Doctrine of Non-Recognition – named after its author, U.S. Secretary of State Henry L. Stimson – which put Japan on notice that the United States would not accept any arrangement that compromised China's "sovereignty, the independence, or the territorial integrity," especially through the use of force.

Roosevelt signed off on the doctrine after taking office in March of 1933, defending it and China more generally in part by pointing to his ancestors' long involvement with the country. His mother's father, Warren Delano, for instance, had been a partner in the American trading company Russell & Company, founded in 1824, which built the first telegraph line in China and established the first steamship company to run regular service up and down the Yangtze River.

In early November 1933, when the SS President Johnson docked in Hong Kong, whose harbor was teeming with American and British warships, its passengers disembarked for a few days of fun. It was also there that Jack Belden decided to jump ship for good.

"I was broke," he told Beatrice Weber many years later. He said it was the ship owner's policy to withhold from the crew one month's pay to discourage them from jumping ship. "So I had no paycheck, and only a dime in my pocket." He planned to stay only a couple of weeks.

He also decided when he left the ship, on November 11, that he would not take a suitcase with him since it would suggest he was not planning to return to the vessel. "So I put on three or four layers of clothing – trousers, sweaters, jackets, socks – and walked off the ship in Hong Kong." [2]

Exhausted, he looked for a place to lie down for the night and, after climbing a hill above the city, he came to a wall, climbed over it in the darkness and found a bit of clear space on the other side, where he fell went asleep. When he awoke up the next morning, he saw he had fallen asleep beside an open reservoir and realized he was lucky he had not rolled off into it and drowned. [3]

Initially, he was forced to beg for money in Hong Kong, which he did, losing it gambling at first, then winning $6 and eventually parlaying it into $50.

With his winnings, he bought a train ticket to Shanghai and spent the next year or so traveling between Shanghai and Peking, learning Chinese and teaching English to the Chinese and Chinese to foreigners. He also played jai alai and gambled some more. "I liked the Chinese," he said. [4]

His slow march to war reporting, meanwhile, picked up steam in the fall of 1934 when he took a job as a proofreader at the *Peiping Chronicle*, an English-language daily newspaper in Peking that was Chinese-owned but run by foreigners.

Among his colleagues at the paper were F. McCracken "Mac" Fisher, who worked in the editorial department while he held down his regular job as a correspondent for United Press, and Israel Epstein, the journalist, author, and war correspondent who lived in China most of his life and was one of the few foreign-born Chinese citizens of non-Chinese roots to become a member of the Communist Party.

Epstein's last book, and arguably his finest, *My China Eye: Memoirs of a Jew and a Journalist,* which was published just before he died in 2005, recounts his time in Peking in the early 1930s and his association with men and women then in their twenties and thirties who were or would become prominent in China-related scholarship, journalism, and politics, including Edgar Snow, John K. Fairbank, Own Lattimore, Harold Isaacs, and Ida Pruitt.

"Then there was Jack Belden," Epstein wrote, "a man without caution or calculation, intense, passionate, a write of major and burning talent, fresh off the ship on which he had worked his passage from the United States....No hanger-on of headquarters or social crony of officers, Jack would always head to places where ordinary soldiers fought and died, and share their dangers." [5]

While he was working at the *Peiping Chronicle* ("for a pittance," according to Epstein), the Chinese Red Army was beginning its Long March (on October 16, 1934) from Jiangxi province to Yenan in Shensi province to escape the Nationalist forces of Chiang Kai-shek. And while Chiang was preoccupied with defeating the Communists, the Japanese were continuing their advance into northern China and breaking their ties with the West.

A few months later, a U.S. army colonel by the name of Joseph W. Stilwell, who had been appointed U.S. military attache in Peking, was writing up his assessment of the situation in a paper called "Future Developments in China."

Drafted as he was traveling to China to take up his new post, the paper said that the Japanese government's ultimate objective was to become "the major power in the Far East," with control over Siberia, Manchuria, Korea, China, Formosa, the Philippines and Netherlands East Indies.

"Is there any possibility that this encroachment will be stopped?" Stilwell asked. "No, not by the Chinese." [6]

Stilwell assumed his new post in on July 7, 1935, and he quickly became the U.S. War Department's eyes and ears on the ground in China as Japan pursued its expansionist aims, with growing implications for the United States. His sources were varied – official and unofficial – and they included journalists, like Belden, who preferred the company of soldiers to that of political leaders and diplomats in Peking.

Barbara W. Tuchman, in her book *Stilwell and the American Experience in China: 1911-45*, wrote that Belden – "moody, driven, alternately gay and despondent" – would become "a close companion" of Stilwell and a "valued informant."

"He would periodically disappear on excursions through the intricate corridors of Chinese affairs," she wrote, "bringing Stilwell reports of Chinese movements and intentions and an abundance of material on the reputations of commanders and the inner relationships that governed them." [7]

His close and life-long association with Stilwell, in fact, began shortly after Stilwell arrived in Peking. But it deepened significantly beginning in July 1937 when a seemingly minor skirmish erupted between Chinese and Japanese troops at Lukouchiao, twelve miles southwest of Peking. It was there, Belden said, that "I saw my first battle...." [8]

The Japanese, who had been staging military maneuvers in the area for two weeks, claimed that they had been fired on without provocation by Chinese soldiers garrisoned in nearby Wanping, so the following morning they launched an all-out mortar and artillery attack against the Chinese.

Little did Belden or anyone else know at the time, however, including Stilwell, that that so-called Marco Polo incident at Lukouchiao would be the spark that ignited formal hostilities between China and Japan, which would last for the next eight years.

Within hours of the incident, Belden was hired by United Press, becoming a war reporter overnight, and a few days later, on cue, *The New York Times* reported (in its July 11 edition) that he had been wounded in battle and was recuperating in a Peking hospital. He was reported missing "all day," it said, after he made an early morning trip to the fighting zone. "He was believed to have been killed," the report said, "until he was found last night in the German Hospital in Peiping. No report on his condition could be obtained."

His stepfather, who read the *Times* report back in the United States, sent a telegram to the State Department in Washington, D.C., requesting "any news of my stepson who was reported in Sundays (sic) New York Times as being wounded. Now in German Hospital Peiping China. Wire my expense any information. I have cabled hospital today for a report on condition. Greatly appreciate prompt reply."

The State Department responded on July 16, saying that the American consul in Peking had confirmed that the report was erroneous. "He is at present in good health in Peiping and not confined to German Hospital," the department said in a telegram signed, "Cordell Hull Secy of State."

Belden was indeed in good health and, in fact, in the process of making plans with a Stilwell aide, Capt. Frank Dorn, to travel outside Peking to check on the military situation first-hand. "Demanding cables and radio messages from Washington were piling up on Colonel Stilwell's desk," Dorn said. "Something had to be done."

On August 3, Dorn and Belden took off with a driver in an old touring car and with only a couple of light knapsacks headed northwest out of Peking with the aim of breaking through the Japanese lines, which encircled the city, and learning what they could about Chinese troop movements.

"Stooped, dark-eyed, and rather gloomy by nature, Belden wore a faded khaki shirt and shorts, low shoes, and an old pith helmut," Dorn wrote. "I had on a pair of old trousers and an open-necked shirt, but no hat." [9]

But only 25 miles northwest of Peking, after they crossed the Sha River, the road came to an end at a stone bridge that had been blown up. Dorn sent the car and driver back to Peking, and he and Belden set off on foot.

Over the next two weeks, the pair would travel through northern China behind Japanese lines gathering intelligence on Chinese troop movements and capabilities – Belden for UP and Dorn for Stilwell.

Dorn said in a letter to Stilwell – addressed to Mr. J.W. Stilwell at his house on Peking's Magpie Lane in order to avoid arousing suspicion among the Japanese – that the Chinese, in his view, were "deploying for a fight." [10]

For his part, Belden would call the trip "somewhat adventurous" – without mentioning, as Dorn did, that the pair had narrowly escaped countless Japanese air attacks and survived death-defying bus rides and "curses of resentment" from the Chinese and "unflattering references to our ancestry, and consignment to all the tortures of the eighteen hells."

After two weeks, the two men parted company in Hsuchow, and Belden headed for Shanghai where, according to Dorn, "bigger events were beginning to shape up" – a not-so-subtle reference to the opening salvos on August 13, 1937, of what would become the three-month-long Battle of Shanghai, one of the largest and bloodiest of the Sino-Japanese war. [11]

Belden filed his first report from Shanghai for UP on August 18, saying he had just arrived in the city after a journey of nearly 1,000 miles through seven provinces over seven weeks.

"What I saw," he wrote, "convinced me that it will be a long struggle."

Belden said that he had eaten and slept with Chinese soldiers during the trip and had been treated well "as soon as I identified myself as an American newspaper correspondent."

His broad conclusions from the trip, he said, were that the Chinese, for the first time, now appeared to be united and willing to obey orders from Chiang Kai-shek; that China had more than 400,000 men in the field, including about 150,000 who are well-trained and -equipped, with the remainder being veteran guerilla fighters and "given enough ammunition, will be able to harass the Japanese army for years"; and that China's provincial leaders north of the Yangtze River were supporting Chiang and the central government despite ancient enmities.

It was in Shanghai, however, where the fighting was the fiercest, taking the war that began outside of Peking a month earlier to a new level and resulting in massive civilian casualties and the virtual destruction of the city. And Belden was in the middle of it.

Yet many military observers told Belden that, while the fighting in Shanghai was, as he called it, "spectacular," it was in the north that the war between China and Japan would be decided. So he headed off yet again to be with the Chinese forces at the front.

Over the next several weeks, he would eat and sleep with the Chinese army as it attempted – mainly in vain – to fend off the Japanese. His dispatch for UP on September 25 from just south of Paoting – China's military headquarters in the north, which had just fallen to the Japanese – was a classic of first-person war reporting.

The report, which ran in dozens of newspapers across the United States, was accompanied by a head note written by UP editors in New York saying that the dispatch was the first about the massive Chinese retreat from Paoting to reach American shores.

"I am retreating with the Chinese army along the Peiping-Hankow railway toward the Yellow River after one of the most disastrous defeats the Chinese have suffered in this war," Belden wrote.

"As I write this dispatch I am sitting in the midst of scores of Chinese soldiers with whom I have been fleeing for forty-eight hours under an all but continuous rain of Japanese shells and aerial bombs," it continued. "The whole countryside is filled with hundreds of miserable, wet, hungry refugees who find it impossible to escape the fury of the Japanese death avalanche....I have slept three hours in the past forty-eight and eaten only once. It is raining and I can't help think of home and the smell of wet grass and leaves in the front of the yard of my mother's home in Summit, N.J. Here it is only the sight of suffering humanity."

The 800-word dispatch was also reprinted in the October 1, 1937, edition his alma mater's newspaper – the *Colgate Maroon-News* – under the headline, "Colgate Grad Swept Into Chinese Rout." It was accompanied by another, shorter dispatch written by the UP staff in New York, saying, erroneously, that Belden was born in Summit, N.J., and that he had gone to China to become a professor of English.

Several years later, Belden would write in *Still Time to Die*, published in 1944, that he had been covering war for more than a decade and had been "nurtured in war by defeat."

"My daily existence was simply that of putting one foot ahead of the other, while keeping my eyes peeled over my should for the blood-seeking thing that was hissing on the trail behind," he wrote. "I knew retreats not just as a pulling back in the night. No, I knew them as mad, chaotic routs, with thousands of soldiers roiling the roads and millions of peasants moving south and struggling ever westward." [12]

For the remainder of 1937, Belden would continue to cover the accelerating retreat of the Chinese army as the Japanese forces stepped up their invasion and occupation of the north. In November alone, the Japanese army would gobble up an estimated 15,000 square miles of Chinese territory.

Belden reported in an October 2 dispatch from Nanking – the Chinese capital at the time – that Japanese were advancing with "astonishing swiftness" down the Peiping-Hankow and Tientsin-Pukow railroads. Just back from a visit to the northern front, he said that Japanese troops were attempting to land at Haichow, on the Chinese coast, in an effort to form a line along the Yellow River and cut China in two.

"Events are moving so rapidly it is impossible to keep track daily of shifts of military positions," Belden wrote, "but in less than a fortnight the Japanese, thrusting southward along the two great railroads, have taken and pushed on from Tsangchow, on the Tientsin-Pukow railroad and are threatening Tihchow—which foreign military experts said would take two years to capture....On the Peiping-Hankow railroad the Japanese have swept past Paoting at least as far as Tinghsien, meeting no resistance.... Military experts believe the loss of the territory north of the Yellow River to the Japanese is imminent."

Another dispatch filed by Belden a few weeks later – this one from Taiyuan-Fu, the capital of Shansi province – said that the "great battle" for control of the province had begun, reaching a "roaring crescendo today when squadron after squadron of Japanese planes rained bombs on this ancient walled city...."

Yet another UP dispatch, from Taiyuan-Fu, said that "scenes of horror marked the retreat of the Chinese, including former Communist corps. Screaming and running like maniacs [were] soldiers whose skin had been burned from their hands and face, splashed by sulphur bombs."

"Speeding military trucks added to the confusion, running down soldiers and refugees who did not step aside in time," Belden wrote. "I saw a munitions truck explode near me and watched an armored car burn. At Fengyang a red-eyed, swollen-lipped figure hailed me. He was General Sun Lien-chung, Commander of the 26th Battalion. He stood disconsolately outside the gate of the city and remarked, 'Things are upside down.'"

But the Chinese continued to resist, and Henry Luce's *Time* magazine reported in its November 1, 1937, edition that Chinese troops were making "brave, effective resistance on a scale the Chinese have not before equalled in the North."

The magazine also quoted a radio report filed by Belden after he interviewed the Chinese general "100 Victories" Wei Li-huang" at his headquarters in Shansi. "I don't consider the withdrawals from Tsian and down the Peiping-Hankow railroad large defeats," Wei told Belden. "We have just begun to fight."

A little over a month later, however, the Japanese army overran the Chinese capital of Nanking in what *New York Times* reporter F. Tillman ("Till") Durdin called "the most overwhelming defeat suffered by the Chinese" to date and "one of the most tragic debacles in the history of modern warfare." [13]

Durdin, born in Texas, had been hired by the *Times* in August of 1937 after working for the *Shanghai Evening Post & Mercury* and later as the managing editor of the China Post. "[*The Times*] needed someone quickly," he said. [14]

Earlier, Durdin, like Belden, had been a restless 23-year-old and left the United States as a merchant seaman to see the world. He had also jumped ship halfway around the world – in 1930, three years before Belden – but not in Hong Kong, as Belden had done, but in Shanghai.

Durdin would say years later that he had arrived in Shanghai "like many others" at the time, "as an adventurer, a hippie of an earlier era," who had left a job at a Houston newspaper to sign on as a "workaway" on the American ship, the SS Scottsburg. His first job in his new career in journalism was as real estate editor of the *Shanghai Evening Post & Mercury*. [15]

His break with the *Times* came several years later when he was taken on as a stringer to fill in for Hallett Abend, its correspondent, when he left Shanghai to report from elsewhere in the country.

By 1937, when the *Times* asked the introspective and taciturn Durdin to join its staff as a full-time correspondent, Durdin and Belden had already known each other for some time and, in fact, had been together when the three-month-plus Battle of Shanghai began (officially) on August 14 with the Chinese bombing of Japanese targets in the city and the opening of a Chinese ground offensive. But the *Times* wanted Durdin to be in Nanking, the Chinese capital, and so he and Belden hired a car and drove together through Japanese lines to get there, some 150 miles to the west.

But Belden – still restless – was soon on the move again, leaving Nanking to roam the north with the Chinese army and file on-the-scene reports for UP on the seemingly desperate struggle by the Chinese to hold off the advancing Japanese.

By mid-November, the Japanese had taken Shanghai and were continuing to thrust westward until Nanking itself was under threat. When the city fell on December 13 – subjected in the process, as Israel Epstein put it, to "a wholesale orgy of rape and slaughter" by Japanese troops – only five Western reporters, including Durdin, remained. The others were Archibald T. ("A.T.") Steele, of the *Chicago Daily News*; Leslie Smith, of Reuters News Agency; C. Yates McDaniel, of Associated Press; and Arthur Menken, of Paramount Movie News. All except McDaniel (who left on December 16) departed Nanking on December 15 on the USS Oahu – a 191-foot-long gunboat built specifically for use on the Yangtze River to protect American lives and property in the 1930s.

The stories filed by the five journalists who remained in Nanking were among the first to appear in print detailing what would come to be known as the Nanking Massacre.

But it was Durdin's reporting that stood out. "Through wholesale atrocities and vandalism at Nanking," he wrote, "the Japanese army has thrown away a rare opportunity to gain the respect and confidence of the Chinese inhabitants and of foreign opinion there ....Wholesale looting, the violation of women, the murder of civilians, the eviction of Chinese from their homes, mass executions of war prisoners and the impressing of able-bodied men turned Nanking into a city of terror."

Durdin also wrote that, just before he boarded the USS Oahu, he witnessed the cold-blooded execution of 200 men. "The killings took 10 minutes. The men were lined up against the wall and shot. Then a number of Japanese, armed with pistols, trod nonchalantly around the crumpled bodies, pumping bullets into any that were still kicking."

The Japanese takeover of Nanking, Durdin concluded in a dispatch filed later from Shanghai, had been marred by "barbaric cruelties, by the wholesale execution of prisoners, by the looting of the city, rape, killing of civilians and by general vandalism, which will remain a blot on the reputation of the Japanese Army and nation." [16]

Durdin, a piano-playing Texan who would never lose his Southern drawl, has often been credited with breaking the news of the Nanking "incident" to the Western world. But it was Steele, in fact, who had managed the trick by bribing an Oahu crew member to send his story ahead of Durdin's, which would run on page 20 of *The New York Times* on December 16 – a day after Steele's piece appeared with much fanfare in the *Chicago Daily News* on page 1.

After McDaniel left Nanking, no Western reporters were allowed to return to the city, and the Nanking "incident" was quickly forgotten. Yet no one could deny the facts: that, in six months, the Japanese had captured Peking, Shanghai and Nanking, and the Chinese government under Chiang Kai-shek was forced to pack up and fall back yet again, this time to Hankow, as the Japanese continued their unrelenting thrust to the south and west.

4

"LAST DITCHERS"

By early 1938, roughly six months after the war had begun, the Japanese were without a doubt on the move, having captured the key Chinese cities of Peking, Tientsin, Shanghai and Nanking. But Henry Luce's *Time* magazine, in its first issue of the new year, said that the Chinese should not be counted out, and in an apparently hopeful gesture, it anointed Chiang Kai-shek and his wife "Man and Wife of the Year."

The Luce-run weekly said that, in 1937, unlike the Japanese, whose rush to war had been driven "much as a hill of ants are driven by their impulses to conquer another ant hill," the Chinese people had been led by "one supreme leader and his remarkable wife. Under this "Man and Wife" team, it said, this historically divided people – millions of whom seldom used the word "China" in the past – "have slowly been given national consciousness." [1]

But Belden and the other war reporters who had decamped with the Chinese government from fallen Nanking to Hankow did not see it that way. It was certainly a time of uncommon unity between the Nationalists, under Chiang Kai-shek, and the Communists, under Mao Tse-tung, and the Chinese had won a series of small-scale but cumulatively significant military victories and were preparing for what would become a major success at Taierchuang. But most observers, including Belden, were not convinced that, in the end, the Chinese would prevail over the advancing Japanese.

Belden's dispatches for UP, in fact, told a story of mounting despair on the part of the Chinese. One of his reports, published in the Portland (Me.) Herald, appeared under the headline, "Rout of Chinese Army At Shansi Witnessed By Correspondent." And the same story, in the Ft. Wayne, Ind., Gazette, ran under the headline: "Million Chinese Flee Over the Mountains."

But for Belden, as well as for the other correspondents assigned to cover the Sino-Japanese conflict, including Durdin, Steele, McDaniel and Fisher, Hankow was the place to be. It was the seat of the Chinese government and the home – albeit temporary – of Chiang Kai-shek and Chou En-lai, second to Mao Tse-tung in the Communist hierarchy.

It was also home a motley mix of journalists, missionaries and government officials including Dorn; Naval Attache Evans F. Carlson; and John P. Davies Jr., Stilwell's political adviser – all "decent, forthright and intelligent men," Belden later wrote.

The noted American historian Charles W. Hayford has said that, in 1938, Hankow was "a world center for the democratic struggle against fascism, and [it became] almost a tourist stop-over for writers and demi-diplomats who swooped through to visit the front." [2] Film-maker Joris Ivens and photographer Robert Capa showed up, as did several leaders of the U.S. Communist movement, including Earl Browder and Mike Gold. Writers like W.H. Auden and Christopher Isherwood also made an appearance.

Durdin said that many of those who were in Hankow had come directly from the Spanish Civil War (1936-1939), which they had "pushed, observed and covered" from the Republican side. "They were also great believers in the Russian Revolution," he said. He said that they felt at home in China because it, too, was fighting a just war. "So at Hankow, with their presence, we had become part of the world scene," he said. [3]

Occasionally, the reporters who were based in Hankow would leave the city to go into the field with the Chinese troops to "see what was going on," Durdin said. But for the most part, he said, they relied on Belden and Stilwell, who cooperated closely in monitoring Chinese troop movements and actions throughout the region.

"Jack and Stilwell would plunge off into the hinterland and come back with information about the situation at the front," Durdin said, "all of which was made available to us." [4]

Only 28 years old, Belden had been covering the war for about six months – since its beginning outside Peking in July 1937. But he had already traveled with the Chinese army some 10,000 miles through nine provinces. His dispatches from the field, while he was based in Hankow, rank among his best and put on full display the powerful immediacy of his prose.

"I'm ripping along the shell-gorged road from Shanghai to Nanking at 3 a.m.," began one dispatch, filed in February 1938. "It is the first time I have driven in six years. A photographer lent me the car after he decided not to make the trip. He was supposed to have been outside Shanghai when planes machine-gunned him and an old woman fell on top of him, saving his life, but losing her own." [5]

From south of Paoting, as he retreated with the Chinese army, he described the nightmarish scene. "Just now," he wrote, "I sit here in a station in the midst of hundreds of soldiers and swarms of miserable, wet and hungry refugees in the mud and muck. There is a dead horse 10 feet away and bleeding soldiers all around me. I slept three hours in the last 48 and ate once during the same time. It is raining and I can't help thinking of home and the smell of wet grass and leaves on our front lawn at home. But everything is different here. There is only the odor of suffering humanity."

Another dispatch, datelined Hsinchow, began: "I walked through fire and water last night and through the dead today. I started without official permission and had to go without a guard. The soldiers cared for me." [6]

One of the more interesting reporters working in Hankow at the time was Agnes Smedley. She had arrived in the city in January 1938 straight from three months with the Communist-led Eighth Route Army in Shansi. There, she worked with and for the Communists and gathered information for her book, *China Fights Back: An American Woman with the Eighth Route Army,* published later that year.

Smedley and Belden had been friends for some time. But unlike Smedley, he would never associate himself directly with the Communist cause and, in fact, took pains over the years to distance himself from any possible political affiliation – although he was consistently critical of Chiang's "inefficient, corrupt and despotic" regime.

U.S. military officers, including Stilwell, drew heavily on Smedley for her knowledge and experience about and with the Chinese Communists. At one point, Stilwell said he enjoyed the company of journalists like Belden and Smedley, who, he said, had learned what they knew through direct contact with the people they covered. It was through Smedley, in fact, that Stilwell came to know Communist leaders like Chou En-lai and Yeh Chien-ying, chief of staff of the Eighth Route Army.

Davies said that Smedley, in fact, was viewed as a Communist agent by the "more anxious intelligence functionaries" in Hankow.

"Agnes loved to wear an Eighth Route Army uniform because she wished she were in Eighth Route soldier– also because she was a militant women's rightser and because she enjoyed shocking the stodgy," he wrote affectionately of her in his memoir, *Dragon by the Tail.* "The getup was a slumped fatigue hat cap pulled down to her ears over her lank bobbed hair, a wrinkled cotton tunic and trousers, neatly wound cotton puttees, and cloth shoes. This ensemble would be unflattering to any woman, but for Miss Smedley, not endowed with beauty of feature or figure, it was aggressively unbecoming." [7]

Davies said that one of Smedley's most ardent admirers was the British ambassador, Sir Archibald Clark Kerr, who appreciated the "valiant spirit of this abrupt woman and saw that she possessed insights into the Chinese Communist movement and burgeoning guerrilla activities that he could not get from his conventional sources."

"[A]gnes was an authentic American in the tradition of Tom Paine, the suffragettes, and the wobblies," Davies wrote. "For a radical, she was curiously unconcerned with doctrine. She said that she was not a Communist.

I supposed that she was probably not, for she was too softhearted and unruly to be a party member. She told me that she admired the Communist soldiers – [Red Army Commander-in-Chief] Chu Teh was her hero – but that she did not like the political leaders in Yenan. With a slight grimace, 'They're too slick.'" [8]

Her professional life aside, however, it was the social side of Smedley's days in Hankow that she would recall with some relish in a June 1939 letter to fellow reporter and friend Freda Utley.

"The last days of Hankow still remain in my mind as rare, unusual days from the psychological and human viewpoint," Smedley wrote. "I still think of [Bernard] Shaw's 'Heartbreak House' when I recall them. As you remarked at the time, no person on earth is more charming than the American journalist abroad, particularly the cultured serious-minded ones. But I wonder what it would be like were I to meet those same men on the streets of Chicago. Gone the Magic!"

"I sort of pine for the magic of Hankow," she wrote. "It was the bright spot in one decade of my life....I wish to retain it as a precious memory. I think often of the play in which many persons of different classes are on a foundering ship in mid-ocean. Class distinctions fall all away as they face death together, drawn closer by humanity."

Smedley also wrote a separate letter to the so-called Hankow Gang, in which she affectionately sketched out the main characters of a play she kiddingly said she would try to write one day:

"I shall one day try to weave you all into a drama–John[Davies], you with your white bowls filled with lovely flowers, with Beethoven's Fifth Symphony in the background. And, I suspect, behind your immaculate life, many dark thoughts and dreams. You are so much a part of this bourgeois, cultured civilization of the present you do not even know other ways of life. Very well, with all that you shall be a leading character in my play. Then there is Evans [Carlson]–where is he? Long and lanky and lovable, he shall be the man unconsciously reaching for the stars–but never touching them I fear. Yet that striving, alone, makes life worthwhile. He shall be the element of tragedy in my play.... Till [Durdin] shall be the psychological case, reticent, fearful of himself as a man, yet trembling a bit at times before the harsh reality of his psychological problems. Arch [Steele] the disciplined–perhaps all too disciplined–looking with amused eyes on the passing scene. Yet at times of which I know so little–deeply moved by joy and sorrow. I shall give him seven wives and one child, but they shall be but the comedy element in the offing, while the real Arch shall be tousled and beaten down at times. Mac [Fisher] of many hidden problems—kind and generous but lovable, and something more, though I have not yet fathomed it. Freda [Utley] shall be the flame, uncontrolled and forever attracting all, instinctively and unconsciously.... And above all [there is] Jack Belden. Jack can be drawn down into chaos or led into a purposeful life, but not in China–at least not the way he is going."

Several years later, however, Belden had become purposeful enough to mount a strong defense of Smedley when she was accused by Maj. Gen. Charles A. Willoughby, who served under Gen. Douglas MacArthur as assistant chief of staff for intelligence, of having worked with the Sorge spy ring (after Richard Sorge, a Soviet spymaster) on behalf of the Soviet Union.

Belden denounced the charges, calling them "so fantastic that the Army had to back down." [9] But in 1949, the House Un-American Activities Committee threatened to call her to testify. By then, however, she had already moved to the United Kingdom, where she died in 1950 at the age of 58.

For her part, Utley, who was British, wrote in her book, *Odyssey of a Liberal: Memoirs,* that in Hankow she and Smedley – not yet but eventually on opposite ends of the political spectrum – were the "best of friends."

"In view of all the suffering around me," Utley wrote, "it may sound callous to record that I had a wonderful time. But everyone who has experienced the heightened awareness of the joy of living war can bring, as also the opportunity it affords of temporary escape from petty cares or the sorrows and perplexities of normal life, will understand why I look back on my experience as a war correspondent in China three decades ago with nostalgia."

Utley said that the "Hankow Last Ditchers" – the name she claims to have invented for the small band of Western correspondents, including Belden, military observers and foreign service officers who stayed on in the beleaguered wartime capital until it fell to the Japanese in October 1938 – were mainly Americans.

"It was now that I first became acquainted with Americans," she wrote, "if I exclude the Communist Party hacks I had know in Moscow, and found I had more affinity with them than with my British compatriots."

As a woman, she said, she was initially dismissed as a nuisance in Hankow by seasoned American correspondents like Belden. But she said she was eventually accepted as a member of the group. "Even Jack Belden," she said, "the most woman-despising of all the newspapermen in China, after accompanying me part of the way on my visit to the front, went so far as to admit that females correspondents might have their uses." [10]

As for Belden, he would insist years later that he had had little use for any of the correspondents who had spent only six months or so in Hankow, including Utley.

"Hankow 1938...had little basic influence on my life," he said. "I certainly was not as 'anti-Communist' as Utley.

I did not like, very unrealistic and irritating, the professional leftists of those days primarily because I had lived a life they knew nothing about except in theory." [11]

As for the Chinese, they were able to hold on to Hankow for another few months following their major military victory over the Japanese at Taierhchuang in April 1938. But any glory that could have come from that success would be short-lived. Within weeks, the Japanese were back on the attack and in mid-May they overran the key city of Hsuchow, which boasted an airfield and an important railway junction.

Belden noted in *Still Time to Die* that the collapse of Hsuchow had come less than a year after the war began.

"Quickly [the Japanese] overran most of China," he wrote, "thrust into the Yangtze Valley and captured and raped the Chinese capital at Nanking." And now the Japanese were pummeling Hsuchow. "From the fifth of May, the attacks were increasingly fierce," he wrote. "Caught between the pilots sights, like a bug under a microscope, Hsuchow was pinned to earth and stabbed with a thousand explosive plummets."

"The destruction was terrific," he continued. "Heavy clouds of smoke occasionally veiled the sun; but they soon passed over, and the sun coming out again glared on the bodies of the mangled people and the ruing homes. Tatung Street, Hsuchow's main thoroughfare, was turned into a field of tile; the steel and mortar wall of the Bank of Communications was pierced with a thousand holes; the second supply station was smashed as flat as a big Chinese cake; the 'Mobilization Daily News' and the 'Hsuchow News' buildings were shaken up one day and knocked down the next; the hospital for wounded soldiers, close by the Catholic mission, was shattered by a direct hit; the patients, unable to escape, were hurled from their beds into the grave; the ammunition dump outside the east suburbs was blown out of existence, whisked into nothingness. The people's homes were burned to ashes, the 'hutungs' were filled with rubble and whole streets were turned into cold, damp fields of tile and charcoal. There was no respite save the night, and then only in work; the refreshing balm of sleep was denied the people, for work had to be performed and it could be performed only when the sun had gone down. As soon as the sun came up, the roads were filled with people. They tramped out on the roads seeking the safety of the country, and if the planes came while they were on the road, they moved off into the fields and lay down until the planes passed over. But each day the planes came earlier. Alarms in the early morning sprang into the people's dreams and kicked them awake, and they ran out in the quivering and shrieking streets, hastily pulling on their clothes as they went. Soon they learned to sleep with their clothes on; soon they learned to get up at four o'clock in the morning and escape from the city before the sun came up over the Dragon Cloud Hill east of the town; soon the people fled altogether, salvaging whatever they could from the wreckage of their homes. One night they were thronging the streets with bags of grain on their shoulders and water and tea jugs in their hands; the next day they were gone. Hsuchow was being destroyed and there was no way to keep the people quiet; almost everyone fled; almost every family moved to the country, to a friend's place, to any place." [12]

Following the fall of Hsuchow, in one of the most bizarre military decisions ever, Chiang-shek ordered his troops to blow up the dikes on the Yellow River at Chengchow in an attempt to halt the rapidly advancing Japanese forces, which were now threatening Hankow.

Reporting from the scene, Belden said that the Chinese army appeared to be in danger of falling apart and dispersing into guerilla bands, while the government and industry remained in Hankow.

"[T]he Republic of China seemed on the verge of disaster," Belden wrote. "Never since the fall of Nanking had the breath of uncertainty so overhung the future of the War of Resistance. Because he literally had nowhere to turn, Chiang Kai-shek in the end turned toward China's ancient nurse and protector – to the Yellow River itself."

He said that Chiang believed that if the Yellow River dikes were not breached, unleashing the flood waters on the Japanese, the entire country might be plunged into swift, irrevocable ruin.

Dynamite was placed on the dikes, and on May 11 it was detonated, allowing the water to rush through the breach with a "terrible roar" and to spread across the surrounding low ground drowning many Japanese soldiers, miring tanks and guns and putting an impassable wall of water between the Japanese army and Chengchow. But the ensuring flood also devastated nearly a dozen cities and 4,000 villages, ruined crops and forced two million people from their homes. The advance by the Japanese had been slowed. But the decision had not exactly endeared Chiang to his people.

By the summer of 1938, it became clear that Hankow could not be saved. It was just a matter of time before it would be overwhelmed by the Japanese. And so, as they awaited the end, the journalists and diplomats who remained in the city established the Hankow "Last Ditchers Corps."

The group, which included Belden, would assemble regularly for dinner to say farewell with great fanfare to what they called the Hankow "deserters." One such dinner was held in September 1938 when Utley and

Carlson were preparing to leave Hankow for Shanghai. A mock "trial" of the "accused" was staged and the charges read:

CHARGE IN THE SUPREME COURT of the Hankow Last Ditchers Corps within and for the District of East Asia, in the first Judicial Circuit, in the year of our Lord one thousand nine hundred and thirty-eight.

THE GRAND JURORS of the Hankow Last Ditchers Corps, duly empaneled, sworn and charged with inquiring in and for the said district, upon their oaths and affirmations, present that Freda Clayfoot Utley and Evans Voice-in-the-Wilderness Carlson during, to wit, the last days of September in the year of our Lord 1000 900 & 38 in the Lutheran Mission Home and Rosie's Dine, Dance and Romance Restaurant in the district aforesaid and within the jurisdiction of this court, did, then, and there, in contravention to the Corps line, knowingly and with force of arms connive to commit—desertion, contrary to the form of the statute in such case made and provided, and against the peace, dialectics and dignity of the Hankow Last Ditchers Corps.

And the Grand Jurors aforesaid, upon their oaths and affirmations aforesaid, do further present that the defendants, on, to wit, the last days of September, of the year of our Lord, etc., in the L.M.H. and R.D.D.R.R., in the district aforesaid, and within the jurisdiction of this court, through their connivance to commit desertion,

2nd Specification

Wreck and create diversion of the defense plans of the Hankow Last Ditchers Corps;

3rd Specification

Sabotage the economic warp and woof;

4th Specification

Sap, gut and scuttle Corps morale; contrary to the form of the statutes in such case made and provided, and against the peace, dialectics and dignity of the Hankow Last Ditchers Corps. A. T. Steele, Presiding Judge.

Throughout the summer and into the fall, as the Japanese bombed the city heavily and unopposed, forcing the Chinese government to withdraw, the "Last Ditchers" continued to enjoy themselves as best they could. They wrote their stories. But they also drank, and occasionally they would enjoy a movie or two, including, according to some reports, the 1935 film "The Last Days of Pompeii."

Stilwell political adviser John P. Davies said that, as residents left the city in anticipation of its eventual collapse, he inherited a cavernous apartment in the Hong Kong and Shanghai Bank Building, where, he said, he entertained "Last Ditchers" that included Belden, Steele, Carlson and Utley ("a confused political gypsy"), as well as Stilwell, Dorn, Snow, and McDaniel. [13]

Also counting himself among the "Last Ditchers" was the photographer and photojournalist Robert Capa, who had come to Hankow to document China's resistance to the Japanese invasion – straight from Spain, where he had been covering the Spanish civil war.

It was in Hankow, however, that he would come up with an idea that would change the way war was viewed. To implement the idea, he wrote to his photo agency, Pix, in New York in July requesting "immediately several rolls of Kodachrome with all instructions about how to use it, filters, etc." He said he wanted use it for a piece specifically geared to *LIFE* magazine.

He had already been in Hankow for several months and had taken hundreds of black-and-white photographs, including one of a 15-year-old Chinese Nationalist boy-soldier that appeared on the cover of the May 16 issue of *LIFE* – one of only two covers for the magazine he ever shot. But color film had only been on the market for a year or so, and color pictures that were used to illustrate editorial content in magazines (as opposed to advertising or art) were rare. Few photojournalists, therefore, including Capa, even bothered to use the film.

His "idea" for *LIFE* using Kodachrome film was to photograph the aftermath of the Japanese aerial bombing of Hankow, which he did in September, a month before the city fell. Shortly after he took the pictures, he left Hankow and returned to Spain. A month later, in the October 17 issue of *LIFE*, four of the color photographs he took of the devastation caused by the Japanese bombing of Hankow were published, and they are believed to be the first color images of war ever to appear in print.

From then on, Capa would carry a second Contax camera loaded with Kodachrome 35 mm film wherever he went, including Europe to cover World War II. He died in 1954, at the age of 40, after stepping on a land mine in Vietnam.

5

JACK IS JACK IN CHUNGKING

Those who knew and worked with Jack Belden in the 1930s called him brilliant, with some even saying he was the finest war reporter of the era. But they also knew him to be difficult, mercurial, moody, aloof and alcoholic.

Not surprisingly, then, his temperament would often come between him and his employer, as it did in the weeks leading up to the Japanese takeover of Hankow in October 1938, when he chose to ignore orders from the home office of United Press in New York and was fired.

It would not be long, however, before he was hired by the English-language *Shanghai Evening Post & Mercury*, where Tillman Durdin had also worked, prior to joining *The New York Times*. Other "China hands," like Harold Isaacs, who would later report from Asia for *Newsweek*, also honed their reporting skills at the "Evepost."

As a new hire, and from his base in the new Chinese capital of Chungking, Belden again took off for the front, as he always had, this time to be with the Communist-led New Fourth Army for a series of "Evepost" articles that were published in January 1939.

The articles – for the first time – described in detail how the Communists, by winning the trust of the people, were able to achieve a measure of success against the Japanese that had been denied to the regular Chinese army.

They also underscored the importance placed by army leadership on maintaining political control over the fighting forces.

"The political system is the life line of the [New Fourth] Army," Belden wrote. "The Army accepts and supports political guidance."

Belden also observed that, in China, soldiers had never been held in high esteem by the rest of society, and as a result gaining the people's trust and confidence in them was difficult. "However," he wrote, "if the soldiers are taught to love the people, the people will generally reciprocate this love, and believe in the Army."

He further noted that the New Fourth Army's political leadership was convinced that "victory in the war depends not only on the force of the army, but on the masses."

Time magazine would later call Belden's "Evepost" articles "classic accounts of the operational tactics of the New Fourth Army ...."[1] But by mid-1939, he had grown disenchanted with the paper and was soon back in Chungking looking for a job – a fact he made known in a letter to his friend and fellow reporter Edgar Snow, whose *Red Star Over China* had been published to much acclaim the previous year.[2]

Recovering from a severe case of malaria, Belden also asked Snow – then in Hong Kong – for help in placing for publication a planned book-length manuscript on China for which, he said, he needed "a wealth of intimate detail that my own personal experiences [in China] don't sufficiently cover." He said that if a publisher could be found to support him for a year or so, he could write a book about China rivaling in breadth and depth William Hickling Prescott's *The History of the Conquest of Mexico*. But no such deep-pocket publisher would ever be found.

Belden also told Snow he had seen their mutual friend Agnes Smedley when he was traveling with the New Fourth Army, and that she seemed sad and lonely because, as a woman, she had not been permitted to visit the front.

Snow, in the meantime, flew to Chungking in the summer of 1939 to join Belden and the other Western correspondents who had made it their base of operation.

He said that Chungking – a place of "moist heat, dirt and wide confusion" – was an "utterly planless overgrown medieval town, sprawling across many square miles," which once had a population of more than 500,000 but was now about one-fifth that size. "Communication had slowed down to a village pace, there were no cars for hire, and a rickshaw – when you could persuade one to pull you – took two hours to pass from one corner of the city to another," he wrote.

Snow said that, in May and June, many acres of buildings had been destroyed in what he called a series of "barbaric" Japanese air raids, which killed more than 4,000 civilians, "and new debris was being added to the wreckage [by the Japanese] during each week of clear weather." [3]

As for Belden, according to Hugh Deane, a friend and long-time admirer of his who reported from China for the *Christian Science Monitor* throughout the 1930s, said that he would lock himself up in the Chungking Press Hostel, pull down the shades in his room and drink himself into a stupor. Only when the blinds were raised did Dean and the other reporters know he was ready to socialize. [4]

Deane also said that, unlike the other reporters, Belden had arrived in Chungking having read Leon Trotsky's *The Revolution Betrayed*, which he used to draw up a series of 30 or so questions to ask officials about the internal situation in China. [5]

"He wasn't a Trotskyite," Deane said. "He just used Trotsky's words to get some basic knowledge about the nature of revolution. Belden sensed that I didn't know very much. He took me in hand, and I went with him to a lot of interviews. He told me things and pointed me in the right direction. I think of him as my teacher." [6]

Few self-respecting reporters, including Deane, really wanted to be in Chungking – except Theodore H. (Teddy) White, who had arrived there in April 1939 straight out of Harvard, having taken the advice of the China historian John K. Fairbank, his tutor at Harvard, to follow in the footsteps of Edgar Snow. His reasoning: "I had the manners, lust and ego of someone who might be a journalist." [7]

White would later call Chungking a "uniquely unpleasant place." For six months of the year , he wrote, "a pall of fog and rain overhangs it," which, of course, protected the city from Japanese bombers but also coated the alleys with slime. The summer heat was intense. "Moisture remained in the air, perspiration dripped, and prickly heat ravaged the skin. Every errand became an expedition, each expedition an ordeal." [8]

Yet White would thrive in Chungking, winning a job as a *Time* stringer, and then eventually as a full-time correspondent for the magazine after working initially for the Ministry of Information feeding information favorable to Chiang and the Nationalists to the foreign press. He would go on to win a Pulitzer prize for his *Making of the President, 1960* and to write three other best-selling "making of the president" books.

It was White, moreover, who played a major role in convincing the powers-that-be at TIME-LIFE to hire Belden, despite his reputation as an exceptionally temperamental employee. Once taken on board, he was praised widely and often as one of the organization's best reporters, including in the September 21, 1942, issue of *Time* magazine, when the editors wrote that Belden had long been a "tower of strength for our News Bureau in the Far East." He was widely admired, to be sure, but not generally well-liked. On several occasions, White, who called Belden "perhaps the ablest of all war correspondents," [9] would be forced to come to his defense and advise the editors in New York to overlook his idiosyncrasies for the greater good.

"As for Jack's four-letter words," White said in a letter to one *TIME* editor in 1944, "Well, Jack is Jack. If he wants to say fuck, shit and piss, that's his business. If you can't publish them because of the law, I should suggest substituting the Chinese equivalent which gives it an oriental flavor and means nothing to the American reader. For example. Wherever he says `fuck,' say `t'sao!'; where he says 'his mother' say 'ma ti pi'."

White had come to China long after Belden had – six years, in fact – armed with a letter of introduction from Harvard president James Bryant Conant; a modest stipend from the university; and a secondhand typewriter compliments of Fairbank. What he saw, after landing in Chungking on its sandbar airstrip in the middle of the Yangtze River, was a city set on a "wedge of cliffs squeezed together by the Chialing and Yangtze rivers...."

He said that the national government had been moved to Chungking from Hankow "because it controlled the entry to the largest and richest province of China–Szechwan. Landlocked by mountains and gorges to the east, backed against the roof of Asia to the west, cupping the most fertile fields of the entire land, Szechwan was a semitropical inner empire of fifty million people, self-sufficient and all but impregnable....[F]rom this natural fortress the Nationalist resistance was to be directed for six full years." [10]

But on May 3 and May 4, less than a month after White had arrived in Chungking, the Japanese bombed the city in what he would later call "at the time...the largest mass slaughter of defenseless human beings from the air...."

"More people were killed that night than ever before by bombardiers," White wrote. "But what was important about the killings was their purpose of terror....There was no military target within the old walls of Chungking. Yet the Japanese had chosen, deliberately, to burn it to the ground, and all the people within it, to break some spirit they could not understand, to break the resistance of the government that had taken refuge somewhere in Chungking's suburbs." [11]

The American writer Emily Hahn – best known for her work for *The New Yorker*, where, beginning in 1935, she wrote more than 200 articles – said that she was not particularly fond of White, who was only 24 years old, on meeting him for the first time upon her arrival in Chungking in December 1939.

"He was very young and cocky, and knew simply everything about everything," Hahn said. [12] "I started out disliking him rather, because he was obviously a bright, precocious boy, and he knew it." But she soon grew to like and admire him. "He was conscientious and in his work he had a broad clear field, without rivals." [13]

While in Chungking, where she remained for about a year writing for *The New Yorker*, Hahn stayed at the Chungking Hostel. It was reserved for non-press visitors to the city, while Belden, White and the other foreign correspondents were housed at the Press Hostel. "I didn't rate as a newspaperman....I fell into the same category as visiting plane salesmen and oil people." But she said that that was fine with her. "The Press Hostel was quite exquisitely uncomfortable," she wrote, "whereas the Chungking Hostel was just mildly awful." [14]

A compound of tumbledown plaster-and-lath buildings, the Press Hostel, in addition to housing foreign correspondents, was also the home of the propaganda offices of Chiang Kai-shek's Nationalist government – a fact that would make Belden and the other Western reporters increasingly uncomfortable.

Recently separated from the "Evepost," he took a job with International News Service (INS), founded by the newspaper publisher William Randolph Hearst in 1909, and he immediately began to look for ways to frustrate the heavy hand of the Kuomintang propaganda machine.

He was joined in that pursuit by, most notably Hugh Deane, who would write a series of controversial articles for the *Christian Science Monitor*, published in 1941, claiming that the Nationalists, or Kuomintang, had lost the support of the people and were on their way out.

"I wound up by saying that the Communists had won the battle for the minds of the peasants," Deane said years later, "and I suggested that this was going to be the decisive factor." [15]

This was not something that the anti-Communist policy-makers at State Department back in Washington, D.C., wanted to hear.

Together and separately, Deane and Belden worked day and night attempting to expose the dark side of the Kuomintang regime, including the systematic suppression of its opponents. Leftists and other dissidents were arrested, and some were even forced to flee Chungking for Hong Kong and elsewhere to escape the wrath of the Kuomintang.

Trust in the "news" being flogged by the Kuomintang, therefore, was declining quickly among the foreign press corps.

Blacklisted in the 1950s, Deane called himself a "minor victim" of the McCarthy era for having allegedly helped the United States "lose" China to the Communists. He could not find work in journalism back in the United States and wound up operating laundromats for a short time to support his family.

A Chinese friend, Shu Zhang, said after Deane died in 2001 at the age of 84 that, along with Belden and Snow, he had "sympathized with and supported the Chinese people's revolution...."

"He traveled far and wide in China," Shu said, "seeing not only greater sufferings of the Chinese people, but also their brave and arduous fight against the Japanese aggressors and under the leadership of the Communist Party of China their determination to overthrow the three big mountains – imperialism, feudalism and bureaucrat-capitalism – and liberate China."

From 1960 to 1986, when he retired, Deane found work in journalism as associate editor and then editor of the Hotel Voice, a periodical publication for New York City's unionized hotel workers. He was also a co-founder of the U.S.-China People's Friendship Association.

In eulogizing his father, one of his two sons, Michael, said that Deane had refused to "name names" or to accept an FBI offer to inform on others during the McCarthy era.

"[H]e was willing to brave the disapproval of his peers, the censure of his colleagues, the wrath of society," the younger Deane said.

Another resident of the Chungking Press Hostel – in addition to the dozen or regulars, including Belden and Deane – was Graham Peck (1914-1968), the American writer and artist, whose classic *Two Kinds of Time* recounted with insight and humor the experiences of "a traveler among the common people," as John K. Fairbank put it, in 1940-1941. Peck had ventured to China first in 1935 after graduating from Yale University, traveling through several provinces, often by bicycle, learning Chinese and making sketches for a possible book. He returned to the United States at the end of 1937 but "determined that China would be my profession." He wrote his first book, *Through China's Wall*, then returned to China via Hong Kong in June 1940. After Pearl Harbor in December 1941, he took a job with the Office of War Information in Chungking, He eventually retired to

Pomfret, Vermont, and wrote a third book, *China: The Remembered Life*, published two months before he died of cancer in 1968 at the age of 56.

In *Two Kinds of Time*, Peck wrote that Chungking, in 1940-1941, was a "backwater if not a dog house for the Americans who were sent there on regular jobs," including businessmen, who, he said, were little more than caretakers for their companies' property.

"The State Department men," he wrote, "might enjoy the protocol and prestige of station in an alleged national capital, but they could not avoid the uneasy feeling that the real work was done, and the careers made, down in the greater occupied cities."

Peck said it was the same for the foreign press corps, who conceded that there was a certain glamor associated with living in the "most bombed-out town in the world." But they knew down deep that they would not be able to really get ahead until they were called back to the coast.

At one point in the book," Peck wrote sarcastically that a series of "prima-donna correspondents" would drop into Chungking "on the Hong Kong plane" and get what he called the quick treatment: lunch with Chiang Kai-shek and/or his wife and then brief visits to a "warphanage," a model factory or a hospital. "Then off they went into the clouds again," he said, "to write their flattering stories."

The rest of the time, Peck said, the news coming out of Chungking was cooked up in the Kuomintang propaganda offices behind the Press Hostel and turned into press releases, which were then tossed into the rooms of the foreign reporters, who would retype the press releases on white or yellow paper for submission to the Kuomintang censors, before they were taken to the telegraph office for transmission to their respective media outlets.

But not all of the reporters were enamored by the Kuomintang tactics. After the so-called New Fourth Army Incident in January 1941, in which Kuomintang forces ambushed the Communist-led army and inflicted heavy causalities, Belden went into a rage on the compound of the Press Hostel, accusing the Kuomintang generals of murder and claiming that the Kuomintang propaganda offices were lying to cover up the crime.

"Big-hearted Belden indeed had a passion for truth," wrote Israel Epstein, the journalist, author and long-time propagandist for the Communist cause in China, who knew Belden well. "From our early days in Wuhan [Hankow] I remember his admonition to me to be more perceptive and less didactic. 'Eppy, if you talked less and listened more you might learn something,' he taught me. And I have since tried." [16]

One of the "prima-donna" correspondents Peck was alluding to in *Two Kinds of Time* was undoubtedly Ernest Hemingway, whose then-wife – novelist, travel writer and journalist Martha Gellhorn – had been sent to China by *Collier's* magazine, and Hemingway went along. Her assignment was to "report on the Chinese army in action and defenses against future Japanese attack around the South China Sea." [17]

"I was determined to see the Orient before I died or the world ended," she wrote, "or whatever came next."

The newlyweds spent the month of January 1941 in Hong Kong, and from there they took off to visit Kuomintang troops at the front in Canton. What followed was an eight-day visit to Chungking in April, where they met Chiang, his wife and other Kuomintang officials.

Hemingway's *For Whom the Bell Tolls* had just been published, in October 1940, but he was already famous around the world for his earlier writings, including The *Sun Also Rises* and *A Farewell to Arms*. So in Chungking, he and Gellhorn were wined and dined and generally treated like the celebrities they were. Agnes Smedley, who met him at a reception, described him as "breezy, self-confident and virile." [18]

But the reporting that Hemingway did from China – for the liberal daily PM – reflected a strong Kuomintang bias since he had decided in advance that it was not necessary to see or visit any Communist troops or officials while he was in the country.

According to Ralph Ingersoll, the editor of PM, who interviewed Hemingway after he returned to the United States in late 1941, Hemingway believed that the Communist side of the story had already been "excellently described" by people like Smedley, Edgar Snow, and others.

"News of the Kuomintang army is important," Ingersoll wrote after interviewing Hemingway, "not simply because it has received no publicity but because the Kuomintang comprises the bulk of the troops on which we, in American, must depend to keep the Japanese divisions occupied in China while we are preparing to defend the Pacific."

Ingersoll said that, while they were in Chungking, Hemingway and Gellhorn spent considerable time with Chiang Kai-shek and his wife, as well as with other Kuomintang officials.

"They stayed about eight days," Ingersoll said, "constantly talking with people." He said that Hemingway had "dined, lunched and breakfasted" with government officials, and that he found the hotels in Chungking to be "excellent – the food plentiful and the water hot." [19]

6

THE LONG MARCH WITH BETTY

The Reuters correspondent in Chungking in late 1940 was a young woman by the name of Betty Graham, a 24-year-old native of Washington State who had come to China three years earlier.

Her father, John Graham, was an architect with offices in Seattle and Shanghai, and his daughter – described as a slender, doe-eyed blond with a wide smile – had fallen in love with China when she first visited him there.

At the University of Washington, where she majored in psychology, Graham was an ace student and a member of Kappa Kappa Gamma. She was as interested in fun and parties as anyone else. But she also had a deeply serious side, as well as a restless mind, with little time for boyfriends or small talk with friends.

Soon telling the story of China to the rest of the world would become her passion, and with the help of her father, she found work, in 1937, as a cub reporter at the *Shanghai Evening Post & Mercury*.

"Tuesday's raid was the real thing," Graham wrote to her alma mater from Chungking in October 1940, describing a Japanese bombing run she had just witnessed. "We heard the planes, but it was a bright day and we couldn't seem to locate them. Suddenly there they were, practically above us and heading straight over. We ran!

The anti-aircraft was firing before we were halfway to the dugout....
The three of us huddled together. Then it came. Whoosh! Whoosh! and
the Japs let go 160 bombs in our end of town....None of us thought we'd
get out alive."

After the raid, Graham and several other reporters toured Chungking
to see the damage. "Bombs certainly mess people up," she wrote. "Probably 400 or 500 killed....The city is beginning to look pretty bad now." But
she said, "believe it or not, I like Chungking very well and wouldn't leave
it for the world. My job is fun...and my living quarters are still standing –
and, all in all, I'm having the time of my life."

A year later, in August 1941, she would team up with Belden – not for
the time of her life but for a reporting trip through Honan and Hupeh that
would test them in ways they could never have imagined.

Reporting for INS, Belden had already been traveling through Shensi
and Szechuan for about four months by mule-drawn cart, bicycle, truck,
river boat and foot. And now he was joined by Graham, who by now had
left Reuters and had just signed on with United Press.

"Betty and I are traveling together through Honan, heading for
Hupeh and the Yangtze River," Belden wrote in his diary on August 27,
at the end of what he called a "hard day's trip." They were staying at the
Round and Abundant Inn between Loyang and Nanyang, he said, and
were planning to return to Chungking overland through the mountains.
"We are moving through military territory....Neither of us have passes, for
Betty lost hers some days ago and the time limit on mine has expired so
both of us are a bit apprehensive."

Belden said that his new traveling companion was "very pretty, very
earnest and very intelligent." He said she could adapt herself to any situation – "policemen, bandits, missionaries, hardship and rotten living conditions."

He said, moreover, that Graham could "sit down on the road and
swap stories with carters, eat Chinese gruel and sleep for nights on end in
bed-bug infested inns. Once in a while she lets out a good American growl
at policemen and special agents who are continually following us. But

always she has nothing but kindness and sympathy for the suffering people of this long-suffering country. And right now she knows about twice as much as most foreign correspondents about the life and blood and heart and soul of China's 'War of Resistance.'"

But Belden's love-charged relationship with Graham would soon take a turn for the worse.

In early September, they arrived at the headquarters of General Sun Lien-chung, the commander of the Kuomintang's 2nd Army Group, near Loyang. Stilwell aide Frank Dorn later complained that Sun was an alcoholic and frequently timid and indecisive, even though most historians consider the burly northerner to have been one of the Kuomintang's most competent generals, noting, for example, the critical role he played in the Chinese victory at Taierzhuang in the spring of 1938.

"Sun gave me quite a welcome the day I arrived," Belden wrote in his diary on September 10, "and [he] seemed quite pleased with Betty too."

But Graham had begun to grate on Belden's nerves. He said she was sarcastic and bitchy and was constantly whining and nagging and "hemming and hawing....I don't want it, or it makes no difference to me bullshit cropping up that I'm at last pretty well through suggesting anything at all....And then she rants at me about being disgusting – I use such naughty words. Whores always have such a delicate sense of morals about speech and manners....She's such a stupid, vicious little animal....I just wanted to get out....Good lord she is terrible."

By the time they had arrived in Loyang, in the summer of 1941, they were at each other's throats – even as fighting between the Chinese and the Japanese for control of the Chungtiao Mountains, which had reached its peak in May with a series of air raids by the Japanese, had subsided.

Slowly, as thousands of evacuees streamed back into the city, Loyang regained a sense of normalcy. Bomb damage was repaired. Shops reopened, with merchandize brought in from the countryside. Electricity was restored.

So-called traitors were blamed for the loss of the Chungtiao. Several men, probably peasants, were driven through the streets of Loyang in June before being executed in public. And the Kuomintang government in

Chungking announced that any general who allowed the Japanese to cross the Yellow River would also be done away with.

Another fall-out from the Chungtiao defeat was that an aggressive anti-Communist campaign was launched throughout Kuomintang-held China, led by the Chungking newspaper "Ta Kung Pao," which accused the Communist forces – still (at least in theory) aligned with the Kuomintang in a United Front against the Japanese – of having failed to attack the Japanese forces from the rear as ordered by the Kuomintang commanders.

On their arrival in Loyang, Belden and Graham were greeted by Graham Peck, a friend from Chungking the previous fall.

A large and gregarious man who found friends easily, according to John K. Fairbank, Peck had come to Loyang from Szechuan Province with Rewi Alley, a New Zealander who was a driving force behind creating the Chinese Industrial Cooperatives (CIC), also known as INDUSCO.

The aim of the INDUSCO movement, whose early supporters also included Americans Edgar Snow, Nym Wales (Helen Foster Snow), and Ida Pruitt, as well as a number of Chinese, such as Hu Yuzhi and Sha Qianq, was to create employment for workers and refugees through the establishment of small, self-supporting cooperatives, mainly in rural areas, that produced uniforms, blankets, and other army supplies to support the national "War of Resistance" against the Japanese. Both the Nationalist government under Chiang Kai-shek and the Communists under Mao Tse-tung initially supported the scheme.

Arriving in Loyang, Belden and Graham joined Peck at the local CIC, where he was staying. But because they were all foreign correspondents, their presence was not appreciated by the Kuomintang, which feared, legitimately, that the Americans would spread the news of Chungtaio defeat to the outside world, notably, the American people, whose financial support it desperately sought. So – officially, persona non grata – they moved from the CIC to the loess caves outside of the city, where they were harassed by the local police and advised to leave Loyang immediately because the Japanese might arrive any day and accuse them of espionage.

The Communists in Kuomintang-controlled Loyang, for their part, understood the importance of entertaining foreign guests, particularly Americans, because they were still under the impression that they could win the backing of the United States in their war against the Japanese.

Peck wrote in *Two Kinds of Time* that he, Belden and Graham attended a party one evening at the Communist offices in Loyang, which included dinner, a one-act play, an operetta, folk dancing and singing. He said that the play concerned a Japanese family that had turned "anti-imperialist" when their only son was killed in China.

"The drama ended when the bereaved mother, wailing pitifully, slowly left the empty stage to join a daughter who had already rushed into the Tokyo streets for an anti-war demonstration," Peck wrote.

After the evening's festivities, which ended with the singing of a half dozen war songs, the three Americans were taken to a briefing by the office commander, who, not surprisingly, described the Chungking battle from the Communist point of view. He criticized the Kuomintang for being overconfident, and he claimed that the Communist forces in the north – despite what the Kuomintang said – had attacked the Japanese supply lines precisely when and where the Chungking government had ordered, and that they had cut both major railways leading from Peking toward the Chungtiao Mountains. But the Kuomintang, he said, had ordered the attacks too late and too far north, hundreds of miles from the fighting.

The day after the party, Belden and a reporter from *Ta Kung Pao* sat down for an extensive interview with General Wei Lihuang, the Kuomintang commander-in-chief of the First War Area, who was obviously in an excellent position to know the truth behind the Communist claim that they had successfully cut off the Japanese supply lines to the Chungtiao. He also had much to gain from denying the claim. But surprisingly, he confirmed the accusation, and Belden put together a story saying so and sent it to the censors in Chungking for retransmission to INS. But the story would never see the light of day – a victim of the Kuomintang censors. A similar report by the correspondent for *Ta Kung Pao*" was also never published, and Peck wrote that he was told several years later it had been killed by the paper's editor-in-chief, Chang Chi-luan, an alleged associate of Chiang Kai-shek.

That, however, was not the only problem that Belden had. On September 10, he wrote in his diary that he had had it with Graham's erratic and tempestuous behavior and wanted to get away. "I got feeling so blue and melancholy last night that I had to go and sit by the door and rest my head against the wall," he wrote. "It seemed at least friendly. One could talk to it without getting slapped, snarled at, lied to and cheated."

The feuding fellow travelers, now heading south back to Chungking, spent the night of September 13 in Nanyang and left early the next morning powered by two "pullers" drawing two separate carts. "Our carts were very uncomfortable," Belden wrote. "Betty's was very narrow and my puller, a wide squat dwarf of a fellow, very dull, kept saying he couldn't pull me."

What the Chinese peasants may have thought about this ever-quarreling Western odd couple is anybody's guess. But the pair were clearly not yet ready to call a halt to their bickering. On September 15, Belden wrote that he had told Graham – after days of "nagging, pulling, demanding" – "to keep her mouth shut."

"She jumped up in a theatrical fashion," Belden wrote, "and rushed away with her cart. I finished shaving and soon caught up with her.... Later told her I was sorry." But she replied, he said, that "there are some things being sorry can't excuse."

A couple of weeks later, after they had made their way overland to Fancheng, in Hupei Province, they hired a junk to take them down the Han River – a tributary of the mighty Yangtze, which led to Chungking – and the couple had apparently come to some sort of truce.

Belden was in a good mood. It was a "marvelous day," he wrote, as they set off from Fancheng, and he and Graham lay on the deck. She told him about a movie she had seen, he said, called "Shanghai," with Loretta Young (1935). In it, Young plays an American beauty, Barbara Howard, who pursues a rickshaw-driver-turned-successful-industrialist, Dmitri Koslov, played by Charles Boyer, up the Yangtze Gorges.

On September 27, according to Belden, he and Graham sat in the prow of the boat and watched the sun go down. "Betty sat under 3/4 moon singing to herself. Romantic atmosphere....[We] studied her Chinese characters. It was nice."

The next day, the couple left the boat at [Liang-chu-kou on the Han River] and began walking south, with two Chinese carriers in tow. A few days later Belden wrote that the moon came up and Graham told him "how nice it was for me to take her for a moonlight stroll and said we would have to do it again when we get back to Chungking."

"The moon rose in the sky...and alone near it was a single star," he wrote. "Walking off the path around the peasants rice plots and into the dark green hills, I suddenly felt melancholy. Here after four years was what I had waited for....I was traveling under a moon with a young girl in exciting times. But there was no feeling of doing something together, of being close together in some big event. We were lose together behind the coolies looking at their backs. It was all so mechanical – no adventure, romance, no passionate understanding. I felt dreadfully lonely. I wanted to pour out my heart to someone and there was no one to pour it out to....This contradiction made everything seem sour. I fell behind to get away from the carriers and wished Betty was a different girl."

Belden said he kept looking back over his shoulder at the single star in the sky and thinking of all he had been through in 1937 and 1938.

"I thought of Lukouchiao [outside of Peking in July 1937] and down through Hopei and Shansi and how nothing stopped me from getting in the thick of things," Belden wrote, "and here I was going back [to Chungking] when I should be going forward going toward an army when I should be going toward the front lines once again getting feelings....I looked at the lone star in the sky and I felt that lonely."

Briefly recalling the trip in *China Shakes the World,* which was published in 1949, Belden said he had traveled through Honan and Hupei provinces in the summer and fall of 1941. But he did not mention that he had made the trip with Graham.

He said that, during the trip, he had witnessed the beginnings of a "catastrophic famine" that had been brought on by the malfeasance of the Kuomintang. "It was depressing to walk along the road day after day and see desolate land, fallow fields and empty houses, tumbling with decay," he wrote. "Since, in many places, there had as yet been no severe drought, I was puzzled to know whey the fields had been abandoned. Then peasants told me they had left their ancestral plots because Kuomintang tax collectors and requisition agents for Chiang Kai-shek's armies were demanding more grain from them than the land could possibly produce."

Belden said that he was approached daily by peasants "crying a new tale of woe" and at night by some county magistrate imploring him "to do something...before it was too late and they all starved to death."

He said he had tried to do something about the situation by writing a story that described the conditions that he had seen. Through it, he said, he hoped to raise awareness of the situation in the outside world and force Chiang Kai-shek – "through either shame or policy" – to act.

But "much to my disgust, but not surprise," he wrote, the Kuomintang censors said that they had received contrary information from missionaries in the interior ("who no doubt were not staring"), so they "completely censored" his dispatch.

"Yet from this famine I was supposed to have conjured up out of my imagination," he wrote, "several million farmers died....The people of Chiang Kai-shek's part of Honan did not die because God sent no rain; they died because of the greed of the men who governed them. Literally, they were taxed to death."

At the end of October, he and Graham arrived back in Chungking, where he immediately met with John S. Service, third secretary at the U.S. Embassy, to brief him on the trip. It was common practice at the time for U.S. diplomats and journalists to share information and to compare notes, particularly concerning military matters.

From a memo that Service wrote later detailing their conversation, it was clear that Belden, in fact, had not been spending all his time on the trip arguing with Graham but had also been gathering important intelligence concerning the economic, political and military conditions of the war-torn country.

Service wrote that he and Belden had been friends for some time and that the reporter, therefore, had talked freely with him. "Having his journal with him," Service wrote, noting that Belden had just returned to Chungking after about six months of travel through Szechwan, Shensi, Honan and Hupeh, "he referred to it continually for the actual details of incidents and conditions which he mentioned."

The memo, dated October 30, was sent to U.S. Secretary of State Cordell Hull with a cover note from the U.S. ambassador to China, Clarence E. Gauss. It arrived on his desk the day after Pearl Harbor.

Service wrote that Belden had traveled simply without official auspices, and because he was fluent in Chinese he had made it a practice of talking to farmers and villagers along the road and in the towns where he stayed. "These conversations, covering such points as grain requisition, food prices, local conscription practice, and so on, he took pains to record," Service wrote. "Although under some suspicion by the Chinese authorities for sympathy with the Chinese Communists, I believe that he is a good observer and has made the most of the rather unusual opportunity which his trip gave him."

According to Service, Belden had noticed a growing food shortage in the areas occupied by Chinese troops – "the importance of which had not been sufficiently realized." But he said that, on the other hand, imports from Japanese-occupied territory were surprisingly high, with the Japanese exacting a "squeeze" on the imports but permitting the traffic. Most of the imports were cigarettes, he said, and large quantities of luxury items, such as toiletry products, cloth and mirrors, were also allowed in. "No evident effort is made to stop this."

Morale among the Chinese troops, according to Belden, was good, and the fighting spirit at Ichang was particularly high despite the recent Japanese attack there, in which Japanese troops had used mustard gas to frustrate a Chinese assault, in violation of international law.

But no mention was made in the memo of the fact that Belden and Graham were the first to verify the claims of the Japanese gas attack at Ichang.

In *Still Time to Die* Belden reiterated what he had filed about the incident at the time for INS, saying that he had come "wandering down across the Yellow River plain, through the mountains to the Yangtze gorges" and had come upon a Chinese division in the midst of launching an attack against the Japanese-held Yangtze River port of Ichang.

"The attack was delivered with such cunning and dispatch that it would have succeeded but for one thing: the Japanese used gas," Belden wrote. "When I saw the Chinese soldiers rolling in agonized pain on the ground, with mustard-gas blisters big as tennis balls on their arms, legs and backs, when I saw and heard them moaning and crawling over the earth to succor each other and when I thought how without planes, guns, tanks or gas masks they had delivered their assault into the face of—this—then I knew that, despite the corruption, the treachery and the malevolent suppression, this race of people concealed within them a simple nobleness beyond all telling."

Time magazine reported in its November 11 issue that "pudgy-cheeked, moody Jack Belden" was the only reporter to verify the Chinese claims of the Japanese gas attack, and it called him the "ablest field correspondent assigned to the China war." It did not mention Graham.

The magazine said that, when the attacking Chinese broke through the Japanese defenses, the Japanese poured in gas shells from the flanks, and that one of the Chinese divisions participating in the attack had reported gas-related casualties as high as one-third of its total strength.

Belden told Service in their conversation in late October that morale among the Chinese civilian population varied widely. If food requisitions by the military were high, morale was low. But if the people had experienced an actual invasion by the Japanese, morale was high. The peasants around Ichang, for example, worked willingly and well in support of the troops, carrying the wounded back from the front. In parts of Honan province, however, where the Japanese had not yet been seen, the people were bitter and wanted the Chinese troops would move on.

Service said that Belden had also told him that he had seen little evidence during his travels of improved relations between the Kuomintang and the Communists. Officers who he had spoken with in Loyang had said that their main job was to suppress and punish members of the "traitor party," including the Communists. Medical supplies for the Communist Group Army (formerly the 8th Route Army) were also not being permitted safe passage, he said.

That Service considered Belden to be a friend is not surprising given that they were both – separately and together – attempting compile as complete a picture as possible of the fast-evolving military and political situation in China – one as a journalist and the other as a diplomat. They were also about the same age: Service was born in August 1909, Belden in February 1910.

But unlike Belden, Service was born in China (to missionary parents) and lived there until he was 15, learning to speak the local Szechwanese dialect and attending the American School in Shanghai. He then moved to the United States with his parents and graduated from Berkeley High School in California and attended Oberlin College in Ohio before returning to China in 1933 (the same year Belden jumped ship in Hong Kong) to begin what would become a long career in the U.S. Foreign Service.

Service was first posted at the American Consulate in Kunming, the capital of Yunnan, then was moved to the U.S. Embassy in Peking, where he met Belden and other Western journalists, including Owen Lattimore and Edgar Snow.

Over time, however, his reports back to the State Department in Washington, D.C., turned increasingly hostile toward the Kuomintang and Chiang Kai-shek. On his return to the United States in 1945, he was arrested and accused of jeopardizing U.S. national security by passing confidential U.S. government material to the editor of Amerasia magazine – a left-leaning publication devoted to contemporary Asian affairs. He was later cleared of the charges but was dismissed from the State Department in 1950 after Sen. Joseph McCarthy (R-Wis.) accused him of being a Communist.

Gauss testified in Service's defense at a Senate "loyalty" hearing in May 1950, saying that he was invaluable in Chungking and that he more than fulfilled his assignment to "cover the waterfront."

"His job was to get every bit of information that he possibly could," Gauss said. "He saw the foreign press people. He saw the Chinese press people....He associated with everybody and anybody in Chungking that could give him information, and he pieced together this puzzle that we had constantly before us as to what was going on in China, and he did a magnificent job."

Service later mounted a legal challenge of his dismissal from the State Department, and the U.S. Supreme Court eventually ruled in his favor, which led to his reinstatement at the agency. He died in Oakland, California, on February 3, 1999, at the age of 89.

While Service and Belden clearly enjoyed a close working and personal relationship over the years – beginning in the early 1930s, when they met in Peking, through late 1942 when Belden left for Europe – it is unclear to what extent Service had known and worked with Betty Graham. But they were probably fairly well-acquainted given that the American community in Chungking was relatively small during the time that they both lived there in 1941.

By then, moreover, Graham's life had already some twists and turns that may have been of some professional interest to Service. After arriving in China in 1936, then working for several months, she traveled to Korea where she soon landed in a Japanese-run jail, charged with espionage. On her release, she returned to Seattle. But in 1939 she again sailed for Shanghai and was soon driving a Red Cross truck into much-bombed Chungking, where she got a job with the Kuomintang government.

In 1942, she again returned to the United States (by way of India), this time to promote the cause of the Chinese Nationalists. While in Washington, D.C., she also covered the State Department for INS before moving to the Office of War Information in October 1944, where she served as a Far

East specialist, posted in San Francisco. But her heart was still in China, and she returned, yet again, in 1946.

Her old acquaintances, however, found her to be changed, saying that her sympathies now lay with the Communists. She was able to pick up some work as a free lance reporter, and she established some friendships with the Communist Party elite, which enabled her to scoop the other Western reporters in late 1946 with the news that Chou En-lai had walked out of a peace conference with U.S. General George C. Marshall.

This won her a job as a stringer for the Associated Press. But she soon left that job and headed off alone into heart of Communist-held China, traveling with the Eighth Route Army. In August 1948, she wrote home that she had had a "moving experience" listening to soldiers "pour out" their "pent-up grievance against the old society....[The] enemy was...a whole class of individuals, plus a class of Americans who were helping the feudal elements in China....Do you still wonder why we will win?"

In early 1949, after the Red Army had marched triumphantly in Peking, *LIFE* magazine correspondent James Burke saw her on a street in Peking bundled up in the quilted uniform of a Communist soldier or bureaucrat. He approached her, reminding her that they had met earlier. But she put him off with polite smile. Later, he tried to reach her at the telephone number she had given him but without any luck, and she did not respond to a message he had left.

In May 1950, she wrote to her family in Seattle saying: "We've all been upset by the news of Agnes Smedley's death ... by persecution....She died in exile from that great land of 'liberty and democracy' of yours.... No, don't ask me to return to such a life ...Whenever I hear from any of my progressive friends it's the same story. Persecution, false accusations, rigged juries, illegal court decisions....How can you want me to return to such a life? It would be like returning to a nightmare world. I am happy here in China and I don't want to leave this wonderful and invigorating place...."

But then, abruptly, in July 1950 she wrote home again saying that "new developments" had prompted her to consider returning to the States. "I have now rather definitely decided on returning," she wrote. But in

September she wrote that she was still "hunting for a ship." Then, in January 1951, with no word from here in the interval, her father received a delayed Christmas card from his daughter that said: "Sorry I could complete my arrangements....to be home for Christmas." A final letter delivered to the family in Seattle on Valentine's Day along with a cable from the Ministry of Health in Peking said in part: "Dear Dad...It seems pretty certain that I'll not be coming back so soon after all...."

The ministry cable said that Graham had died the previous night at Peking Central Hospital. "SHE WAS FOUND IN ADVANCED COMA AT 8 A.M. YESTERDAY AND INSTANTLY RUSHED TO HOSPITAL WHERE OUR DOCTORS WORKED HARD TRYING TO SAVE HER LIFE," the cable read. "COMPLETE INQUIRY IS BEING MADE...HER FRIENDS IN CHINA WOULD PREFER HER REMAINS WERE GIVEN FITTING BURIAL IN COUNTRY ...SHE LOVED SO WELL...." [1]

It is unclear exactly how Graham, at 34 years old, met her fate. But Hugh Deane, who knew her in Chungking, claimed that she had fallen in love with Alan Winnington, a left-wing British journalist who, like her, had accompanied the People's Liberation Army on its march into Peking. When he jilted her, Deane surmised, she committed suicide. Winnington died in East Germany in 1983, at the age of 73. [2]

LIFE magazine reported in its March 12, 1951, issue that Graham's fate "was even more tragic than that of" other left-leaning American reporters of the time, like Agnes Smedley and Anna Louise Strong. "For Betty Graham symbolized a new sort of American tragedy in its ultimate form," it said. "A young American intellectual, she had fallen in love with Communism; she was apparently her alien lover's captive when she died."

Chinese radio reported in March 1951 that Graham was interned at "the sanctuary of eternal repose" in the Western hills overlooking Peking – a reference to Babaoshan Revolutionary Cemetery, where Smedley's ashes were interned the previous year.

7

WITH "VINEGAR JOE" IN BURMA

On a sunny Sunday in early December 1941, General Joseph W. Stilwell and his wife were relaxing at their home in Carmel, California, when the phone rang with the news that Pearl Harbor had been attacked.

The next day, President Franklin D. Roosevelt, calling December 7 a "date which will live in infamy," asked Congress to approve a declaration of war against Japan, which it did, bringing the United States officially into World War II.

"Vinegar Joe" Stilwell, who was then commander of the U.S. Army's newly reactivated 7th Infantry Division at Fort Ord, was as shocked as everyone else. He believed that the Japanese might launch a surprise attack somewhere in Southeast Asia. But he did not foresee such an operation being launched more than 3,000 miles across the Pacific. On December 22, he was summoned to Washington, D.C., to discuss a possible new assignment. [1]

On his arrival in the nation's capital, Stilwell was told by the deputy chief of the War Plans Division – a former classmate of his at Fort Leavenworth's Command and General Staff College by the name of Dwight D. Eisenhower – that he had been selected to lead an Allied military operation in French West Africa, which had long been considered to be a possible jumping-off point for a Nazi attack on South America.

Over the next few weeks, while the plan was being fleshed out in the corridors of government, Stilwell began to worry about the fate of the Far East, where the Japanese had achieved a number of major victories in frighteningly quick succession – Guam and Wake; Hong Kong; Manila, Thailand.... And now they were threatening Burma, which separated China, already under siege by the Japanese, from India, an ally, to the West.

On New Year's Day, Stilwell met in Washington, D.C., with Army Chief of Staff George C. Marshall to discuss his concerns. He said later that their conversation had been all about "troubles in the Orient." [2]

After the meeting, Stilwell sent a memo to Marshall outlining his plan for U.S. engagement against the Japanese, arguing that the United States should begin by developing "maximum offensive power" in China involving one U.S. Army corps, at a minimum. Three weeks later he was named Commanding General of U.S. Army Forces in the China-Burma-India theater. [3]

The Japanese, meanwhile, were on the move in Burma, taking Moulmein in late January 1942 and threatening Rangoon, which fell on March 8. But Stilwell, who had arrived in China on February 25, was still stuck in Chungking discussing the details of his new assignment with Chiang Kai-shek and arguing that Burma could be rescued from Japan's grip by going on the offensive.

He said in his diary on March 6 that Chiang clearly was "fed up with the British retreat and lethargy" in Burma and was prepared to turn over command of the Chinese Fifth and Sixth Armies to him.

Later that day, Stilwell met Belden – an old and trusted friend from Stilwell's days as military attache at the U.S. Legation in Beijing (1935-1939)– along with F. McCracken Fisher, of United Press, to discuss the situation, and on March 11, when Stilwell flew to Burma to set up his headquarters at Maymyo, Belden went along.

In Maymyo – operating from the Baptist Mission Compound – Stilwell immediately went on the attack, ordering the Chinese Fifth Army's 200th Division to hold fast at Toungoo and the 22nd Division to advance.

The plan: to hold a line against the advancing Japanese between Toungoo and Prome, 150 miles north of Rangoon. [4]

Belden reported at the time that Stilwell also dispatched Major Frank Merrill to Prome to ask the commander of the British 1st Burma Corps, Lieutenant General William J. Slim, to join the attack.

"What is Stilwell's objective?" Slim asked Merrill. "Rangoon," he replied. "You tell Stilwell that he can count me in," Slim said. And so the attack was launched with an allied force consisting of Chinese, British, Indian and Burmese troops. [5]

Impatient as always, and eager to again see action at the front, Belden headed south from Maymyo, past Mandalay, toward Toungoo in car that Stilwell had made available to him. But halfway there, the car and driver were ordered back to Maymyo, leaving Belden stranded on the road in the middle of nowhere surrounded by Chinese soldiers.

Eventually, a Chinese general took him under his wing and invited him to ride with him to the front in a U.S. Army scout car packed with five soldiers armed with rifles and tommy guns. "This is not China," the general told Belden. "People are unfriendly."

Near Pyinmana, about 60 miles north of Toungoo, the car suddenly came to a halt. "An orange glow tinted the sky," Belden wrote in a cable to *Time* magazine, which had recently taken him on as a full-time correspondent. Japanese bombers, he said, had set the town on fire. "In the woods, tall, straight trees formed pillars in the column of fire, and stood trembling silently for a few moments, then crashed to earth," he wrote. "The whole town was going up in a great conflagration. The fire heated the steel of the scout car and we detoured around the lake, which reflected the fiery glow." [6]

The driver of the car was able to skirt the fire and find an opening in the flames, where the road turned, and out of nowhere a British captain – a liaison officer with the Chinese 96th Division – appeared and took them in a bus that he had commandeered to a makeshift "hospital" nearby, run by Gordon S. Seagrave, a Baptist missionary surgeon.

At the facility – a small stucco house surrounded by a wire fence – the British officer deposited Belden and five wounded Chinese soldiers he had picked up along the road.

"I peered through the fence with astonishment," Belden wrote later. "On the front and left side of the house was a small unroofed porch with a cement floor. On this porch, lit by a glaring gas-pressure lamp as if it were a stage, a strange tableau presented itself. In a group at one end of the porch, appearing to bend over something beneath them, were three young brown-skinned girls....Facing the girls and on the opposite side of a table between them was a white man, bared to the waist."[7]

On the table, he said, lay a waxen-faced Chinese soldier, half naked, with a jagged gash in his arm down which blood was pouring.

"As the white man made swift incisive cuts into his arm, the soldier stirred, his arm flew straight out into the air and blood streamed down one finger, which pointed at the girls like an accusing red arrow," Belden wrote. "They flew to his side, uttering little cries of sympathy and attempting to hold him down, but he writhed on the table, opened his eyes once, and moaned load enough for me to hear: `Ma! Ma!'"

Belden said that hearing those "universal words" – the same in Chinese as in English – and seeing that soldier struggling through a mist of torture and pain, he turned away.

When he turned back, he said, the white man – i.e., Seagrave – had picked up the soldier and was carrying him to a bare spot on the porch, which was now crowded with twisted human shapes. "Gently, like a mother, he laid him down and then picked up another soldier and put him on the table. Over his nose he placed a rag, and the soldier soon lost consciousness. The doctor then picked up another shape from the forms on the hard cement and placed it on another table table, alongside the first. When this man was under chloroform, he began operating on the first, alternating between the two and performing two operations at once."

Two more jeeps, meanwhile, pulled up behind Belden and deposited for Seagrave's care more Chinese soldiers they had collected from the side of the road.

"Is there anything I can do for you, Dr. Seagrave?" one of the drivers shouted over the fence. "My God," he replied, "get me some food. Some of these men haven't eaten for three days, and I have not a drop of food left in the house." Then, Belden wrote, Seagrave went back to work "with the sweat glistening over his bared torso and the flames forming an orange umbrella in the sky over his head."

Seagrave, a chain-smoking surgeon known to the Burmese simply as "Dr. Cigarette," was born in Burma to missionary parents in 1897. After medical school in the United States, at Johns Hopkins University, he returned to Burma with his wife in 1922, and they settled in Namkham in northeastern Burma. There, they ran a 100-bed hospital with a staff of two doctors and 11 native nurses who had been personally trained by Seagrave, providing medical care to anyone who happened to need it.

Unorthodox, outspoken and uncompromising, with something of Stilwell's caustic temperament and a distain for pretension, Seagrave had been assigned by the British to provide mobile medical support to the Chinese Sixth Army. After Stilwell arrived in in Burma in mid-March, however, he offered his services to the Chinese Fifth Army, which was under Stilwell's command, and Stilwell accepted the offer.

Immediately, Stilwell ordered Seagrave and his nurses to move their operation to the American Agricultural College, near Pyinmana, which was being run by Breedom Case, who, like Seagrave, was an American missionary born in Burma.

Working with Seagrave was another American, John Grindlay, a 1935 graduate of Harvard Medical School who had recently been at the Mayo Clinic in Minnesota.

Grindlay, who arrived in Pyinmana on April 1, had been in Asia since September of the previous year, serving as a first-lieutenant medical officer with the American Military Mission to China (AMMISCA), commanded by Brigadier General John Magruder. He was promoted to captain in early 1942.

"Another captain turned up today while I was matching nurses for blood transfusion," Seagrave told his diary. "Captain Grindlay trained in the Mayo Clinic....Looks just like a Mayo man, too!"

Grindlay's told his diary that he had reported to Seagrave in Pyinmana after a hot, dusty jeep ride from Maymyo, and that no sooner had he joined the unit than two truckloads of wounded Chinese soldiers – victims of Japanese bombing – also arrived compliments of the British Friends Ambulance Unit.

"One had two legs off at thigh and horrible burns," Grindlay wrote. "Sick at stomach. Scrub. Just started amputating the legs of this case when he died. Then I took one [with] shrapnel [wound in] buttock. Found it passed in front of sacrum. Opened belly–full of blood. Ten holes in p.i. [proximal ileum, i.e., the small intestine] and probably pelvic vein torn. Died." [8]

But while Seagrave and his team, which included forty Burmese nurses from his hospital at Namkham and an American dentist, Capt. John O'Hara, were caring for the wounded at their makeshift hospital near Pyinmana, the attack that Stilwell had ordered against the Japanese at Toungoo, 50 miles to the south, was not going well.

The 200th Division, whose commander, Major General Tai An-lan, had seen service in the Chinese victory at Taierchuang in 1938, was holding on bravely in Toungoo, according to Belden. But the 22nd Division was not up to the task to which it had been assigned, arriving at the scene of battle later than had been planned – "tired out, and with uncertain morale."

"Thus the first and last offensive tried by the Allies in Burma died almost before it was born," Belden wrote. [9]

Belden said that a sense of desperation was now setting in as the 200th Division – partially cut off by the Japanese in Toungoo – was forced on April 1 to retreat across the Sittang River, back to Yedashe, where it was met by the remnants of the retreating 22nd Division. [10]

"He had lived on the verge of death for almost five days," Belden wrote of General Tai, "with no sleep, little water and less food....At the commencement of the battle the 200th Division had about 8,000 men. On its return to the main Chinese line it had a thousand less....With red eyes and a grim, far-away expression on his face, [Tai] entered the little muddy depression where the 22nd Division headquarters was and in which men had anxiously been waiting for him, and was promptly hailed by his Chinese comrades as a hero."

But Tai brushed off the praise, telling Belden that he had lost the battle. "It's always hard to lose a battle," he said. "Let's remember the lessons, but forget the politeness." [11]

At Stilwell's headquarters in Maymyo, meanwhile, the mood in the American delegation was souring by the minute as the Chinese failed to hold the Prome-Toungoo line. Contempt for the Chinese and British, in particular, began to intensify, with the Americans saying that some British soldiers, in fact, had already deserted their units and were heading for Mandalay, hoping to escape Burma for China to the east.

Stilwell's aide, Lt. Col. Frank Dorn, said that the British were dispirited and tired; the Chinese were uncertain and frightened; and the Japanese were determined, merciless and cruel, torturing prisoners and killing the wounded. Water was also scarce and food was running out. [12]

For his part, Belden had especially tough words for the British, saying that the "meat of the matter" was that the British soldiers and diplomats in Burma were afraid and unable to draw the Burmese people into the war.

"By adopting a negative policy of repression and anti-fifth-column work instead of adopting a positive policy for the unleashing of the energies of the people against the invader," he wrote, "the British authorities, and in fact all members of the United Nations responsible for fixing policies, sealed the doom of the Allied Armies in Burma." [13]

Stilwell had also had it with the British, who, he said, did not seem to care that their empire was beginning to crumble beneath them. And he was miffed by Chiang's contradictory and/or capricious orders.

"Am I the April fool?" he asked in his diary on April 1. "From March 19 to April 1 in Burma, struggling with the Chinese, the British, my own people, the supply the medical service, etc. etc. Incidentally with the Japs."

The Japanese forces, in fact, were encountering little resistance as they raced north through Burma, and Belden said that the anti-Allied movement in the country was now gaining momentum. On the morning of April 4, without warning and unopposed, Japanese planes struck Mandalay.

"The pilots leisurely fixed the town under their sights, as a scientist fixes a bug beneath a microscope, pinned it to earth, and stabbed it with hundreds of explosive plummets," Belden wrote. "Out of each plummet rose a splash of flame; fires sprang out of wooden houses, and soon half of Mandalay was ablaze....Soon whole streets were roaring with an angry orange fire." [14]

Witnessing the raging nightmare, Belden said that the flames were so long that they reached out and licked the clothes off the people running in the streets. "[T]hey staggered down the hot roadway, like moving exclamation points of fire, collapsing, and dying where they collapsed," he wrote. "Others, singed and burned by the terrific heat, managed to escape the flames and stumbled on with agonized faces toward the city hospital, only to learn that its buildings had been demolished in the very first blow from the air." [15]

Belden was clearly horrified by what he saw as he made his way around the city with his colleague Darrell Berrigan, of United Press. He said that a tall man with a cigar raised to his lips and a smile like Goofy the Dog on his face leaned against a tree, "frozen dead like a figure buried in Pompeii." Another man sat on the ground with an umbrella over his shoulder in one hand, "his other hand gesticulating and his mouth open, killed in the act of saying something." [16]

At least four hundred people were killed in the raid and an untold number were injured. The city hospital and the railroad station were also destroyed, and the 18th-century Palace of the Burma Kings was smoldering. The Japanese had started the burning, Belden said, but the looters and the Burmese fifth-columnists finished the job. For twenty-seven days and nights, "the city was to burn, the fire never ceasing."

Depressed and exhausted, Belden returned to Maymyo with Berrigan. There, they found fellow correspondent Martha Gellhorn – but now without her husband, Ernest Hemingway, who had returned to the United States – working on a long piece for *LIFE* magazine. After dinner on April 9, the three Americans, along with the British photojournalist George Rodger drove to the Maymyo Country Club for a party in honor of the foreign women who were being ordered to leave Burma in light of the rapidly advancing Japanese. [17]

But the discussion, despite the festive mood, quickly turned serious, with Belden, Berrigan and Rodger telling Gellhorn that they were fed up with Burma and wanted to leave.

"I asked Belden what he thought of the American mission [in Burma]," Gellhorn wrote. "He said, 'God, they're good eggs! And Stilwell's a honey!'" But he and the others, she said, agreed that Burma was being overrun through inertia in India, obstinacy in England, ignorance in the United States. [18]

Gellhorn wrote that Berrigan, for his part, said that "war...is hell for a correspondent [especially] when your side is losing."

"You can't say how badly you're losing because that just depresses everybody and you can't tell why you're losing because that's either comfort or information to the enemy," Gellhorn quoted Berrigan as saying. "All you can do is wait until the whole thing is lost and then you file one big exciting story on the blowup, and then go to some other front."

The next day, Belden and Berrigan headed for the oil fields at Yenangyaung, southwest of Maymyo, which had supplied the fuel for the Allied campaign but were now about to be set on fire by the retreating British forces. On April 15, as the Japanese were breaking through the Allied defenses to the south and heading toward Yenangyaung, the order came.

"The glare from the burning oil inside five great storage tanks, each of them containing over a million gallons of crude oil, cast a yellow glow on the green trees hanging over the highway," Belden wrote, "and the air above the city was disturbed by five tremendous streamers of smoke that climbed to a height of nearly two hundred feet above the tanks, and in huge spiraling ribbons moved parallel to the ground for many miles." [19]

But as Belden and Berrigan were congratulating themselves on being the only correspondents left in Yenangyaung, a man ran up to them and as they inched their jeep past the abandoned British Club and shouted at the top of his lungs, "Road block!" From the darkness on the other side of their jeep came a whisper: "The Japanese have put a block across the road at Pin Chaung. We are cut off." [20]

Also cut off was the 1st Burma Division, under the command of British Major General Bruce Scott. On the morning of April 17, he was told that Allied tanks were attacking the road block and that his rear would soon be freed. But the attack failed, and hope soon gave way to the realization, Belden said, that they were all now in an "actual state of siege" on the Rangoon-Mandalay highway.

"The block at the Pin Chuang [river] had cut us off from our ammunition, medicines, and food and, worst of all, from the only available water save for the Irrawaddy River," Belden wrote. "[T]o break out of our predicament involved difficulties of a high order."

Scott ordered the group to disperse and to head south toward the main Japanese force, and in the mad rush of cars and trucks that ensued, Belden and Berrigan lost contact with the general as a squadron of Japanese planes found them and forced them to run for cover through 100-degree-plus heat and jagged gulches and up steep dusty hillsides. "That afternoon," Belden wrote, "I knew what it was to...lie panting on the ground and not care whether I was bombed or not," Belden wrote. "I learned what a swollen tongue really was, what in actuality were lips cracked so thick that it was painful to speak. For the first time I learned the real meaning of thirst."

Eventually, Belden and Berrigan caught up with Scott, who by then had asked General Sun Li Jen, commander of the Chinese 38th Division, to send in a rescue team to help break the blockade.

"We had to break through or die – die of either thirst or hunger," Belden wrote, "while being slowly cut to bits by an enemy whose campfires were at the very moment drawing closer around us." [21]

But his own personal courage was found to be lacking in the midst of battle.

"I lay by the side of the road, for the most part too witless and exhausted to move," he wrote. "I, for one, though I was engaged in no violent action, was completely done for. My ankles had swollen to twice their normal size, my legs were rent by painful cramps, and my whole body was limp and feeble. Above all, I could not stand the glare of the sun, which many time had me on the verge of fainting and made my breath come in little quick pants. I found it absolutely impossible to sit in the jeep, even though I had a battered hat of [Berrigan's] on my head and sometimes a blanket on top of that to cover me from the sun." [22]

He could not believe how helpless he felt, given all that he had been through in China. "Here I was," he wrote, "the experienced war correspondent, the tough guy who had gone through five years of war in China, tramping from the plains of Peiping to the mountains of Shansi and the guerilla areas around Nanking, undergoing every kind of hardship, subsisting on the barest kind of food, suffering every kind of danger, being surrounded and cut off by the Japanese four or five different times – here was I completely helpless, done in, almost without the physical guts to go on, while Berrigan, who had seen little of war, and [Reggie] Edwards [ministry of information photographer from Australia], who had never seen a battle before in his life, were marching about the road, making themselves useful, joking with the soldiers, watching the battle, and keeping their depressed spirits in decent check. And now they came and said a kind word, told me of the progress of the battle, sought to find me water – me, a wretched, feeble, useless creature who had no place and no value in this battle, who could offer no help and who could only lie there and wish it was all over."

For the rescue mission, Sun had offered up his entire division. But his commander, General Lo Cho-ying, allowed only a regiment of 1,121 men to take on the task, and for the next three days, a combined force of Chinese and British troops attacked southwards, inflicting heavy casualties on the Japanese and allowing the British 1st Burma Division to fight its way across the Pin Chaung river, where they were met by a Chinese relief column on April 19.

"A tide of overpowering joy flooded through my veins as I recognized the insignia of the Chinese Army," Belden wrote, "and I stood up, clenching my fist and wildly shouting: Chung Kuo Wan Sui!" Or "China Forever!" [23]

8

"WE'RE GETTING OUT OF HERE"

For the Allied forces following the rescue at Yenangyaung, the battle cry became "Hold Mandalay!" It was the junction of all the main roads and rail lines in the country, and all the telephone and telegraph lines also passed through the city. But by mid-April 1942 it was under siege. "Some junction," joked Frank Dorn to Stilwell. "The roads are jammed with refugees. The trains have quit running. And the electric lines have been cut by the Burmese."

Choking the streets of the city were rotting corpses, which were being gnawed on by black crows, mangy street dogs and stray pigs. "Yes," Stilwell replied to Dorn, "and it begins to look as if the British Army is about to run out on the whole damned mess." [1]

Even the war correspondents were fleeing to the north, to Shwebo, leaving only Belden, Berrigan, Dan Deluce, of AP, and William J. Munday, of the *London News Chronicle* to report the news from the front for people back home.

"When Berrigan and I escaped from Yenangyaung and reached the other side of the Pin Chaung," Belden wrote, "a few Gloucester soldiers had called to us: 'Good-by, Yank. See you in India.' And they were right. The whole campaign was rapidly falling apart, and all that was needed was a sudden blow to bring about a complete collapse." [2]

From April 22 to April 26, the Japanese had managed to take Taung-gyi and Loilem, southeast of Mandalay, and were quickly moving in on the key city of Lashio, with its large airfield. "The advance of this column was amazing," Belden observed. "It proceeded with such rapidity along the road that even radio intelligence reports could not keep up with it." [3]

It appeared that there was no stopping the Japanese advance, so it was decided to hold a conference of all Allied commanders at Kyaukse, 20 miles south of Mandalay, to set a strategy for future action.

On the morning of April 25, as Belden and Berrigan were lounging on the porch of the designated meeting house on the edge of town, the commanders began to arrive: General the Right Honourable Sir Harold Alexander, commander-in-chief of the allied armies in Burma; Chinese General Tu Li-ming, along with his chief executive officer Lo Cho-ying; and Stilwell. A bevy of aides – more than 20 in all – dutifully followed their bosses into the meeting.

It would not take long, however, for the group to decide to take the only path that was realistically open to them: a general retreat north of Mandalay.

Alexander's chief of staff, Major General T.J.W. Winterton, requested time to return to Maymyo to issue a formal general order in writing. "What for?" Stilwell asked. "We haven't time." Alexander agreed, saying that the movement of troops could not be delayed. "It'll be difficult to get some units out as it is," he said. "I'm afraid a few may be cut off." [4]

Belden said that, after the meeting, he and Berrigan quickly retreated to Maymyo, which by now was in a state of panic, with everyone associated in any way with foreigners, including servants, taking flight.

He said that there was also a shortage of food, and that he, Berrigan, Deluce and Munday were forced to capture chickens or stray pigs or whatever else they could find by forming a circle in the bushes. "No one was actually hungry," he said, "but much effort had to be made to get little food." [5]

The day after the meeting of Allied commanders in Kyaukse – on April 26 – Stilwell issued an order to move all American personnel and equipment across the Ava Bridge, which spanned the Irrawaddy River a few miles south of Mandalay, before dawn the next day.

On hearing the order, Belden grabbed a rifle, shouted good-bye to the headquarters staff and, throwing his luggage into his jeep, drove off to the press hostel to warn his colleagues. They agreed that they should leave as quickly as possible, with Deluce and Munday saying they would cross the bridge that night and Belden and Berrigan deciding to make for Stilwell's advance headquarters in Kyaukse.

Just after midnight the four reporters, plus Berrigan's Indian "bearer" Jimmie, headed off into the darkness in four separate jeeps. At a bend in the road leading to the Ava Bridge, they saw British forces already retreating by truck, and after hesitating briefly – wondering whether to take the relatively safe road over the bridge or the one leading south to Kyaukse – Belden and Berrigan decided to take the road to Kyaukse as originally planned.

The city of Kyaukse, in fact, had been heavily bombed the night before, and when Belden and Berrigan arrived after an all-night drive they found a deserted city except for hoards of retreating stragglers – Indian, Chinese and a few British soldiers – some of whom sat on the ground with a "dull, far-away look in their eyes, seeing nothing and comprehending less."

"There is something awesome and chilling in the atmosphere that is quite above and apart from the emptiness of the towns themselves," Belden wrote. "It is the retreating soldiery that lends an air of dread to such places. Some of them have a wild look in their eyes that seems to say: 'One word out of you and I'll kill you.' And others have that dazed appearance which just as clearly states: 'I don't care if you kill me.' Such a town was Kyaukse on the morning of April 27." [6]

Just outside the city, in a two-story stucco building, Stilwell had set up a small provisional headquarters, from which he would direct the retreat to the north. Resting, in addition to Stilwell, Belden and Berrigan, were several members of Stilwell's staff, including Major Frank Merrill and Stilwell's trusted driver Sgt. Frank Astolfi.

Belden said that Astolfi was a "raw-boned, six-foot-two ex-butcher boy" who had joined the army when his boss had refused to give him a raise.

"Astolfi was a queer case," Belden said, noting that he repeatedly asked Belden and Berrigan to write about him. "It was funny the way he talked. He seemed half conversing with himself."

"The Army gets me," he told Belden. "Before, I used to feel I was free, and if anyone had talked to me then like they do in the Army now, I would have smashed them in the face. I don't know what it does to you – I suppose it teaches you a lot and makes a man out of you – but somehow it twists you and tears you....I don't know what it is. Ever since I've been out here there's something eating me, something happening to me. Sometimes I don't feel just right...."

Clearly intrigued by Astolfi, Belden said that, for him, it was embarrassing to look at this hulking boy from Plains, Pennsylvania, with his twisted facial expression and only twenty-two years old. He seemed to be on the verge of tears. "Life, the war, the East, the American Army – something – was just too much for him," Belden wrote. A month later, he put a bullet through his head to end his misery. [7]

The British, meanwhile, were planning to blow up the Ava Bridge at midnight on April 30, so Stilwell ordered the immediate evacuation of his staff from Kyaukse to ensure their safe passage across the Irrawaddy River. He conceded that the Japanese were giving the Allied forces "a bad licking." [8]

Late the night of April 28, as Stilwell and the others, including Belden, approached the mile-long structure, which was being prepared for demolition, they spotted a deserted police station.

Stilwell and Dorn looked at each other and grinned like scheming schoolboys. "Go on," the general said to his aide. "Give it the works. I know darned well you're itching to do it....For once in your life, you can set fire to a police station without going to jail. Hurry up. We have to get moving."

Knocking over a kerosene lamp, Dorn set fire to a pile of fuel-soaked paper and within minutes the small building went up in flames. "Thus," he wrote many years later, "we thumbed our noses at Burma, the Japs, the war and all the frustrations of the past few weeks."

Belden said it was dawn when they drove across the bridge. "The pink sky threw long shadows across the Irrawaddy swirling far below us," he said. "As we crossed, I felt as if we had put a barrier between us and the Japanese." [9]

The road on the other side of the river, however, was clogged with trucks, carts, troops and thousands of native refugees, along with tens of thousands of defeated and fleeing British troops. It took seven hours to make the 70-mile trip from Mandalay to Shwebo.

Belden said that, in the wake of the retreating Allied armies and the advancing Japanese forces, lay a wilderness of destruction, "a veritable wasteland of ruin."

"Every town for a distance of two hundred miles on the two highways up the Sittang and Irrawaddy river valleys leading to Mandalay was by now completely burned to the ground," he wrote. "Pyinmana, Pyawbwe, Meiktila, Magwe, Kyaukse, and dozens of pretty market towns, jungle cities, and river marts set amid groves of trees like oases in the desert heat of Burma had been wiped off the face of the earth and now no longer existed except as place names."

Barely a building remained standing. "Trees had been burnt to ashes and covered the ground with a black soot, or stood like burnt matches of purest charcoal," he wrote. "Everything was a graveyard, and in the graveyards sat Burma's vultures and buzzards picking on the corpses of towns.... The Japanese Army had blazed a trail of conquest with fire....Mandalay was no longer a city, but a field of tile and charcoal." [10]

The head of the American technical mission in Burma, James Wilson, was caught in his car during the final Japanese bombing of the city and was killed seeking shelter. Another American, Tommie Thompson, a young mechanic working for the Chinese, later found his compatriot's body, along with that of a British oil executive, and while he was digging a hole to bury the two men, a figure emerged from the shadows and raised a long knife to cut off the ring finger of one of the corpses. Calmly picking up his machine gun, Thompson shot and killed the looter, then returned to digging the grave for Wilson and the British executive, who he buried side by side. [11]

The Japanese, meanwhile, continued their attack, bombing and strafing the American compound and the surrounding area at Shwebo shortly after Belden, Berrigan and Deluce arrived and killing dozens. Among the injured was Berrigan's boy Jimmie, who was taken to a hospital but never found when Berrigan returned to visit him later that day. [12]

Dorn said that the complete collapse of the Allied forces now appeared to be at hand, as the Japanese captured Lashio, which protected the only road to China, and moved quickly to take Hsipaw and Bhamo. After Alexander ordered the evacuation of all of Burma, Stilwell told his staff: "It looks like we're getting out of here. To India for most of you. A plane is on the way now, but it can't carry all of us. I'm going to Myitkyina. That's where most of the Chinese troops will be, and I belong with them." [13]

Belden said that an estimated twenty thousand refugees were already pouring across the Irrawaddy River near Shwebo, heading for India, although there was no solid information on where the roads, if they existed at all, might be. The British had been in northern Burma for nearly sixty years, but maps were incomplete or inaccurate.

The lack of information about roads consequently placed a high premium on jeeps, which could negotiate any type of cart track or path, and Berrigan and Deluce decided that they would use theirs immediately to escape the advancing Japanese.

Several days later, on their arrival at the British base in Imphal, India, someone questioned whether they, in fact, had actually made the journey by jeep, pointing out there were no roads in the area that they supposedly traversed. "Shhhh! Not so loud," the *Chicago Daily News* quoted one of them as saying. "Our jeep hasn't found out about roads yet, and we don't want to spoil it."

It was the last time that Belden and Berrigan would see each other.

Born and raised California, Berrigan had fallen into reporting as a profession in much the same way that Belden had. In 1939, at 23 years old, he took a job as a merchant seaman after attending college in Bakersfield, washing up basically broke in Shanghai, where he talked his way into a reporting job with UP. Soon, he was setting up a UP bureau in Bangkok. But in early December 1941 when Thailand surrendered to the Japanese and declared war on the Allies, he was hustled out of the country by Thai friends concerned about his safety.

For the next three years he reported from Asia. Edgar Snow, who worked and traveled with him in the Philippines, called him "irrepressible" – someone who had a "gift of friendship for all the strays of Asia." [14]

His series of "I-was-there" reports for UP on the British retreat from Burma were particularly compelling. After the war, he returned to Bakersfield to spend time with his ailing mother. But the lure of the Far East was too strong, and, having quit UP, he returned to the region, where he made a modest living as a freelance reporter from his base in Bangkok, writing for *The Saturday Evening Post*, *The New York Times* and other media. "I went back to the U.S.," he once said, "but I could not get un-Oriented."

At 41, and still in Bangkok, he acquired a local, English-language weekly newspaper, *Bangkok World*, in 1957. It had been launched by Thailand's police chief and deputy interior minister, General Phao Sriyanond, who hired Berrigan initially to edit the publication after seeing an article he had written claiming that Phao, in addition to being the country's top cop, was also its top opium smuggler.

Impressed with Berrigan's reporting skills – and just before being kicked out of the country following a coup d'etat – Phao put aside enough money for Berrigan to run the paper until the relatively young American could scrape enough money together to buy a controlling interest in the product, which he did.

Quickly, the *Bangkok World* became what *Time* magazine in 1958 called a national institution and "one of the genuinely cultured pearls of the East" – despite the fact that most of Berrigan's reporters could not speak or write English very well.

Returning to the office after covering a story, a reporter would be asked where he had been and the reporter would reply: "We go Sanam

Luang [site of an election rally]." Berrigan would then ask: "What did you do?" The reporter would respond: "We look all the Sanam Luang." Berrigan would press the issue further: "Did you see something?" And the reporter would end the exchange with: "Yes, but I don't know what."

Yet Berrigan would later insist that putting out the newspaper each week was by far the most satisfying work he had ever done. [15]

Part of the satisfaction, he said, came from writing a column six days a week on subjects as varied as the heat in Thailand ("A neighbor's pig was unwise enough to walk into the sun, and the sun rendered him down to a shoat.") and the joy of ignoring the dictates of a clock ("We sit here thinking we have plenty of time because the sun is where is is, and the shadow of our pencil is falling at the plenty-of-time angle.").

In 1958, Peter Arnett, a 23-year-old aspiring journalist who would later win a Pulitzer Prize for his reporting from Vietnam, was hired by Berrigan to report for the *World*. By then, according to Arnett, Berrigan had become "a touchstone for all American journalists who were passing through the Orient and needed an experienced brain to pick and hospitable company to enjoy." [16] And indeed the long line of visiting heavyweight American reporters was impressive: Snow, Teddy White, Keyes Beech, Robert "Pepper" Martin, Tillman Durdin and others.

But in the fall of 1965, tragedy would strike. On October 4, the *Bangkok Post* – a rival to the *World* – reported that Berrigan's body had been found in the back seat of his car, which was parked only 30 yards or so from his house in central Bangkok. He had been killed by a single bullet to the back of his head.

9

THE WALKOUT

The options facing Stilwell in early May 1942 were not good, and they were growing worse by the minute. His initial plan was to head north from Shwebo to Myitkyina by train, truck, jeep or whatever other means possible to meet up with the Chinese and regroup.

But the situation was becoming increasingly dire, leaving Stilwell with little room for maneuver. "It's a great May Day," he said to Belden. "Down with everything. Down with everybody." [1]

In the east, the Japanese had captured Lashio, closing off the only highway to China, and they were moving rapidly toward Bhamo and Myitkyina, where the airfield was still operational, with the aim of preventing the allies from escaping to the north and east. They were also making gains in the west, reaching the confluence of the Chindwin and Irrawaddy rivers by early May. Their ultimate objective was clear: to bottle up the British, Indian and Chinese forces in the malaria-ridden jungles of northern Burma in what Belden called a "death embrace."

"[The Allied Armies] were being enclosed in a smaller space," he wrote, "the hole of escape was narrowing, and the noose was being gradually drawn tighter."

The allies, therefore, had no other choice than to begin two separate marches to escape the "rough edges of this noose across their necks," as

Belden put it, with the British and the Indians heading west toward India and the Americans and the remaining Chinese, under Stilwell, heading north along the Mandalay-Myitkyina railway in a bid to beat the Japanese to Myitkyina and open a window of opportunity to decide where and when to establish a new base of resistance.

For Stilwell, a trip upstream on the Irrawaddy River would be too slow, and there was no known highway leading north along the Mandalay-Myitkyina railway, which was hopelessly jammed with wrecked and derailed locomotives and railcars. So, in the meantime, as he contemplated his options, he ordered a plane to take the bulk of his staff out of the country and on to India.

He sent the order initially to General Henry H. (Hap) Arnold, commanding general of the U.S. Army Air Forces, who in turn relayed it to Colonels Caleb V. Haynes and Robert L. Scott Jr., commander and chief executive officer, respectively, of the new Assam-Burma-China Ferry Command, at the Yunnanyi airfield in China. It said, "proceed immediately receipt this message transport aircraft vicinity Shwebo Burma effect evacuation Stilwell and staff most urgent acknowledge." [2]

Belden, on hearing that an aircraft would be coming, began composing a message he would send on the plane back to the editors at *Time* in New York. [3]

"This is probably my last message," Belden wrote. "The Japanese are driving with incredible speed, swinging wide of both our east and west flanks and somehow we have got to get the troops out of this closing-in trap." He said that the roads were clogged with thousands of refugees, and that the Japanese had advanced some 350 miles in two weeks, or about 25 miles a day. "All about me is utmost misery. Roads are lined with belongings abandoned by refugees, 20,000 of whom crossed the Irrawaddy [River] only yesterday, hoping to get to India, but their chance is very slight. Evacuation to Bhamo via river route is practically useless with the Jap capture of Lashio."

"Must go," he wrote. "Goodby." [4]

As he was typing, he heard the sound of an airplane overhead and then shouts of joy from the Americans. He ran outside, looked up and saw a green Douglas C-47 (DC-3) circling to land as the headquarters mess officer sang "God Bless America!"

Col. Haynes, the plane's pilot, told Stilwell after landing on Shwebo's gravel runway that the Japanese were preparing to launch yet another air raid in the region and that he had to leave immediately.

Belden handed his hastily written message to Col. Frank Roberts, an intelligence officer on Stilwell's staff, and asked him to deliver it to the censors in Calcutta. Then Stilwell approached him and asked him if he wanted to leave on the flight out with the rest. "Are you going?" Belden asked the 59-year-old three-star general. "No," Stilwell replied. "Guess I better stay, then," Belden said. [5]

Later, he summed up the overall situation in Burma on May 1 as the overloaded C-47 lifted off the runway at Shwebo and headed west. "In January," he said, "the problem of the war had been how to get out of Moulein; in February, how to cross the Sittang; in March, how to get out of Rangoon; in April, how to get out of Yenangyaung; by the beginning of May, the problem was how to escape from Burma itself." [6]

Exactly how that escape would occur, however, was still unclear. Stilwell's transportation officer, Col. Paul L. Jones, had spent three days personally trying to move the stalled railway equipment off the tracks with a crowbar. He had also noted that all the river boats were sunk or had disappeared – to which Stilwell replied that, therefore, the escape would have to be made by road. Reminded that there were no roads, he said, "Then, dammit, we'll go by track or trail."

Major Frank D. Merrill had already explored one cart path by jeep through a dry bamboo forest for fifty miles north and reported that it might be passable. But beyond that, he said, it was unknown territory.

On the morning of May 1, Stilwell's small caravan of vehicles headed north on the road from Shwebo to Zigon, some 30 miles away, with Merrill's jeep in the lead, followed by Stilwell's sedan, driven by Frank

Dorn; another sedan carrying Major General Franklin Sibert and Col. Willard Wyman; and a third sedan with Col. Robert P. Williams, the senior doctor.

Following in a column were three or four jeeps that had been commandeered in the streets of Shwebo the day before, along with a radio pickup and nine trucks interspersed with more jeeps carrying the Seagrave medical unit, baggage and rations. A truck carrying oil and gas held up the rear.

Dorn counted about eighty men and women in all: twenty-eight American officers, enlisted men, doctors and mechanics; one American reporter (Belden); nineteen Burmese nurses; a Chinese guard of sixteen; seven British Quakers from the ambulance unit; eight or nine Malay, Indian and Burmese cooks and helpers. [7]

After reaching Zigon at sunset, the Stilwell party spent the night camped on a grassy slope by a small stream, and on the morning of May 2, "with the Japanese seeking to cut us off," it headed off on what Belden called that "rutted cart track in that burning, arid desolate country.... [W] e struck northward, following the railway, moving without information of the enemy and driving toward an undetermined goal." [8]

Get in behind me, Jack, with your jeep," Merrill called to Belden. "I'll lead the way, and you keep the column closed up." [9]

By 9 a.m., they had only made five miles. But by 7 p.m. they had reached Pintha, and by 9:30 p.m. the next day they were in Wuntho, having made roughly 100 miles in two days, causing the Americans, according to Belden, to develop a "profound affection" for their jeeps.

"Ugly, ineffectual-looking green boxes on wheels," he wrote, "they proved themselves the salvation of our column, ferreting out pathways through woods, pulling sedans out of ruts, hauling trucks through streams and up slopes too steep for them to negotiate under their own power, and rushing back along the track, bringing aid and succor to other stricken cars. All in all, we decided they were the toughest, handiest all-purpose car yet built, admirably suited to war and especially adapted to the primitive roads and tracks of Asia." [10]

On May 4, Jones reported to Stilwell that the railroad north was still jammed and impassable, noting that fourteen railway cars somewhere south of Myitkyina had been let loose down a grading and smashed into a bridge and killed a number of people, either through sabotage or careless-ness. [11] "Hell," Stilwell wrote in his diary. [12]

After hearing Jones' report, Stilwell called a meeting of the Americans to tell them that he had decided, rather than to turn westward, to keep heading north toward Neva and perhaps as far as Indaw, where the party would come out above the Japanese and could make their way west toward the Chindwin River and across to India. But he said that there was still some "small hope" of getting around the railway blockade and keeping to the original plan of heading to Myikyina.

From the start of the trek north, Stilwell had insisted on the need to hurry since the Japanese were in a position to take Bhamo and head toward the Mandalay-Myitkyina railroad in an effort to cut them off the while continuing to threaten their rear.

"Disintegration at Shwebo," Stilwell wrote in his diary on May 4. "Chinese out of control."

Belden said that the younger Americans in the group – to ease their discomfort – spoke incessantly about Coca-Colas, ice cream sodas and the everyday luxuries available in the United States. "But all this meant noth-ing to me," he said, "as I had not been home in nine years." [13]

On May 5, four days after leaving Shwebo, the Stilwell party, which now numbered around 100, experienced what Jones called a "rough river crossing" near Meza over a "shaky" bamboo bridge. "We lost one truck in the river," he told an interviewer in 1992, "[and] we were only a little ahead of the mobs of refugees and deserters that were clogging the roads everywhere in Burma."

Belden described the scene a bit more eloquently, saying that the road to India on the night of May 5 was "flooded by the ebb-tide of the British Empire."

"Officials, refugees, soldiers were pushing through the dust in columns and groups," he wrote, "trampling on the grass beside the road, knocking over children, stumbling on wounded, jumping into halted trucks, streaming, swirling, and ebbing westward." [14]

On the night of May 5, after passing through Indaw and turning west, the group made camp eight miles beyond the village of BanMauk. The next morning they got what Stilwell called a "late start" at 3:30 a.m. "Lost four trucks yesterday and one sedan," he said, "but [we] have the food and the jeeps and the party is together, and still ahead of the deluge [of refugees]." [15] But later that day they were forced to abandon what trucks they had left after only the jeeps were able to make it across the flimsiest bamboo bridge just east of Magyigan.

"We are off the main refugee route," Stilwell reported. "We are ahead of the Chinese horde....If we push hard we can make it."

In the afternoon of May 6, Stilwell assembled the group for a pep talk, telling them that the plan was now to walk or ride in jeeps along and in the shallow Chaunggyi River, then transfer to rafts at Maingkaing on the Uyu River, which they would use to float down to Homalin, where they would cross the Chindwin River into India.

The group formed a circle, with Stilwell in the middle wearing a light khaki windbreaker, khaki pants and army boots. On his head he wore a battered, flat-brimmed campaign hat from World War I. A cigarette-holder with a burning cigarette dangled from his mouth, and he was chewing gum. [16]

Belden described the group in a chained circle as "American, Englishman, Chinaman, Burman, Indian, Chin, Karen, Kachin, Malaysian, Anglo-Indian, Anglo-Burman, half-breeds from all of Asia. A motley crew. Generals, colonels, young privates, radioman, mechanic, cook, servant, dishwasher. American preacher, British Quaker, Karen nurse. Men, women, and a dog."

Stilwell knew most of them except several who were "filthy, unshaven, emaciated, and tired-looking." British commandos, it turned out. "Where did you come from?" he asked. "Just picking up a ride, huh? I don't mind you hopping a ride, if you only come and ask first." He glared at them for a minute or two, then asked, "Got any rations?" There was no answer. But Stilwell let them stay, bringing the total number in the group to 114. [17]

"The bridge ahead can only take jeeps," Stilwell said. "We will abandon the transport here. We will stay together in one group. But we must have better discipline."

He said that, in particular, they had to be cautious with the food. "We don't know what is ahead," he said. Rations of porridge, rice, corned beef, and tea would be pooled. And he ordered the assembled men and women to discard whatever baggage they had and keep only what they could carry on a four-day march. He said that they may be able to take a couple of jeeps to Homalin – out of the eleven that they now had – but clothes and other personal items would have to be shared or thrown away. Weapons and ammunition, of course, would be retained.

"By the time we get out of here," Stilwell concluded, "many of you will hate my guts but I'll tell you one thing: you'll all get out." [18]

The clearing where Stilwell had addressed the group, meanwhile, quickly took on the appearance of a rummage sale. "Everything is a kaleidoscopic, colorful mess," Belden wrote. "Pink brassieres hang on thorns, Oxford-gray pants like on top of olive-green car radiators, gray steel helmets tumble in the weeds. Whisky bottles, whose presence heretofore has been unknown, mysteriously disappeared. Heads are tilted back, the bottles emptied, thrown away. Blankets full of cigarette tins are opened; they are bought and sold, traded for a pair of khaki shorts....Bulky belongings thud onto the ground, lighter things rain through the air, catching on the branches of bushes....Only the Chinese have nothing to throw away." [19]

That evening, Stilwell sent a radio message to the War Department in Washington, D.C., via Chungking, saying that the 100-plus party was heading for Homalin and Imphal. "We are armed, have food and map, and are now on foot fifty miles west of Indaw. No occasion for worry....Will endeavor to carry radio farther, but believe this is probably last message for a while. Cheerio, Stilwell."

But another message, this one to Major General Lewis H. Brereton, commander of the American Tenth Air Force, in New Delhi, which was under Stilwell's command, took on a more ominous tone: "Hope to make Homalin May Tenth. If possible, send five hundred lbs of food from Imphal by carriers to meet us at Homalin. India govt. should be warned rice, police, and doctors urgently needed by refugees on all routes to India from Burma. Large numbers on way. All control gone. Catastrophe quite possible. End." [20]

Then, Stilwell ordered the bulky radio transmitter, which weighed no less than 200 pounds, to be destroyed and the codes and file copies burned to lighten the load and to ensure that allied communications would not fall into the hands of the Japanese if they were to beat the party to Homalin, as they might. He said the Japanese were already making their way up from the south in gunboats on the Chindwin. He told Belden, however, that the greatest danger facing the group in the hot, insect-infested jungle was the dual threat of rain and the shortage of food. [21]

From Magyigan, as they set off on foot early on May 7, having been forced to abandon their jeeps, Stilwell's rag-tag party of escapees now comprised, according to Belden, 18 American officers and five enlisted men; Seagrave's medical unit of two doctors and 19 nurses; 16 Chinese soldiers; seven members of the British Friends Ambulance Unit, who had worked with Seagrave in Pyinmana earlier in the year; nine Indian, Malayan and Burmese cooks and porters; several stray British officers and civilian refugees; Rev. Breedom Case, an American Baptist missionary and president of the Agricultural College at Pyinmana; various stragglers; and, of course, Belden himself, the only correspondent on the trip. [22]

"Hard going in the river all the way," Stilwell reported in his diary on May 7. "Cooler. All packs reduced to ten pounds."

But soon, heat exhaustion would claim several members of the group, including Col. William H. Holcombe, who had to be revived with ammonia crystals after falling out of line, and Merrill, a West Point graduate. Staggering, Merrill had fallen face down into the mud, half in the water and half on the bank, apparently a victim of a heart attack. He would recover, but Stilwell was obviously concerned. "Christ, but we are a poor lot," he wrote.

The next day, arriving in Saingkyu at 10:15 a.m after several hours of walking, Stilwell expressed frustration with the physical prowess, or lack thereof, of his motley charge. "Limeys' feet all shot. Our people tired. Damn poor show of physique." But he would also add: "Merrill and Holcombe better."

At the urging of Col. Williams, his chief medical officer, Stilwell therefore decided that they would not walk during the hottest part of the day.

Capt. Jones reported on May 7 that the trail had crossed and re-crossed small streams and that the party spent more time wading in water than walking on land. His ingrown toenails bothered him so much that he walked barefoot part of the time – a move he paid for a couple of days later with debilitating foot pain. Leech bites had also caused weeping ulcers to erupt on his legs.

Belden said that the bow-legged Stilwell, leading the long column through the shallow water, counted out 105 steps to the minute, "with men and girls stretched out in single file behind him as far as the eye could see – a magnificent sight." [23]

Seagrave's nurses, he said, were the perfect companions, and he began to fall in love with them, "not singly, but as a group." Their high-pitched, girlish voices were frequently raised in song and echoed through the cliffs enclosing the stream provided relief in moments of sagging morale and fatigue. Aside from Stilwell's dogged perseverance, he said, the nurses were the sole source of "invigorating influence" on the march. [24]

Late in the afternoon of May 9, the party reached the village of Maing-kaing on the Uyu River – a larger body of water than the Chaunggyi – where Stilwell had hoped to send his people downstream to Homalin and the Chindwin River for the crossing into India. But when they arrived in Maingkaing, only three rafts had been prepared on orders from the village chief, who had been advised of the need for water transportation. Six more were needed, and promised by the following morning. "Had a swim," Stilwell wrote. "We can start tomorrow."

At mid-morning on May 10, after the nurses had installed bamboo roofs on the rafts – now numbering thirteen – to protect the group from the tropical sun, the flotilla pushed off. "Nice ride," Stilwell reported, "but too damn slow." [25]

Capt. Jones said that, instead of drifting speedily down the river, the groups had to pole in many places to achieve the forward momentum necessary to make any progress at all. "Poling a boxy, home-made raft on a sluggish river under the hot, Burmese sun," he said, "is the kind of work that could cause a man to give up soldiering."

All night they poled and pushed their way down the Uyu, which wound through a series of bends but then straightened out on May 11 and found its way between two narrow sandbars, where the party now suddenly spotted a plane flying low overhead. At first, they feared it was a Japanese bomber but on a closer look it bore the red and blue markings of the British Royal Air Force.

"The drone of a plane sent us scuttling for cover," recalled Martin Davies, a member of the British Friends Ambulance Unit, "and American tommy guns pointed skywards. But as it approached low, I could see that it was a [twin-engine] Vickers Wellington. I shouted the news out, and the guns were tentatively lowered and everyone ran out of cover and waved, and from the plane came tumbling sacks and sacks of food. My former life in the aircraft industry had, at last, come in useful." [26]

Belden said that this sudden and somewhat unexpected assistance from the outside world was like a shot of adrenalin, raising the spirits of men and women alike, who now believed that a rescue party would indeed be meeting them at Homalin.

But on their arrival at Homalin on May 12, they found nothing. "No one in Homalin," Stilwell reported. "Telephone office shut. Suspicious." [27] No messages came in response to the radio message he had sent several days earlier. And no food and no one waiting for them.

For another three miles, stumbling over tree roots and stones in the dark, the group walked toward the Chindwin River and camped for the night at a Buddhist temple above Homalin, depressed and disappointed that their hope of rescue had turned out to be a mirage.

To lighten the load he was carrying, moreover, Belden was forced to discard his ground sheet and his treasured correspondent's typewriter, keeping only a blanket, an extra pair of shorts and a musette bag with a shaving kit and his notes on the Burma campaign.

"I look sadly at my typewriter," Belden said. "Soldiers are court-martialed when they thrown away their weapons, but this is my weapon, effectual as it may be, and I hate to see it go." [28]

Traveling day and night had also taken its toll. Three cases of dysentery and three cases of malaria had taken hold. Many in the group had developed skin diseases and streptococci infections. Even Seagrave had fallen ill: his ankles and feet had become corroded with sores brought on by a wounded soldier's blood dripping on him. [29]

Also negatively affecting the morale of the group was the prospect of scaling the Naga Hills on the other side of the Chindwin River in India, which they could clearly see ahead of them from Homalin, with their numerous passes of 7,000 feet or more.

"All of us on seeing the mountains this afternoon have been taken a little aback at their seeming endlessness, at the range upon range of peaks, fading off into the distance," Belden wrote. "It is bitter to think you have arrived at the end of the trail only to see that trail winding out of sight on the other side of the Chindwin, into the deep jungle and across those steep and forbidding-looking mountains....It is bitter, but what else is there to do but go on? It is not heroics that leads us on, but only a desire to escape." [30]

But escaping would first mean crossing the swiftly flowing, three-quarter-mile-wide Chindwin River without mishap – a formidable challenge for a party of more than 100, whose resistance and morale had been whittled down by more a week of treacherous travel through the Burmese jungle. The Rev. Breedom Case, looking out over the river and then turning back to Stilwell, said, "Now we have come to the Red Sea." [31]

Psychologically and strategically, the whole journey, in fact, had been aimed at the river because it was the most dangerous barrier lying between the group and India, and it was where the Japanese most likely would seek to cut them off.

But just then, the "miracle of the Chindwin," as Belden put it, appeared around a bend in the river. As Case spoke, several dugout canoes and behind them a kind of sampan or junk slid up in the water beside the beach. On orders from Stilwell, everyone fell in line, and they boarded the canoes six at a time before being shuttled across the river quickly and without incident.

Still lying ahead, however, were the Naga Hills, which were possibly inhabited by head-hunting tribes known as Nagas that plied their trade when one of their members wanted to take a wife. Belden found this to be a "queer impulse to mayhem." He also noted that while the Nagas apparently did not see anything wrong with stealing someone's head every so often, their punishment for the theft of anything else was death. He suggested that perhaps the Stilwell-led group could make a deal with the head-hunters: exchange the heads of the more unpopular members of the group for food or whatever else the Nagas had to offer.

"In this frame of mind and still feeling weary," Belden said, "we marched into the jungle and immediately went up the side of a mountain." [32]

Stilwell said that, on May 14, the group had made three slow marches through the cool, shady jungle after he had removed from his person a large leech, which he described as a "big bright green sucker about 8 inches long." Then they made a long climb to the village of Kawlum on the Burma-India border, arriving in a heavy rain. There, the party was met by a British district official from Imphal, Tim Sharpe, who had been sent to meet the group with some four hundred porters, live pigs for dinner, a doctor with medicines, other food, cigarettes, whisky and Indian rum. "Food, doctor, ponies, and everything," Stilwell wrote. "Quite a relief." [33]

Sharpe met the group at a thatch hut, where he had taken shelter from the heavy rain. "We are from General Stilwell's party," said Case. "Yes, I know," Sharpe replied. "We came to meet you." [34]

But Stilwell barely reacted, asking only how long it had taken him to get there. "Five days," Sharpe replied.

Belden said he was shocked at Stilwell's sangfroid – "at his lack of excitement, his almost lack of – interest. It was as if he almost did not care about being rescued. As if he were only concentrating on one thought: how much longer it would take us to get back to civilization; how much longer before he could report to the War Department; how much longer before he could get to Delhi, get to Chungking, see [British Field Marshall Sir Archibald] Wavell, see Chiang Kai-shek, forget about the past, make another plan for the future. Not a thought about the man who had come to meet us. Not a word of welcome. As if all this did not matter." [35]

Capt. Jones said that the celebratory dinner that evening with Stilwell and the British had gone well until Sharpe broke out the rum, which Jones guzzled down without thinking. "I was in no physical condition to drink much of anything except water, and not much of that," he said. "A single sip [of rum] would probably have been too much." On the way back to the camp after dinner, he said, he veered off the trail several times and fell down twice. "A bit slippery, isn't it, Captain," Stilwell said.

Jones said later that, to his surprise, he had been rescued and gotten soused all within three hours. "I slept outside that night and didn't know it had rained until I woke up, soaked, the next morning," he recalled.

The next day, the sick and disabled in the group traveled by pony and horseback, thanks to the British rescue, while the others continued to walk. But there were still steep mountains to climb.

As they made their way toward Imphal, with Sharpe as a guide, they were frequently met by village elders who offered them gifts. At Chammu on May 16, for instance, after a four-and-a-half hour climb straight up, they were greeted by a village chieftain in a bright red blanket who presented Stilwell with a bottle of rice beer. At another village, the headman offered him a goat. He reciprocated with cigarettes. Other villages offered cider, chickens and rice wine. "Getting to like the wine," Stilwell, normally a teetotaler, told his diary on May 18.

Dr. John Grindlay – Seagrave's assistant – said that the climb up to Chammu had been up "the longest, steepest, hottest, grinding trail," which put a terrible strain on everyone. "[T]he men all nearly collapsed," he wrote in his diary, "several of the girls very weary, and I had to have them await the ponies." Even Stilwell, usually stoic about such things, would call the hill "a bitch."

Grindlay said that, after a 21-mile hike on May 18, the group reached Ukhrul, at an altitude of 6,500 feet, where they took baths "in icy air in [a] well, and girls washed clothes. Had clinic for feet and drying clothes by roaring fire in our house. Picked fleas...." [36]

That evening, Sharpe put on another celebratory dinner for Stilwell and the other officers in a house with a flower garden and a fireplace with a fire. "Tim broke out the scotch and water," Jones recalled, "and we thought we were back in civilization."

On May 19, after having traveled for 18 straight days, the group came to a narrow steel suspension bridge near Litan that linked up with a real road to Imphal. Seven trucks arrived to meet them the next morning, along with two American officers in a jeep bearing chocolate, cigarettes and whiskey and the news that "Doolittle Raiders," under Lt. Col. James H. "Jimmy" Doolittle, had bombed Tokyo...on April 18.

The next day, the party arrived in Imphal after pulling and pushing the trucks through knee-deep mud en route. "We got in at 3:00 and had chow at the old fort," Stilwell told his diary. "Cordial reception by the Limeys." The following day: "Rain. Breakfast at 'A' mess. Not such a hot impression. Indefinite about transportation....Feeling like hell with a cold....In bed all afternoon." [37]

From Imphal, Stilwell traveled by truck to Dinapur, then on by train to Dinjan and Tinsukia, where the airfields of the Air Transport Command were located. On May 24, he flew to New Delhi in General Brereton's plane. A flock of photographers greeted him at the airport. That evening he held a press conference at the Imperial Hotel. [38]

"I claim we got a hell of a beating," Stilwell told the assembled reporters. "We got run out of Burma and it is humiliating as hell. I think we ought to find out what caused it, go back and retake it." [39]

10

FROM THE JUNGLE
TO THE DESERT

The Allied retreat from Burma was one of the most horrific military withdrawals ever in terms of physical hardship and duration, and it continued well into the fall of 1942. Thousands of soldiers were simply lost in the dense jungles and swamps and died of malaria, exhaustion and starvation, including an estimated 5,000-6,000 Chinese.

But those losses, while important, were relatively insignificant, Belden argued, compared with the thousands upon thousands of men and women who staggered in small groups for days, weeks and months through the forests, mountains and jungles of northern Burma without food as they sought to escape the Japanese.

"These were the heros of the retreat from Burma," Belden wrote. "These, the unnamed and unsung, were glorious, the martyred, and the damned. And not we, who thought we suffered, but didn't; who talked glibly of courage and adventure when there wasn't any; who paled at dangers that were never there. These are the people whose pictures should be in the magazines, but aren't; these are the people this book [*Retreat With Stilwell*] should be about, but isn't; these are the lost children of Burma who got killed." [1]

The book, written in the fall of 1942 while Belden, seriously ill, recovered from the Burma "walkout," was published in March 1943 to rave reviews, with *The New York Times*, for instance, calling it a "solid piece of workmanship, wrought by an assured hand which vividly evokes the odors, heats, sweats, thirsts, fatigues and heroisms of that weird and, at times, positively spooky campaign which was the opening of the war in Burma."

The *Saturday Review* said that, in the book, Belden had told a story as gripping as any swift-moving piece of fiction. But in it he had also crafted a penetrating analysis of the follies and weaknesses of imperialist colonial policies.

"The story ... would be incredible if poorly told," wrote the book's reviewer, Hallett Abend, who reported for *The New York Times* from China and Japan in the 1930 and 1940s. "Jack Belden has told it surprisingly well. In his hands it becomes high tragedy; it becomes a soul purge of pity and anger and terror; it even becomes a tale of shocking beauty coupled with bitter disillusionment."

From Burma, with only a week's rest, Belden went to China to cover the exploits of the "Flying Tigers" (formally known as the American Volunteer Group, or AVG, of the Chinese Air Force), under Brigadier General Claire L. Chennault – eating, bunking and flying with Chennault's group of fighter pilots as they engaged Japanese aircraft and strafed Japanese ground forces and other Japanese targets throughout eastern China.

A Cajun from Waterproof, La., Chennault had been hired as an adviser to Chiang Kai-shek and his air force in 1937, when he was forced to retire from the American Army Air Corps for medical reasons. He was known in the early 1920s as one of the world's top aerobatic pilots, and in January 1941 – after Japanese aircraft had been pummeled Chinese cities with incendiary bombs almost unchallenged – Chennault won the approval Chiang and President Roosevelt to recruit retired American fighter pilots to join his all-volunteer air force. [2]

The financial rewards for the pilots were substantial: $600 to $750 a month, or two to three times what they were paid in the U.S. military, plus $500 for each Japanese aircraft they blew out of the sky. About 100 pilots and another 200 or so mechanics, radio operators and other ground personnel were sent to Burma and China in late summer 1941 for training. And on December 20 – 12 days after Pearl Harbor – the pilots of a fleet of aging P-40s originally destined for England were engaged in their first combat under AVG command, attacking a flight of unescorted, twin-engine Mitsubishi bombers near Kunming, China, and scoring a major success.

For the next seven months, the "Flying Tigers" would shoot down a confirmed 299 Japanese aircraft (and probably another 150 or so), providing a significant boost in morale for the allies before they were absorbed into the newly created 23rd Fighter Group in July 1942, where they went on to achieve similar combat success.

On July 4 – the last day as commander of the "Flying Tigers" – Belden visited Chennault at his office at the edge of the airfield at Peishihyi, outside Chungking, and asked him how he felt about the unit being disbanded and folded into the regular army air force.

"You know," Chennault told Belden, "I have had the greatest opportunity an air officer of any nation ever had. To collect and train a group like this with complete freedom of action caused me supreme enjoyment. Not only was I able to satisfy my desire to prove my methods sound, but I was able to contribute to the common cause." ³

Chennault said that the "Flying Tigers" had been lucky. "But individual courage and the willingness to carry the battle to the enemy against any odds were the real secret of our success," he said. "The AVG is the world's finest bunch of fighting airmen. I regret their disbandment. Now I only look forward to meeting the enemy."

Several of the "Flying Tigers" went on to sign up with 23rd Fighter Group, also under the command of Chennault, who had been recalled to active duty with the rank of brigadier general and made head of the China Air Task Force.

One of those pilots was David Lee "Tex" Hill. Born to Presbyterian missionaries in Korea in 1915, he moved with the family to Texas when he was six years old. In 1938, he graduated from Austin College, then completed naval flight school and served in a torpedo squadron on the USS Saratoga and in a dive-bomber squadron on the USS Ranger before being recruited by Chennault for the "Flying Tigers" in 1941. During his service with the unit, he was credited with destroying 10.25 Japanese aircraft (second only to Robert Neale).

In July 1942, after the "Flying Tigers" had been absorbed into the 23rd Fighter Group, Belden flew in a group of bombers and pursuit aircraft, including one piloted by Hill, on a mission whose intended target was a large Japanese base below Hankow on the Yangtze River.

Belden wrote in an article published in *Time* on August 3 that he flew in another aircraft piloted by Col. Caleb V. Haynes, who had been sent into Burma to evacuate an unwilling Stilwell three months earlier.

"There's certain to be plenty of antiaircraft there," Haynes told the pilots at a pre-mission briefing. "We'll come in high. Tex, you follow behind us with your boys, and if you see anything worth strafing, have a go at them."

Hill said that he would, adding in his Texas drawl, "It's going to be tough on rabbits."

Nearing the target, according to Belden, the hills and trails over which he had retreated with Chinese forces in 1938 spread out below. "It was almost like coming home."

Haynes's plane soon let loose its cargo of Chinese-made incendiary bombs, setting fire to piers, warehouses and other targets on the ground. Then, ack-ack guns and pom-poms on a large Japanese ship on the Yangtze – perhaps a light cruiser or destroyer – began "throwing everything but the kitchen sink at us," Belden wrote, to which gunners on the Haynes plane responded, silencing the ship.

Behind the ship were two gunboats, toward which Hill now led his fighter aircraft in a large swooping dive.

"He made a pass at a destroyer," Belden wrote, "but, on getting closer and looking at it, he saw that it was armed to the teeth, so he swerved off, made a sharp bank and came down within 50 feet of the water, with all guns wide open shooting lead into the first gunboat. Before we could get to the second gunboat the deck was swept clean – figures threw themselves into the water as Tex's guns poured cannon shells into the water close by the side. Bullets skidded of the top of the water and struck the ship near the water line. The fire burst out and the ship started listing."

After the planes returned to their base in China, Hill walked toward Belden – "his long wiry body moving with a roll that held a kind of threat in it" and looking like a "steely-eyed Texas cowboy." A broad grin was splashed across his face. "Sure was rough on rabbits," he said.

Belden also flew with another crew, which raided the main Japanese air base at Canton. Again, in early August, it was the same routine: "Hurl a few score bombs, dive into a whirling Richthofen Circus with 30 Jap Zeros. Home again, grab yourself a plateful of chow. Flop in your bed at ten. And here is the boy again calling you at a quarter to two in the morning." [4]

But the weather this day was hazy and rainy, and the leader of the mission, Major Del Baily, of Spokane, Washington, suggested that he go up and take a look, and if it was clear he would flash one navigation light.

"I climb into the bomber with him," Belden reported. "Above, we find a clearer spot in a squall and flash on one light. Up after us come the rest of the bombers and peashooters [P-40 fighter aircraft]. As dawn breaks we are off for Canton."

Over the Canton airfield, Belden heard the rumble of the bomb doors opening, and soon bursts of smoke popped out of the ground as the bombs hit the warehouse docks. On the airfield itself, Japanese planes were lined up in neat rows. And behind Bailey's plane another bomber unleashed its load, which decimated six Japanese aircraft on the ground below.

Leading the fighter escort was Captain Charles W. Sawyer, one of the five "Flying Tigers" who had signed up with the Army Air Force after the all-volunteer unit was disbanded on July 4. He was towheaded, Belden reported, and he walked aimlessly around with a haunted look in his eyes. Three weeks earlier, he had gotten lost in a storm and crashed his plane in the mountains near Tibet, escaped three firing squads of hill tribesmen and walked back into China proper.

Now, Sawyer and the other "peashooters" were being attacked by Japanese Zeros and their newer I-97s, which had been scrambled to counter the American raid on Canton. "I see six go at Sawyer," Belden wrote in an article in *Time* on August 24. "He makes a head-on run at the leader, pours in a couple of bursts. The I-97, camouflaged with bright green paint, falls away in smoke. Five others do a quick flip to get on Charlie's tail, but he dives and pulls rapidly away and then comes up again on the corner of our tails....We roared homeward, landing safely while our top cover stayed up to protect us. But the Japs did not come."

Time said in its August 24, 1942, issue that, in Asia, never had so few done so much as the American pilots in China, and no correspondent had reported their activities so thoroughly as Belden had.

But by early September, the Burma "walkout" had begun to take its toll on Belden, and *Time* reported to its readers that his pulse was running at a rapid 110-130 beats per minute and that he had gone into the hill country of India – to Srinagar in the Vale of Kashmir – "for a rest he badly needs....[H]e has to take it very easy for a while."

This was a period, to be sure, when Belden, who had turned 32 in February, was one of *Time's* golden boys. A letter to subscribers from the magazine's publisher, P.I. Prentice, in its September 21 issue said that Belden was a "tower of strength" in the magazine's Far Eastern news bureau, noting that he had been in the "thick of the fighting" in almost every critical campaign since China was invaded by the Japanese in 1937. He was, according to Prentice, the ablest correspondent covering the China war.

Prentice said that the strain of Burma, however, had finally gotten the best of Belden, and that he was enjoying a well-deserved "war correspondent's holiday" in India. "But he is far too tough to let even a half dozen diseases keep him down," he wrote. "Odds are he will be back at the front for you before the fall campaigns really get going."

By the end of October 1942, and still in India, Belden had recovered from the "half dozen diseases" that had kept him down. He had also finished writing *Retreat With Stilwell*, and he was now ready to travel again – to wherever the TIME-LIFE organization chose to send him. This time it was North Africa.

The allied invasion of Algeria and Morocco, designated Operation Torch, which began on November 8, had prompted the TIME-LIFE editors to move about a dozen of its crack correspondents, including Belden, to the region.

Among the transferees were reporters like Harry Zinder (who joined the *Time* Cairo bureau after having been with the British Eighth Army during its triumphant run from El Alamein, Egypt, to Derna, Algeria), Will Lang Jr. (who landed with the American troops at Oran), and Line Barrett (who sailed with the British forces from England, landing near the Mediterranean port city of Bone, Algeria).

Time said in its November 30, 1942, issue that the correspondents had not been sent to North Africa to duplicate the news that came across the wires of Associated Press but to "dig up background information and usually-overlooked detail," so that *Time*'s editors could give their readers some of the taste and smell and feel of the battles taking place around Africa's rim, as well as of the quality and flavor of the men who are fighting those battles and preparing for new ones.

Equipped with a new passport, which he had obtained in Calcutta, Belden headed for North Africa in early November. He said later that, at the time, he felt he was reaching new heights as a writer and was filled with the excitement and promise of continuing his career as a war correspondent – with his own unique style on a new continent. [5]

Arriving in Cairo, he set up shop at the TIME-LIFE bureau. But soon he was off to report from the strategically key island of Malta, where a two-year-long siege was in the process of being lifted.

The failure of German General Field Marshal Erwin Rommel to subdue the island, Belden wrote, would allow the Allied air forces to use it as a base from which to strike south, west and north against Tripolitania (northwestern Libya), Sardinia, Sicily and Italy and to cover the Allied invasion of North Africa. It would also provide impetus to British Field Marshall Bernard Montgomery's march out of Egypt across the Sahara Desert to

Tripoli and Tunisia, which included his Eighth Army victory over Rommel at El Alamein in October-November 1942 – the first large-scale Allied land victory of the war and a major turning point in the conflict. [6]

"Montgomery had cracked Rommel at Alamein and [Lieutenant General Dwight D.] Eisenhower had landed in North Africa," Belden wrote. "For the first time in many months the Maltese said: 'There is hope.'" [7]

Back in North Africa – at an unidentified Allied air base somewhere in the desert – Belden prepared in early December to board an American B-24 Liberator bound for Italy. Its mission was to attack the base near Naples used by the Italian navy to protect ships loaded with war material destined for Rommel's forces in North Africa.

"At noon on Dec. 4," Belden wrote in *LIFE* magazine, "unshaven crewmen filed their bottles with lemonade, pulled down baseballish caps over their eyes, swarmed across the desert airfields, crawled under the bellies of their B-24's and turned over their motors. They were ready for the first American air raid on Italy." [8]

The four-engine bombers – relatively new, having been flown for the first time in 1941, and "clumsy and pregnant with heavy-caliber bombs" – lumbered down the long runways and rose slowly from the desert. Above the field they rendezvoused with the lead aircraft, "Shanghai Lil," piloted by Major C. H. Rueter, of Waco, Texas.

"We followed Lil out along the coast road," Belden wrote. "We passed trucks carrying supplies to Montgomery's Eighth Army in western Libya, struck out over the Mediterranean and headed toward Italy."

The bombers skimmed over the sea and toward mid-afternoon began to climb, as the air grew colder, prompting the passengers to don flight suits and oxygen masks. Suddenly, a slight clearing in the overcast sky appeared, and ahead Belden saw a brown mass of mountain and then an open crater with smoke ascending from it. "Vesuvius. In back of it, Pompeii. Ahead, Naples. There, around the volcano, lay our goal. There lay the target."

Then someone shouted, "Open the bomb-bay doors," and an icy blast of air shot up through the open belly of the aircraft.

"We began to lose altitude," Belden reported. "Three to five thousand feet below us other formations followed after us and we all dipped downward. Suddenly we swept around Vesuvius, shot through a hole in the clouds and descended on Naples....[T]he target was clear. Naples lay helpless and beautiful under our advancing wings and we broke into our bombing run and made for the target."

Together, in a wide circle, the B-24s flew over the hills below and the houses than ran down toward the heart of the city, passing over railroad yards, factories and warehouses and advancing on the Italian fleet – destroyers, cruisers, battleships and submarines – lying still in the Naples harbor. "Toward a group of six ships we loosed our bombs," Belden said. More B-24s took a run at the target. "Smoke and flame were rising from the quay. Where once had been six ships was now only a blot of smoke." More explosions shook the low-flying B-24s, and a large spurt of orange flame rose up 2,000 feet from the harbor and the quay of Naples glowed.

Guns from the ground opened up. But the B-24s were soon out of range of the ack-ack guns and passing over the island of Capri heading back over the mountains of southern Italy. "We struck out over the Mediterranean and headed for home. The mission to Italy was over."

Time Publisher P.I. Prentice, meanwhile, said that December 25, 1942, would be a strange Christmas for many of the organization's war reporters, including Belden. The least "Christmasy Christmas" of all, he said, would probably be spent by George Johnston in New Guinea. "Steamy jungles, evil-smelling swamps and man-high kunai grass are no substitutes for holly wreaths, nor the whine of Jap bullets for jingle bells," he wrote.

The coldest and snowiest Christmas, Prentice wrote, would probably be experienced by James Aldridge in Moscow. "He will probably hear plenty of droshky sleigh bells, as the Russians have a lot more to celebrate this year than the Germans," he wrote. "But even so hungry Moscow must be a pretty grim place to spend Christmas." The thirty-odd people in *Time*'s London office, he said, were looking forward to England's best Christmas since the blitz in 1940.

As for Belden, according to Prentice, he hoped to have Christmas dinner with Zinder at Shepheard's Hotel in Cairo – "where Rommel planned to have his headquarters by now" – assuming that Zinder made it back from the desert in time. "And I will be surprised if Will Lang and Lincoln Barnett don't have a really royal feast with the American troops in North Africa," he said. But Carl and Shelley Mydans, who were captured by the Japanese during Christmas week 1941, were beginning their second year in a prison camp. "I hope the Japs know this is Christmas and give them a break." [9]

11

VICTORY IN NORTH AFRICA

The successful landing of 73,000 American and British troops on the beaches of Morocco and Algeria in early November 1942 – an operation code-named Operation Torch – had cleared the way for an Allied push into Tunisia, where Erwin "Desert Fox" Rommel's Axis armies were preparing for a major offensive.

British Lieutenant-General Bernard Montgomery, with his tide-turning victory at El Alamein, Egypt, had forced Rommel to retreat across Libya to Tunisia, and Hitler ordered him to defend it at all costs. For the Axis powers, he said, Tunisia would be the "cornerstone of our conduct of the war on the southern flank of Europe." [1]

Softening up Tunisia from the air – and denying the Axis forces a supply route from southern Italy – fell to the U.S. Army Air Force's 98th Bombardment Group, which would fly heavy, four-engine B-24 Liberators on some 417 missions in North Africa and Europe throughout the war.

After Christmas, Belden traveled to the British Royal Air Force base at Fayid, northeast of Cairo, to join the group, describing one raid in January 1943 on the port of Sousse, 85 miles south of the capital of Tunis, as "not exciting, not heroic, but the kind of dull, monotonous, hard, nerve-straining work American bomber pilots have been doing for five months now in the Mid-East." [2]

He said that the crew on the Sousse raid had become irritable and impatient at Fayid "as only bomber pilots can be when bad weather holds them from their target." Finally, the order came: "Bomb the quays and shipping at Sousse."

Major S.R. Patterson, the flight leader, told Belden as they took off in his B-24 "Pink Lady" that if the sky were clear and the moon bright, "that harbor ought to be framed like a picture." But Belden said that that would also mean that "we'll be framed, too," recalling how "Flying Tigers" had shot down Japanese bombers in China several months earlier. "Yeah, that's right," Patterson said. "But I hope we get in and away before those night fighters can rise and meet us."

Settling in for the long, monotonous flight to the target ("Ten hours of boredom; five minutes of excitement – that's the life of bomber crews."), Belden introduced himself to the crew: Lieutenant F.A. Miller, the bombardier, who passed the time reading the popular Western potboiler "Singing Guns," by Max Brand; Technical Sergeant Anton J. Budgen, a gunner; Lyle Winchell, another gunner; and Pilot Virgil M. Anders.

Approaching the target after hours of flying over the Mediterranean Sea, donned in life vests and fleece-lined flying suits to protect against the cold, a vague outline of the Sousse harbor appeared. Miller guided the plane toward the target, which only he and the navigator could see from the front of the aircraft.

"The plane was shuddering and shaking," Belden reported. "The bomb-bay doors were opening. The wind blew out of the purple night and flew at our hands eagerly. It pounced on the windows, frosting them up, and turned the plane into an icehouse. I looked down through the bomb-bay doors into nothingness. The bombs glinted icy grey as they fell into the blue, bleak blackness." And then the plane turned back toward Egypt, several hours away.

"I took off my oxygen mask and curled up to sleep," Belden said, "and the bombardier came out of the nose of the plane and said: 'That was a son of a bitch of a monotonous mission.' 'Yeah,' I answered.'"

Two months later, in another bombing run – this one at Naples, Italy – several members of the crew who had participated in the Sousse raid, with Belden, including Anders and Budgen, were reported missing in action and eventually declared killed when their B-24 crashed at sea.

Tens of thousands of U.S. airmen, in fact, were killed during World War II, and some 65,164 aircraft, according to the Department of the Army, were lost between December 1941 and August 1945, including 22,948 in combat.

By late February 1943, meanwhile, Rommel had strengthened his position – albeit tentatively – with his victory over the Americans under Major General Lloyd Fredendall at Kasserine Pass, a two-mile-wide gap in the Grand Dorsal chain of the Atlas Mountains in west-central Tunisia. Belden wrote that Rommel had simply "beat up" the "weak and inexperienced" Americans, who were pushed back fifty miles to the west from their positions at Faid Pass. But he said that the Rommel's success was short-lived, noting that in the process Montgomery had been able to bring up part of his "far stronger and more experienced" Eighth Army to prepare for an assault on the Mareth Line to the south. [3]

Commanders on both sides of the war – the Allies and Axis – were convinced that the final fight for North Africa, and indeed for the entire southern Mediterranean, would take place on an ever-shrinking, fifty-mile wide-by-300-mile-long strip of land in the eastern third of Tunisia. [4]

Covering the endgame for the American media, in addition to Belden, were several reporters who were or would become legends in their chosen profession, including the AP's Don Whitehead, who later would win a then-unprecedented two Pulitzer Prizes.

Another Pulitzer Prize winner, Rick Atkinson, author of the much-lauded *An Army at Dawn: The War in North Africa, 1942-1943*, has praised Whitehead for possessing what he called the "priceless impulse to go to the sound of the guns." No one, he said, "bore witness" better than Whitehead did. [5]

But Whitehead himself would say that, in fact, he had not obtained that "priceless impulse" on his own but had learned it from Belden.

He said that during his first few weeks in Egypt he noticed that Belden would disappear from time to time, and one day Whitehead asked him where he had been. He said he had been at the front with the troops. At that moment, Whitehead said, he realized that he had not been covering the war "as it should have been covered."

"From that time on," Whitehead recalled several years later, "I decided I would use the Belden approach to reporting and get as close as I possibly could to the fighting." [6]

Whitehead was born on April 8, 1908, in the coal-mining town of Inman, Virginia, and was raised in Kentucky. As a 10-year-old boy, he witnessed a murder in his hometown of Harlan and wrote a story about the incident. When he submitted it to the local newspaper several days later, however, he was told by the editor it had been turned in too late. "Can't use it, son," the editor said, seeking to teach the youngster an early lesson about the importance of timeliness in journalism. "Everybody in town knows about that shooting." [7]

After two years at the University of Kentucky, the future Pulitzer Prize winner took a job at the "LaFollette Press" in LaFollette, Tennessee, published by his brother Kyle. He returned to Kentucky in 1930 to become managing editor of the "Harlan American." Four years later, he moved to the "Knoxville Journal," and in 1935 he joined the Associated Press, working first in Memphis and then in Knoxville.

But by early 1941 his feature-writing skills had earned him a promotion to the AP's New York bureau, and in the fall of 1942 he was sent to North Africa to cover the British Eighth Army's make-or-break overland pursuit of Rommel's Afrika Korps. [8]

On October 9, after arriving in Cairo after a 10-day trip from New York, he had dinner with fellow AP reporter Toby Wiant at the Doll's Cabaret, which he said had a very good orchestra and floor show. "The place [was] jammed by men in British uniform," he wrote in his diary. "In the gaiety and brilliance of the cabaret, it was hard to realize that only eighty miles away the British and German armies face each other. It's a fantastic city but then this is a fantastic war." [9]

Although new to this "fantastic war," he wasted no time heaping scorn on the British for what he considered to be their mixed-up priorities. He said, for instance, that they displayed "an amazing and sometimes infuriating show of unconcern which bordered on disregard of the realities. Chin up. No necessity, really old man, to change the GHQ office hours of 9 a.m. to 1 p.m. and 5 p.m. to 7 p.m. The heat y'know." [10]

Whitehead also said that, in his view, the most effective way to defeat the British would be to cut off their supply of tea. "British troops can do without proper weapons, food or clothing," he wrote. "They will hang on with their bulldog tenacity when everything seems lost. But I believe they would disintegrate, division by division, without the stimulus of the little leaves marketed by Sir Thomas Lipton." Every day at teatime – 10 am. and 4 p.m. – British trucks, guns and tanks ("the entire desert war") would come to an screeching halt, he observed, as the British army enjoyed its cup of tea – "a strong scalding brew that lifted one's spirits by the nape of the neck and shook them vigorously."

With or without his tea, however, Montgomery would eventually prevail in the Second Battle of El Alamein (October 23 to November 5, 1942), turning the tide in the North Africa campaign by ending Rommel's hopes of occupying Egypt, taking control of the Suez Canal, and obtaining access to the oil fields in the Middle East.

Belden arrived in Cairo shortly after El Alamein to take up his post at the *Time* news bureau, and he and Whitehead would meet there for the first time, probably over drinks at the Shepheard's Hotel, a residence and informal gathering place for the Americans and Brits who were condemned to serve in North African desert in the early 1940s.

But by early February 1943, Montgomery's Eighth Army had driven Rommel west across Libya, meaning that Cairo would soon become merely an Allied supply base in the North African campaign. On February 10, General Harold Alexander, commander of the British Near East Command, announced to a standing-room-only crowd of some 50 reporters that he would be moving his operation to Tunisia to take charge of the new 15th Army Group, which had been created to assume overall control, under Eisenhower, of the Eighth Army and the Allied forces already engaged in battle in Tunisia. [11] So, with Cairo now becoming a veritable news backwater in the Allied-Axis conflict, there began an en masse exodus of war correspondents from the Egyptian capital.

On the morning of February 24, Belden and Whitehead – joined by George Lait, of International News Service, and Ned Russell, of United Press – left Shepheard's Hotel and boarded an American DC-3 bound for Tripoli. Shortly after noon, the plane made a refueling stop at Benina airport near Benghazi, a port city in northeast Libya, before resuming its flight to the Royal Air Force base at Castel Benito, near Tripoli, where it landed at about 6 p.m.

Among the other passengers on the flight was Clare Hollingworth, a British reporter for *The Daily Telegraph*, whose presence in Tripoli prompted Montgomery to say, according to reports at the time, "I'll have no women correspondents in my army. Don't let her into Tripoli. Get rid of her. I don't care if the Americans did bring her up, she can't stay." And without much ado, she was subsequently put on a flight back to Cairo. [12]

Montgomery apparently did not know, or care, that Hollingworth – on her first assignment for the *Telegraph*, at 26 years old in 1939 – had broken the news that Germany was about to invade Poland. Her front-page article, based on eyewitness reporting from the border, which was published in the August 29 issue of the *Telegraph* under the headline "1,000 tanks massed on Polish border. Ten divisions reported ready for swift stroke." It has since been called the scoop of the century. [13]

The Germans, meanwhile, must have thought that they were being short-changed in the American media because shortly after Belden, Whitehead and the other American reporters arrived in Tripoli on February 24, they launched an intensive air raid on the harbor lasting about 30 minutes. But the next day, driving around the city, the reporters noticed that, far from suffering, the residents were beginning to live a normal life again – in contrast to a month earlier when the city's economic life had come to a halt with the arrival of British troops, tanks, trucks and guns. A huge bomb crater disrupted traffic near the Grand Hotel, and a German bomb had torn up the sidewalk along the harbor front. But overall, the city was now regaining a sense of normalcy. [14]

That was not the case, however, 175 miles or so up the Mediterranean coast at Medenine, where Rommel was preparing for what would turn out to be his last engagement with the Allies in North Africa, before being replaced as commander of the Afrika Korps by General Hans-Jürgen von Arnim.

In late February, after British intelligence had decoded German radio transmissions confirming Rommel's planned to attack at Medenine, Belden and his fellow American war correspondents, including Whitehead, moved up the coast toward the expected battle site, and on March 3 they pitched camp outside of the now-deserted Tunisian town.

Belden later reported from the scene that Rommel, unaware of the preparations that had been made by Montgomery in advance of the attack, had arrived in El Halouff in the Matmata Hills west of Medenine on the night on March 5. "We will attack at dawn and take Medenine by dusk," he confidently told his assembled tank crews. [15] At dawn on March 6, he moved out.

"A heavy dew glistened on the ground and the haze was just lifting from the lower slopes of the Matmata Hills, when British patrols heard a faint clank of metal hitting the ground," Belden reported. "Nearer and nearer, faster and louder, louder and faster the sound came. Suddenly, at a distance of 3,000 yards from the British lines there emerged from the mists one hundred of Rommel's tanks deployed for action along an eight-mile front." [16]

Montgomery's officers watched first with curiosity and then with disbelief and finally with joy as Rommel's cavalcade advanced – not concentrated but dispersed over a wide area. "It seemed as if Rommel, the leading exponent of armor concentration, in his last desperate gamble had lost his nerve and hedged," Belden wrote. "This is what the British with their antitank guns wanted, and they coolly held their fire."

Soon a line of German tanks headed straight toward the British forces, which opened fire and destroyed seven tanks in a matter of minutes. Another twelve tanks were taken out when they were caught in a British ambush. Yet it was a few hundred yards away in the middle of the battlefield – a dry river bed since nicknamed Panzer Gulch – that the main action would take place, with Rommel throwing in an armor and infantry "spearhead" supported by dive bombers attacking the British units.

By evening, however, Montgomery had repelled the assault and inflicted debilitating damage on the Afrika Korps, without significant losses to his own forces or equipment.

"The sun sinking toward the Matmata Hills was shining in the British gunners' eyes as German lorries drove across the plains and disgorged 1,000 shock troops just southwest of Elephant Hill," Belden wrote. "Perhaps Rommel was counting on the setting sun to blind the British gunners, but the only thing blind in the plains that day was Rommel's own folly."

He said that even before the German infantry had taken one step forward, 150 British guns began lobbing shells on the amassed German troops at the rate of 200 a minute.

"Within a few moments hundreds of slain and wounded lay in the arid, inhospitable plain before the British positions," Belden reported. "When dawn came the next morning, there was scarcely a living member – soldier or tank – of the German Panzer host left in the plain. Rommel, who suffered the quickest and sharpest drubbing of his desert career, had given up and withdrawn to the hills to lick his wounds."

On March 9, Rommel flew to Rome and would never set foot in Africa again.

Toward midday on March 6, meanwhile, Whitehead, who had viewed the battle from Elephant Hill 800 feet above the plain, made his way back to Medenine and ran into Belden, Lait and Russell. "Where were you today?" Belden asked. Whitehead said he had been on Elephant Hill during the shelling. "I knew that's where you would be," said Belden, who had watched the battle from a nearby ridge, which had a lesser view. "That's where we should have been."

Time reported in its March 22 issue that Belden had visited the battlefield after it was all over and counted 52 German tanks that had just been left on the arid, rock-strewn plain between the Matmata Hills and the Mediterranean Sea. Some were blackened by fire. Turrets were torn off, and the fronts of some tanks had been blown in.

"Tanks!," Belden exclaimed in a cable to *Time*. "How futile they appear face-to-face with these ambush-placed guns. Like paper mache boxes they are strewn across the Medenine plain."

Now the campaign for control of North Africa, after Rommel's debacle at Medenine, would move to the so-called Mareth Line – a line of fortifications arching twenty miles from the Matmata Hills north to the Mediterranean Sea. It had been built by the French in the 1930s to forestall Italian advances from the east, and now in March 1943, it was held by the Germans and Italians.

On March 17, Hitler had ordered the Axis army, now under von Arnim, to defend the Mareth Line to the end. But Montgomery had other ideas, vowing to launch an attack against the line that would be the final blow to Hitler's forces in North Africa – his confidence stemming from, among other things, the overwhelming strength of the Eighth Army, which had a two-to-one manpower advantage over the First Italian Army and five to one advantage in tanks. [17]

The day the attack began – Saturday, March 20 – Montgomery delivered a message to his troops saying that the days of the Axis forces in North Africa were numbered. The Eighth Army, he said, would destroy the enemy at Mareth, then break through the Gabes Gap and drive northward through Sfax, Sousse and finally into Tunis.

"We will not stop, or let up, until Tunis has been captured," Montgomery said, "and the enemy has either given up the struggle or been pushed into the sea. The operations now about to begin will mark the close of the campaign in North Africa." [18]

But after an initial British foray, the 7,000-strong 15th Panzer Division counterattacked on March 22 and drove the British infantry back across the water-filled gulch known as Wadi Zigzau. Soon, no fewer than thirty-five Valentine tanks were obliterated, and bodies were seen beached or floating in the stream. For the first time in ten months, the Eighth Army was forced to withdraw. Their attack on the Mareth Line, at least for now, had failed. [19]

"Crowds of men, wounded and unwounded with scarcely distinguishable faces, flitted like wraiths through the haze," Belden wrote. "Some crawled. Some stumbled. Some marched, erect. Some moved forward in a zigzag path." [20]

The next day, awakened at 2 a.m. and told the news, Montgomery revamped his plan for fighting until "the enemy has either given up the struggle or been pushed into the sea." He would recoup his fortunes, Belden wrote, by reinforcing his left flank, sending the X Corps under Lieutenant General Brian Horrocks, who had been waiting, in vain, for the expected breakthrough on the Mareth Line, to the south and around the Matmata Hills to catch up with the advancing New Zealanders under Lieutenant General Bernard C. Freyberg. Together, the two generals would be ordered to break through the Tebaga Gap – fifty miles as the crow flies west of Mareth – and to capture Gabes on the sea before the Germans were able to evacuate from the Mareth Line.

At nightfall on March 23, Horrocks moved through the fort town of Foum Talahouine – some 30 miles south of Medenine – and by the morning of March 24, he had arrived at the edge of the desert, where he unloaded his tanks from the twenty-four-wheel transportation trucks and headed out across the sand in battle formation."Scout cars first," Belden reported, "swarming over the high ground and reconnoitering, followed by light Honey tanks, then heavy Shermans and Grants and finally guns and supply trucks – all moving in five or six parallel columns, raising clouds of dust and following the tracks made by Freyberg before them." [21]

By March 26, Horrocks had caught up with Freyberg's forces, which were being held up by significant Axis opposition at the Tebaga Gap. But he decided nevertheless to attack that night through the gap toward the oasis town of El Hamma and directly to Gabes in one blow. It would be the first mass tank attack at night in history. [22]

His tanks, in the end, were were quickly able to overwhelm the enemy at the Tebaga Gap, including, most notably, a number of field guns that would have been able to easily knock them out during daylight hours. At dawn on March 27, his forces were within five miles of El Hamma, and the road to Gabes was clear. "It was the most enjoyable battle I have ever fought," Montgomery said later. [23]

Abandoning the Mareth Line, the Axis forces began an orderly retreat north along the coast, through Gabes as far as the Wadi Akarit, and over the next few days and weeks, the Allies made steady but halting progress toward their ultimate objective of taking Tunis, as well as the key port city of Bizerte, north of the Tunisian capital.

As for Belden, who was always looking for ways to be "at the front," he would track the Eighth Army through Gabes to Wadi Akarit – a four-mile-long gulch heavily fortified by the Axis forces – where on April 6 the British attacked the new Axis line, held by Italian Lieutenant-General Giovanni Messe, with a tank advantage alone of 462 to 25.

But according to Belden, who reported on the conflict for *Time* magazine, it was the Gurkhas of the Eighth Army – with their long, curved-bladed knives called kukris – who would inflict huge, initial damage on the Italian troops.

Time said in a report from the battlefield based on Belden's cables that Gurkhas were "dark little men from Nepal who take to slopes like goats. There is a saying that the only thing which tires a Gurkha is walking along a flat place."

"In Nepal they use kukris to cut their enemies' heads off," *Time* said, again quoting Belden, adding that just after midnight the Gurkhas moved forward quietly toward the 800-foot hill known as Djebel Fatnassa. "At Djebel Fatnassa they reached their objectives with hardly a sound; dying Italians made the only noises."

Belden then reported that, from a ridge overlooking the battlefield, he heard a voice call out, "Look, prisoners, thousands of them." Below him he saw a mass of black figures advancing from a smokey grove of olive tree. A British soldier with a grin on his face headed a column of about 2,000 of them. At the rear of the column were about 50 Germans "as unhappy about being captured as the Italians were happy." [24]

The Allies, meanwhile, were also engaged in heavy combat with the Axis armies northwest of Wadi Akarit. British General Harold Alexander, who in February had assumed command of the Allied ground forces in North Africa, had ordered the Americans – specifically, the II Corps under now Lieutenant General George S. Patton Jr. – to take Gasfa, which they did before moving quickly south and east to overwhelm the Axis armies at El Guettar and Sened Station, covering a total of 75 miles in five days.

South of El Guettar, Brigadier General Theodore "Ted" Roosevelt Jr. repelled a spoiling attack by the Germans and won what Major General Omar N. Bradley called the "first solid, indisputable defeat we inflicted on the German army in the war." But the U.S. forces were stopped for a week in the midst of an attempted drive due east to meet up with Montgomery's Eighth Army, which continued to push north along the coast.

By the end of March, however, the tide had turned as the Americans successfully carried out an order from Patton to attack the Axis north-south line of defense between them and the Eighth Army. [25] As the Axis forces melted away, the Americans were able to break through – but only after massive shelling – and Highway 15 was soon filled with American tanks, half-tracks, jeeps and trucks pressing rapidly eastward. As the first week of April drew to a close, American scouts and British troops met each other for the first time in the desert of North Africa, setting the stage for the British Eighth Army to to capture Tunis while the Americans focused on Bizerte. [26]

Traveling with the Eighth Army, Belden reported to *Time* in New York that the British now believed that the Axis forces were about to be defeated. "It begins to look as if they are right," he wrote. [27]

But in a series of battles over the next two weeks, while the Allied forces continued to advance, Axis troops escaped their grip – a fact that did not escape the attention of the correspondents covering the war for the American media, including *Time*, which suggested that the Axis had made fools of the Allies. [28]

Time reported in its May 24 issue that the battle for Fondouk, for instance, had been downright embarrassing for the Americans, notably the 34th Division under Major General Charles W. Ryder.

"Those who watched a brigade of [British Eighth Army troops] take the dominant hill north of Fondouk in half an hour, who later saw the British armor plunge through a 450-yard-deep minefield covered by twelve anti-tank guns and speed for Kairouan," *Time* said in a piece written from the field by Foreign News and Battlefronts Editor Charles Wertenbaker, "felt that there was something essentially wrong with the 34th, which had been unable to take the hills on the south side of the pass."

Still, an Allied final victory in North Africa was now close at hand, with more than 200,000 Axis troops cornered in a relatively small, 240-square-mile patch of northern Tunisia. Heavy fighting would continue over the next couple of weeks. But von Armin, who had replaced Rommel in March as commander of the Axis armies, would eventually surrender on May 12 at Ste. Marie-du-Zit, 15 miles south of Tunis, which had fallen five days earlier.

The Americans – now under the command of Bradley, who replaced Patton in April – took Bizerte on May 8.

"The enemy had neither the courage nor the skill for Dunkirk," Belden wrote in an on-the-spot analysis of the collapse of Axis forces, published in the May 24 issue of *Time* magazine. "He couldn't take it. He wilted. He collapsed swiftly, miserable and ingloriously....The Germans, the authors of blitzes, could not understand a blitz in reverse. The quick push on Tunis, though it was an obvious move, gave the enemy a shock greater than that of all our shells and bombs. From that shock the Germans and Italians never recovered."

Belden wrote, moreover, that the Axis intelligence apparatus was "unbelievably" bad – a fact that also contributed to the Axis collapse. Many German officers, for instance, were not aware that Tunis had fallen, and on May 11, four days after it had been captured, the officers continued to drive their soldiers toward the capital right into the hands of the Allies.

Wresting North Africa from the Axis armies – in a campaign that had begun in November 1942, when the Allies landed in Morocco and Algeria, and ended with the surrender of Hitler's commanders in May 1943 – had been achieved at the cost of more than 70,000 Allied casualties, including some 20,000 Americans, of which about 7,000 had been killed in action.

British Prime Minister Winston S. Churchill, however, in an address to the U.S. Congress on May 19, suggested that the price of victory in North Africa had not been too high.

"One continent at least has been cleansed and purged forever from Fascist or Nazi tyranny," Churchill said. "[F]or us, we can say at this stage...`One continent redeemed.'"

With the redemption of a continent, and with fellow war correspondent and close friend Don Whitehead, Belden would now head to Algiers, where Eisenhower had set up his headquarters to prepare for the upcoming Allied invasion of Sicily, code-named Operation Husky. It would be the largest amphibious operation of World War II – surpassing by two divisions the Allied landing at Normandy, which would come eleven months later.

12

LANDING AT GELA

On July 9, 1943, as the sun was setting over the Mediterranean Sea, Jack Belden, of *Time* magazine, stood with his legs wide apart on the swaying upper deck of the USS Barnett, en route from North Africa to Sicily.

"The sea ahead of me was an undulating, dappled path, where heavy transports, dripping and rolling, chased one another in a wavering battle column," he wrote. "On the rest of the sea, thousands of warships of the British and American Navies, swaying in sinuous and menacing lines, ploughed deeply through the water and showed now their rising, pulsating bows and now the tops of their spray-clouded masts." [1]

Belden was one of three correspondents who had been assigned by *Time* to cover the Allied landing at Sicily, where the Americans would assault the southwest coast at Gela and the British would attack along southeast coast south of Syracuse.

Time Publisher P.I. Prentice, writing in the magazine two weeks after the operation, said that the task of the correspondents was to provide American readers with a "first-hand feel" for the Sicily invasion: Reg Ingraham, "our naval expert," on duty with the American warships off shore; John Hersey, a veteran of the Guadalcanal Campaign in the Pacific from August 7, 1942 to February 9, 1943, who flew into Sicily with the American transport aircraft; and Belden, "a veteran of four years' fighting in China, companion of General Stilwell in the retreat from Burma [and] often under fire with the British Eighth Army as it swept across the Mareth Line and up through Tunisia," who would go ashore with the U.S. Seventh Army's 1st Infantry Division.

Commanding the division was Major General Terry Allen, whose assistant commander was Brigadier General Theodore "Ted" Roosevelt Jr., the son of the ex-president. Both were veterans of the Tunisian campaign.

Belden had been assigned to accompany Roosevelt on the USS Barnett, and his friend and colleague Don Whitehead was with Allen on the USS Samuel Chase, which also carried the commander of the DIME task force, Rear Admiral John L. Hall Jr.

Commanding the overarching U.S. Seventh Army was the brilliant but abrasive tank-warring master strategist Lieutenant General George S. Patton, Jr., who sailed on the operation's flagship, the USS Monrovia. His "Order of the Day" was to the point: "When we land we will meet German and Italian soldiers whom it is our honor and privilege to attack and destroy. Many of you have in your veins German and Italian blood, but remember that these ancestors of yours so loved freedom that they gave up home and country to cross the ocean in search of liberty ....Remember that as attackers we have the initiative. We must retain this tremendous advantage by always attacking rapidly, ruthlessly, viciously, without rest. However tired and hungry you may be, the enemy will be more tired, more hungry. Keep punching. God is with us. We shall win." [2]

Allied planning for the invasion had begun immediately after the Casablanca Conference in French Morocco, which took place from January 14 to January 24. There, U.S. President Franklin D. Roosevelt and British Prime Minister Winston S. Churchill, meeting with their senior military advisers, had decided on the next steps for prosecuting the war, which included invading Sicily and then moving on to the Italian mainland.

It was agreed that the Sicily invasion, initially set for June but later moved to July 10, would involve nearly 3,000 Allied ships and landing craft that would leave from staging ports in Algeria, Tunisia, Libya, Egypt and Lebanon – as well as from the United States and Scotland – and rendezvous off the Mediterranean island of Malta before heading in a massive armada to the Sicilian coast.

Roughly 160,000 Allied personnel from the United States, the United Kingdom, Canada and Free France would take part in the attack.

Patton chose to organize his forces around three assault divisions: Major General Troy Middleton's 45th Division, newly arrived from the United States, would wade ashore on the right near Scoglitti; on the left, Major General Lucian K. Truscott's Third Division would land at Licata; and in the center, in what was expected to be the most difficult of the three assaults, Allen's First Division would seek to secure Gela and its nearby airfields, including Ponte Olivo, just northwest of the city, and then to move north to Niscemi.

Supporting Allen would be two battalions of Army Rangers under the command of Lieutenant Colonel William O. Darby and two regiments of paratroopers from the 82nd Airborne Division, commanded by Colonel James M. Gavin.

All three amphibious landings were scheduled to take place at 2:45 a.m. on July 10. But Gavin's paratroopers were ordered to land on the island a few hours ahead of the waterborne assault to seize the high ground north of the beachheads occupied by Allen's forces and to block the road south from Niscemi.

Following the Axis surrender in North Africa in mid-May, Belden and the other war correspondents working in the region were sworn to silence about future operations and prohibited from filing reports from the field.

This turned out to be particularly difficult given that General Dwight D. Eisenhower, who had been chosen as the supreme Allied commander of the Sicilian operation, had called a press briefing at Allied Forces Headquarters (AFHG) at the Hotel St. George in Algiers on June 13 and made an announcement that would otherwise have been front-page news – that the Allied invasion of Sicily would take place in early July.

Eisenhower's director of information, Brigadier General Robert A. McClure, had suggested that Eisenhower brief the correspondents concerning the Allies' future plans. But he was shocked to hear him plainly state that the next objective would be Sicily. After the press briefing, McClure told the correspondents that many Allied officers had still not been made privy to the plans, so he cautioned them to keep what they had just heard strictly to themselves. [3]

After the war, in his book on the European campaign entitled *Crusade for Europe*, published in 1948, Eisenhower wrote that he had decided to take the unprecedented step of informing the press of a military operation in advance "paradoxically, to maintain secrecy." He said he had to stop the speculation that had been mounting among the reporters regarding the future intentions of the Allied forces.

"At the moment northern Africa was a hive of preparation for the Sicilian invasion," Eisenhower wrote. "At every possible spot along the beaches we were holding exercises; ports were being stacked with needed supplies, and harbors and inlets were receiving landing craft. It seemed certain that if reporters seeking items of interest for their papers and radio networks should continue to report upon activities throughout the theater, the enemy would soon be able to make rather accurate deductions as to the strength and timing of our attack, even if we should be successful in concealing its location." [4]

Eisenhower said that during periods of "combat inactivity" reporters tended to fill their stories with speculation. So he decided to take them into his confidence. Still, he said, "mouths fell open" when he began the press briefing with the news. But he said that the exercise – although one he would not want to repeat – was a complete success.

"From that moment onward, until after the attack was launched," Eisenhower wrote, "nothing speculative came out of the theater and no representative of the press attempted to send out anything that could possible be of any value to the enemy." [5]

The correspondents were also expected to keep quiet about the training exercises that had taken place in June along the North African coast. As Whitehead put it, the invasion of North Africa and the subsequent fighting in Tunisia had revealed that basic training for the troops was inadequate for the tasks ahead, including the Sicily operation. And the pre-Operation Torch training in the United States had clearly not been realistic enough to condition the troops, either physically or mentally, for live warfare. [6]

So, between the conquest of Tunisia and the invasion of Sicily, an "Invasion Training Center" was set up and brought into full operation along a 100-mile stretch off Mediterranean coastline west of Algiers, near the village of Arzew, to which correspondents such as Belden and Whitehead were invited. But they were sworn to refrain from writing home about it until after the Sicily operation.

Here, division after division were schooled in street and house-to-house fighting and in amphibious landings under fire, employing lessons learned from the North Africa campaign.

At one landing rehearsal, near Arzew on June 23, a group of top commanders, including Eisenhower, Bradley and Patton, watched in amazement as troops from Allen's First Division stumbled up the beach a half mile from their intended mark.

"And just where the hell are your goddamned bayonets?" Patton shouted at them from the water's edge. Watching the spectacle, Major General Harold R. Bull, an officer on Eisenhower's staff, whispered to Bradley: "Well, there goes Georgie's chance for a crack at higher command. That temper is going to finish him yet." [7]

It was decided, meanwhile, than no more than a dozen reporters – out of the 100 or so American and British correspondents who had covered the North African campaign – would be allowed to land in Sicily with the first wave of troops, including, as *Time* magazine put it, "burly, silent, broody Jack Belden." [8]

Two weeks after Eisenhower's press briefing, with Belden securely on board, the 486-foot-long, 9,750-ton USS Barnett left Oran, Algeria, and headed for Sicily along with the other Allied ships participating in the operation, steaming east along the North African coast for three days, past Tripoli, before turning north – a diversionary move intended to confuse the Axis commanders about Allied plans.

Belden reported that before reaching Malta, the USS Barnett had sailed for four "idyllic days," with the Mediterranean Sea exhibiting "all her fabled, summer-time charms, with the blue ocean carpet scarcely once wrinkled by an untoward wave." His conversations with Roosevelt in his cabin at night, however, were unsettling.

"[W]ith solemn faces," Belden wrote, "we had declared that the failure of our invasion would be a fatal blow from which the American people, desiring action against Japan and not Germany, might never recover." [9]

On board the ship, under Roosevelt's command, were two battalions of the First Division's 26th Infantry Regiment, being led by Col. John W. Bowen, a West Point graduate who had turned 33 years old on July 3 and, according to Belden, was a skilled technician and a "cool, resourceful leader."

Belden said that, prior to the Sicily operation, Bowen had been "baptized in defeat" during the American debacle at Kasserine Pass, in February, but then he and his soldiers had been victorious at Djebel Tahent (Hill 609) two months later. [10] He would eventually attain the rank of Lieutenant General, and his decorations would include the Distinguished Service Medal and the Silver Star. He retired from the military in 1968 and died in San Francisco nine years later.

As they prepared to arrive off the coast of Sicily on July 9, 1943, Bowen's soldiers gathered one platoon at a time on the sun-drenched top deck of the Barnett to study a relief model of the town of Gela, which they would soon assault. None of them, Belden said, showed any sign of nervousness. On the contrary, he said, everyone was in good spirits, "acting more like tourists going on an excursion to a foreign land than soldiers preparing to assault a hostile shore....In the calmness of the sea everyone undoubtedly had found a sedative for whatever turbulence lurked in his spirit. Briefly, we had been at peace." [11]

But then, as if on cue, at noon on July 9 – on the eve of the invasion – a fresh breeze kicked up out of the north and swung around to the west. Toward the middle of the afternoon, Belden said, it "lashed the sea into a froth."

"[T]he whole sea, mounting higher and higher," he wrote, "had at last assaulted our fleet, rocking the transports from side to side, crashing down with an angry venom over our low-slung destroyers and all but swallowing the small tank-landing craft....We call it 'Mussolini wind.' "

Belden said that Bowen's soldiers were growing increasingly pale and seasick and preferred to stay in their bunks, fearing that if they were to venture on deck, they would vomit over the rail.

On board the USS Samuel Chase, Don Whitehead noted during a meeting in the skipper's cabin that Admiral Hall and Major General Allen were concerned. He said that many officers were convinced that disaster would be the end result if the invasion were to continue on schedule in such rough weather, noting that they learned later that the Allied high command in Algiers, in fact, were considering delaying the mission, even though doing so would give the Germans and the Italians more time to prepare their defenses.

"Small landing craft could not possibly carry troops and equipment through a stormy surf," Whitehead wrote. "They were certain to be capsized or strewn along the beaches in wild disorder." [12]

But at dusk on July 9 the strong Mediterranean winds began to die down, and the seas subsided in what Whitehead said appeared to be a sign that God was taking mercy on the Allied warriors. Spirits among the soldiers rose as they took the change in the weather to be an omen of good luck.

The plan of attack called for the Third Infantry Division to land at Licata; for the Rangers, led by Lieutenant Colonel William O. Darby, of Fort Smith, Ark., to attack the town of Gela and a battery of enemy guns near the town; for the First Infantry Division – with Belden, Whitehead, and H.R. Knickerbocker, of the Chicago Sun, who was on board the USS Samuel Chase, representing the press – to land just east of Gela; and for the 45th Infantry Division to launch an assault on the beach to the right.

Just before 3 a.m. on July 10, troops from the USS Barnett, with correspondent Belden in tow, hit the Gela beach. Troops from the USS

Samuel Chase, along with Whitehead and Knickerbocker, followed just after dawn, at about 5 a.m.

"I tried to appear calm and indifferent to the sounds of battle before these veterans of Tunisia," Whitehead wrote, "but my heart was pounding with excitement." [13]

Belden was equally concerned, and he even began to doubt the wisdom of accompanying the troops ashore. But he took courage from the soldiers around him, including Roosevelt, who, with his ruddy face and walking stick, had a word of encouragement for each and every soldier.

"[H]ad he not been in the last war," Belden asked rhetorically about Roosevelt, "gone to Europe with the very same 26th Infantry Regiment of the very same First Infantry Division with which now twenty-six years later he was returning to Europe?"

Roosevelt wrote to his wife Eleanor from the USS Barnett on July 7 that the officers and men on board were not young anymore. "They're not the fresh, smooth-cheeked boys you saw at a dance more than two years ago," he wrote. "They've got a hard-bitten look." Later, he wrote: "The sea is mill-pond still....Everything is battened down, port-holds are closed, lights doused, no smoking on deck....There's a sort of dead hush over the ship now. No one is moving on deck." [14] And on the night of July 9, he wrote to her that the ship was dark and the men were moving to their assembly stations. "Soon the boats will be lowered away. Then we'll be off." [15]

For his part, Belden was exhilarated by the prospect of the upcoming assault – at least for a moment. "A flush of thrill and excitement shot through me like flame," he wrote. "It was wonderful. It was exhilarating. Smash! Pound! Roar! Rush! – toward the goal. Here we come! Whee! My mouth was open and I giggled with insane laughter." [16]

But he also was overcome not by what he called the terrible knowledge that "on that waiting shore there was nothing but a yawning, empty void and not a single thing I wanted."

Soon, however, he would be climbing down the net on the side of the ship into a small, flat-bottom landing craft with the other men, who, as it roared for shore, were "sicker than ever. They held their heads in their hands. They moaned. They vomited." [17]

The landing craft – designated a Landing Craft, Vehicle, Personnel (LCVP), which was one of 20,000 or so such vessels designed and built specifically for the war by New Orleans boat-builder Andrew Jackson Higgins to typically carry a platoon-sized complement of 36 men – plowed through and over the waves at nine knots and eventually came to a violent halt as it hit the Gela beach in the early morning darkness.

"Glancing fearfully toward the bow of the boat," Belden wrote, "I saw it swinging down, like a huge jaw opening....I advanced to the ramp. 'Here it comes,' I thought and jumped."

With the water now up to his neck, he pushed forward keeping only his helmet-covered head above the water and made out a sandy beach ahead of him, rising slightly. "Figures were crawling on hands and knees up the slope. Every few minutes they halted and lay flat on their stomachs. By now the water was really shallow. I straightened up and dashed for the beach. Bullets snapped overhead. I threw myself flat on the sand. At last, I was on dry land." [18]

Other men, however, were less fortunate, as the LCVPs they were in struck sandbars or reefs. Ramps stuck. Some men jumped too soon or too late. And some drowned.

Belden and Whitehead observed separately that the enemy resistance was surprisingly light. "This is not as bad as the Mareth Line," Belden wrote. But both men were also aware of how useless they were to the cause as typewriter-totting war reporters.

"To what purpose did I," Belden asked, "an unarmed man, scribbling undecipherable words on a notebook, follow ridiculously these soldiers, heavily accoutered for murder, so frightfully cautious, so terribly earnest about everything?" [19]

For his part, Whitehead said that one of his main concerns had been to ensure that his typewriter remained operational, and that to protect it from sea spray he had wrapped it in a piece of rubberized material made from contraceptives, which the troops also used to keep moisture out of the barrels of their carbines and rifles. They were also employed to waterproof money, cigarettes, pictures and letters.

"I found the number of contraceptives issued by the army to the troops had no relation to morals," Whitehead wrote. [20]

Belden's typewriter, he said, was supposed to have been brought ashore during one of the later assault waves. But it had not shown up. But the day after he landed, he took a walk along the beach and happened to see an abandoned, nearly submerged jeep about twenty yards from shore. On a whim, he searched the vehicle and found his typewriter, which was covered with a thick, gooey white substance that clogged all the keys. It was, he said, hissing as if some chemical reaction had been triggered by the water.

"Feeling downhearted because I now could not write any story, I shoved the useless typewriter in my musette bag, and we ploughed on in search of the headquarters of the First Division," he wrote in long hand. [21]

At the division's advance command post – set up by Roosevelt in a small lemon grove about 400 yards from the beach – Belden met up with Whitehead as the Germans were beginning to counterattack, launching heavy artillery against the Allies and sending waves of fighter aircraft through heavy anti-aircraft fire to attack Allied ships and the beach crawling with Allied soldiers.

The next day (July 11) Belden, Whitehead and Knickerbocker made their way to the hilltop town of Gela, where Darby and his Rangers, within seven hours of landing on the island, had beaten off an attack by eight Italian tanks and had taken the town ahead of the First Division.

In a building with "DUCE!" scrawled on one side, Belden found Darby sitting behind a desk acting as if he were the mayor of the town, and he asked the 32-year-old officer what had happened.

"Well, it was sort of rough for a while," Darby said. "About nine o'clock I thought we had resistance stamped out, so I sent the town crier through the streets to shout the news and tell the people that we were Americans that had come to help them. "[T]hen eight Eyetie tanks...came down the hills and started zoomin' through the streets. They raised hell....I saw one tank coming down a street and I chased it around the block in my jeep, swung around a corner, ran up on a sidewalk and started shooting at him with my 30-caliber machine gun. I must have fired 300 rounds at him. It wasn't doing any good and the tank still kept coming on. I ran like hell." [22]

Darby said that he then drove down to the beach, where he found an antitank gun and loaded it on to his jeep. There, he picked up Capt. Charles M. Shunstrom, and together they went after the recalcitrant Italian tank.

"Every time we slammed a shell in that dismounted gun," Darby told Belden, "she recoiled on Shunstrom and knocked him ass over teakettle into the back seat. But we hit the tank and knocked it out. After that we got another tank cornered right in the middle of the street. We must have put it out of commission because it wouldn't move. But nobody would come out of it either....I said, 'Here, let me fix 'em' and I fired an assault grenade at the tank, but that didn't budge 'em either. They were trough guys all right! Seeing they wanted to play rough, I thought I'd play rough too. So I took an incendiary grenade and walked up and slapped it on top of the tank. It began dripping inside, and we saw a little smoke coming out of the tank; then the turret opened and they all poured out screaming like they were made. After that we got another tank, and the rest went away. It's been pretty quiet since then."

Darby, who graduated from West Point in 1933, when Belden was jumping ship in Hong Kong to begin a new life, was killed by gunfire near Torbole, Italy, on April 1945 while attached to the U.S. 10th Mountain Division. He was posthumously awarded the rank of Brigadier General – the only U.S. Army officer so honored in World War II.

To Belden, meanwhile, it was becoming clear in early July 1943 that Sicily was not where he wanted to be. On a knoll overlooking the Gela beach, where he, Whitehead and Knickerbocker had slept the night before on flea-infested mattresses salvaged from an abandoned Italian army barracks, he mumbled curses to himself as he awoke on the hot Sicilian morning of July 11.

"Jeezus," he growled. "What am I doing here? I could have gone home for the first time in eight years – and I turned down the chance." [23]

Whitehead tossed him a cigarette, recalling later that Belden never had cigarettes or matches of his own, and he asked him why he had not gone home.

"Well, I saw the Chinese being beaten by the Japs and I was with Stilwell on his retreat from Burma," Belden replied. "I figured I'd like to be with the winner for a change. You get awfully tired writing about retreats."

Knickerbocker told him to quit his complaining, saying he was lucky to be alive. "Maybe," Belden said with a grin. "But it would help to see a good-looking dame occasionally."

That, of course, did not happen even as the three reporters, after piling their bedding and typewriters on a passing jeep, made their way down the hill to the First Division mess for breakfast. And as they did – unbeknownst to Belden at the time – enemy aircraft were attacking the USS Barnett. One bomb detonated just off the ship's port bow, ripping a hole in the hull and causing heavy flooding.

Subsequently, the ship was made to list to starboard to bring the hole above the waterline. Seven men had been killed in the attack, and 35 were injured – all Army personnel. The next day the ship left Sicily under its own power and returned to Algiers for repairs, arriving there on July 15.

But more bad news was yet to come.

On the evening of July 11, while Belden, Whitehead and Knickerbocker were sitting on a hillside above the beach discussing the day's events, they were also listening for the sound of airplanes, since at 11 p.m. U.S. paratroopers were scheduled to land on the beachhead to support the advancing First Division. [24]

German aircraft had been active over the American sector for most of the day, so senior Army and Navy officers went to some length to inform anyone who needed to know that Allied aircraft were planning a nighttime paratroop drop over the area. But in what Whitehead later called "one of the most blood chilling sights I have ever seen" nervous anti-aircraft gunners ashore and afloat opened fire on the American transport aircraft as they arrived over the beaches in the wake of a brief German air raid.

"O, God, No!" Belden yelled. "No! No! Stop, you bastards, stop! Stop shooting!"

But the planes kept coming, and the gunners kept shooting. Some planes fell into the sea; others crashed on the beachhead. Some amazingly flew through the hail of gunfire; others crash-landed safely; and still others flew around the fleet to escape the friendly-fire attack. But in the end, Allied antiaircraft guns shot down a total of 23 planes and damaged another 37 out of the 144 American paratrooper-carrying aircraft that comprised the mission. A follow-up investigation would reveal that not everyone, in fact, had been informed of the impending American paratroop drop despite the best efforts of the Seventh Army command.

By the morning of July 12, when Eisenhower came ashore for the first time unaware of the previous night's debacle, the Allies had landed some 80,000 troops on the Vermont-size island, along with some 7,000 vehicles, 300 tanks, and 900 guns. [25]

Patton had come ashore the previous afternoon, no longer able to bear, according to Belden, "the stillness of command offshore." He was seen by U.S. troops in Gela riding in an armored command car with his three-starred flag flying up front – "beautiful and battle-fevered in boots and whipcords." Just as he arrived, Belden reported, German bombers viciously attacked the town of Gela, killing 70 civilians. [26]

The next day, Belden and Whitehead joined Darby's Rangers for an assault on the hill-town of Butera, 10 miles inland, which was held by the Germans with some less-than-willing Italian soldiers under their command.

From their observation post in the hills outside of Gela, Darby looked up the twisting valley that led toward Butera, where he would set up a command post for the operation. "I know your boys are tired," Darby told Capt. Shunstrom, whose company would lead the operation. "But they are the best for this job." [27]

Darby told Shunstrom, only 22 years old at the time, to hold his men back a mile from Butera until he was ordered to attack. "If you are not fired on, do not fire," he said. "If you get in trouble, fire a steady stream of red rockets. That will be the signal for our artillery. If you are successful, shoot two green flares. That will be the signal for all the Rangers to move on the town."

No one knew what to expect as the men set off on foot at about 10:30 p.m., although there were intelligence reports suggesting that about 400 enemy troops were garrisoned in the town.

At about 12:30 a.m., the Ranger detachment of 50 or so men reached the top of a ridge, where they could see Butera straddling the hill ahead. "It was dark and forbidding against the starlit sky," Whitehead wrote. By about 4 a.m., the town had already been secured – not the result of a major battle but through the courage of two men: Army Privates John C. See and John Constantine.

With Shunstrom looking on in a small square on the edge of Butera, Belden and Whitehead asked the two men what had happened.

See told them that he and Constantine were the lead scouts in Shunstrom's first platoon, led by First Lieutenant Collins Kendrick, and were ahead of him on the road leading into Butera when they saw several Italians lolling around and chatting beside their guns and trucks. Constantine shouted to them in Italian to surrender or be killed. Two German officers were also there and ordered the Italians to stop when they moved to give up to the Americans. But in the confusion someone fired a shot, and Constantine quickly fired back and killed the man who had shot at him. Then the two German officers fled on foot and See chased them firing his tommy gun as he ran. [28]

Belden later wrote that, in fact, only a small part of the town had been occupied by the Americans, so Shunstrom walked the streets with two riflemen "poking a gun around street corners, then darting quickly across open spaces and constantly whirling and turning to face any possible ambush. He looked like an agile young killer."

A veteran of North Africa, Shunstrom would go on to distinguish himself in future fighting at Salerno and was known as "The Wild Man of the Anzio Beachhead," where he was one of a small group of Rangers who escaped a German trap that wiped out most of his fellow soldiers.

He reportedly was taken prisoner by the Germans but escaped and spent five months on the run before gaining safe haven with the British forces.

Whitehead said he often wondered what happened to this "handsome, fierce young Captain Shunstrom" after the war, and one day he saw a news report saying that Shunstrom had been brought before a Superior Court judge in Los Angeles on charges of armed robbery. He pleaded not guilty, and not guilty by reason of insanity, on all ten counts.

The judge was quoted as saying that Shunstrom had changed from a "daring reckless young officer that his comrades knew, to a man filled with discouragement, disillusionment and even hatred for people who he thought would not allow him to earn a livelihood."

He was set free "to begin a new life," the judge said. "A nation cannot train a man to kill his fellow men without developing dangerous tendencies which often break out after he has returned from the combat areas. The passion to kill, rob or plunder, when developed, cannot be shut off like a faucet." [29]

Whitehead wrote that, in his view, Shunstrom – a hero of Sicily Salerno and Anzio – deserved a new life as payment for the one he had lost when he saw his best friends die in battle around him. He died in Buffalo, N.Y., in December 1972 at the age of 51.

13

TAKING SICILY

It is not surprising that Lieutenant General George S. Patton Jr., who commanded the U.S. Seventh Army's, successful invasion of Sicily in July 1943 would express deep frustration with what he saw as the relatively minor role he had been assigned to play in the ensuing campaign: to protect the left flank of Montgomery's Eighth Army as it moved up the east coast of the island toward Messina and the Italian mainland.

Patton thought rightly that his forces could be put to better use, and he also feared he would be deprived of any glory that might accrue from the expected Allied victory in the Sicily campaign.

So with map in hand on July 17, he flew unannounced to Tunis to make his case directly to the commander of the Allied ground forces, British General Sir Harold Alexander – a case that would later be buttressed by Montgomery's painfully slow advance up the coast and his encroachment on Patton's forces north of Gela.

Belden explained that Patton's plan was simple: to send one of the Seventh Army's divisions north and another up from the southwest, both meeting in the capital city of Palermo.

Reluctantly, Alexander, who doubted the ability of the Americans to carry their weight in the fight to come, agreed to give Patton more latitude with respect to pursuing the campaign.

After the meeting, according to Belden, Patton climbed into a British command car, slapped his leather-bound swagger stick into the palm of his hand and urged an accompanying correspondent to return to Sicily with him or risk missing the action. "You better come now," he told the reporter, "or my men will have killed all the bastards." [1]

Later, Alexander would wonder whether, following the meeting, the highly explosive American general might have decided just to take off across Sicily on his own without his permission, recalling that, in the meeting, Patton had angrily pulled out a map of the island, jabbed at it and said: "Have I got to stay here and protect the rear of [the] Eighth Army? I want to get on with this and push out." [2]

In fact, Patton's "push out" had already begun. On July 14, three days prior to his meeting with Alexander, he had met with the commander of the Third Infantry Division, Major General Lucian K. Truscott Jr., and ordered him to take the port city of Agrigento, ten miles up the coast from Gela, which he did with the help of Darby's Rangers on July 16, taking 7,000 Italian prisoners in the process. [3]

From Agrigento, the division, which was merged with the 2nd Armored Division and the 82nd Airborne Division to form a provisional corps under Major General Geoffrey Keyes, made a dash west and north through the Sicilian countryside, covering 30 miles or more in a day – through Sciacca, Castelvetrano and Prizzi and eventually into the outskirts of Palmero on July 22.

Among the division's hard-charging troops was an 18-year-old Texan who, in the next two years, would become the most decorated American soldier in World War II. His name was Audie Murphy, the son of sharecroppers, one of eleven children, whose father walked out on the family when he was 11 years old and was never heard from again. His mother died when he was 16.

"My temper was explosive," Murphy recalled in his 1949 autobiography, "To Hell and Back," which was made into a movie in 1955, in which Murphy played himself. "And my moods, typically Irish, swung from the heights to the depths. At school, I fought a great deal. Perhaps I was trying to level with my fists what I assumed fate had put above me." [4]

After completing eighth grade, Murphy left school to work and support his family, and after turning 18 years old, he applied to join the Marine Corps and the paratroops but was rejected because of his diminutive size (5' 5-1/2") and weight (112 pounds). He was eventually accepted by the Army, but he was not happy about it. "I was not overjoyed," he said. "The infantry was too commonplace for my ambition." [5]

His hopes for overseas service were also frustrated by his youthful appearance, which, he said, caused "much shaking of heads." But finally he was successful in winning an assignment to North Africa in early 1943 – just as full-scale combat there, as fate would have it, was winding down.

It would not be long, however, before the future winner of the Congressional Medal of Honor – the highest award available to military personnel – would see his first day of combat when he landed with the 15th Infantry Regiment of Truscott's Third Infantry Division near Licata on July 10. But there, too, assault troops had already taken the beach, and the battle had moved rapidly inland, leaving Murphy and the rest of the unit to tramp over the hills and fields without coming into direct contact with the enemy. "So far," he wrote, "the action of the unit has been undramatic and disappointingly slow." [6]

But soon the horror of war would hit home, when later in the day, as his unit was resting on the slope of an inland hill, an enemy shell whistled in out of nowhere – the explosion, he wrote, was "thunderous" – killing an unnamed, redheaded soldier who tumbled from a rock not far from Murphy with blood trickling from his nose and mouth.

"So it happens as easily as that," Murphy later ~~wrote~~ recalled. "You sit on a quiet slope with chin in hand. In the distance a gun slams; and the next minute you are dead."

For its part, the 1st Infantry Division, meanwhile, to which Belden was attached, would encounter stiff resistance as it moved inland from Gela, particularly in the hills around the central-island town of Barrafranca. By July 14, its 26th Infantry Regiment under Col. John W. Bowen had moved toward Mazzarino after Darby's Rangers had taken Butera to the south, and before noon it had consolidated on the high ground north and west of the city. But Belden reported in *Time* magazine that, at midnight on the night of July 15-16, near Barrafrana, the regiment was startled by the sound of machine-gun fire, which one soldier said clearly "ain't ours."

Introducing Belden's 2,300-plus-word report on the battle for Barrafranca, published in the August 2, 1943, issue of *Time*, the magazine's editors said that, in the article, Belden had uniquely described what war was like from the ground-zero perspective of the foot soldier, "with all its desperation, irrelevance and confusion."

At dawn on July 16, Belden wrote, the lieutenant colonel commanding the 2nd Battalion ordered another officer and five soldiers to follow him up a ridge off the road where a battle was then raging. Belden scrambled up the hill after them. Two other companies were ordered to take a higher hill ahead.

By 5:15 a.m. it was light enough to see a number of U.S. light tanks – M-3 Stuart "Honeys" – coming up the road from behind them and moving into position.

Near a house at the end of a cliff on the higher hill, Belden saw a machine gun and enemy soldiers moving toward it. He and soldiers from the 2nd Battalion tried to warn the Americans who were making their way up the hill and were not in a position to see the enemy, but to no avail. Artillery was ordered. But from the hill a curious guttural howling and yelling was heard, and just below the house figures were seen rushing down the slope. "They were our men, the men of the 1st Battalion's Company A," Belden wrote. "The German machine gun had found them."

"Heartsick, we watched those broken ranks stumbling down the slope," Belden reported. "It was worse when mortar shells landed in the middle of them. Beside me an awed voice said: 'They're getting hell kicked out of 'em, aren't they?' One of the figures suddenly fell over, then gripped himself between his legs. Men tried to reach him but were driven off, and he sat there alone on the slope of White House Hill."

Rocket shells began hitting slope and the hill crest, and the 1st Battalion began withdrawing as German tanks also opened fire. "The valley was shaking with heavy gunfire," Belden wrote. "Close at hand, above the heavy sound of artillery, came the sharp crackle of machine guns. Bullets whined through the trees."

"Dozens of voices were shouting at once," he wrote. "The fog of war had descended on us in earnest." Sweeping out of Barrafranca, he said, were thirteen German tanks that overran the 3rd Battalion in the plain. "Temporarily unopposed by infantry, the tanks came down the valley between the hills, shooting up at us as they came."

But from a high hill, American artillery began to rain down on the valley increasingly, and the light U.S. "Honey" tanks, which had hidden in a draw out of reach of the superior firepower of the German tanks, now began to pour diagonal fire across the German vehicles. A U.S. artillery observer, watching the tanks go at each other from a seat high above the valley, murmured to Belden in awe: "You'll never see anything like this again in 20 years."

The U.S. tanks, for their part, were briefly able to take the wind out of the German sails. But the 3rd Battalion was driven back, leaving only the 2nd Battalion in a position to take what was now being called by the soldiers White House Hill.

With his company of 2nd Battalion soldiers, Capt. J. Kelly, in fact, had already arrived at the top of the hill and was coming under heavy fire from at least one German machine-gun. From the crest of the hill where the other members of the battalion – and Belden – were still positioned, Lieutenant Walter Bowland began to direct mortar fire at the Germans until Kelly radioed frantically that the shells were falling on him. "Cease fire," Bowland yelled, even as the German machine gun continued to bark.

The remaining 2nd Battalion soldiers – seeing no other choice – rushed the hill. "As we climbed," Belden wrote, "everyone grew faint, turning pale and looking at each other in the naked frankness of misery....Soldiers were slow in reaching the top of the hill. They had not slept all night. They had marched a long way into battle. They had had the toughest fight of the Sicily campaign."

But in the end the men came through. "Trucks rushed ammunition to tanks which had no ammunition," Belden wrote. "White House Hill was taken. The assault there broke the back of the German resistance. All except a few stragglers pulled out. That evening, with the 1st Battalion and the tanks, we drove into Barrafranca."

By early the next morning, July 17, the 1st Infantry Division had passed through Pietraperzia, and on July 18 Caltanissetta was secured. Three hours later Santa Caterina fell.

Belden wrote from Enna on July 20 that "nothing but smiling faces and declarations of joy" had greeted the Americans' arrival. The same was true at San Giuseppe, he said, where "on balconies inclosed by iron railings, girls and old men screamed and yelled and waved white flags and handkerchiefs as if they were banners of joy....On the ground a man was rushing up to all halted vehicles and pouring out huge tumblefuls of wine, begging American soldiers to drink."

With H.R. Knickerbocker, of the Chicago Sun, Belden continued in a jeep driven by Whitey Beckman through San Giuseppe and into the hills outside of Palermo, where they encountered Lieutenant Colonel Paul A. Disney, commander of the 82nd Armored Reconnaissance Battalion, who told them that the road ahead was not clear.

Disney said that a scout car with six U.S. soldiers had just been struck by an artillery shell, and a U.S. counter-artillery response was being initiated. "[W]e didn't know what to do," Belden wrote. "But it is the job of the reconnaissance unit [to which he was attached] to find out for the rest of the army what is ahead, so we went forward."

After a two-hour battle, the offending German 155 was discovered and taken out, and the reconnaissance unit proceeded through the tiny village of Giacalone – with three or four houses and white flags flying – and down the hill behind a column of tanks into a valley leading to Palermo.

But the welcome they had received until now would not compare to the embrace that greeted them in Monreale, just outside of Palermo.

In a scene documented by award-winning photographer Robert Capa in the August 23, 1943, issue of *LIFE*, "a flood of people threw themselves in front of our tanks and around our jeeps, completely stopping us," Belden wrote. "Men and children rushed up to grab our hands and then as the crowd thickened, a strange, wild frenzy seemed to grip everyone and we were hugged and squeezed and kissed by men delirious and babbling incoherently with joy." [7]

Capa later wrote that the road into Palermo was lined with tens of thousands of frantic Sicilians waving white sheets and homemade American flags with not enough stars and too many stripes. "Everyone had a cousin in Brook-a-leen," he wrote. [8]

For his part, Belden said while people in other towns had begged the U.S. soldiers for cigarets, "here cigarets were showered on us. Grapes, wine, watermelons were poured into our laps by hundreds of hands....Conquerors that we were, we could not escape. Only when a voice yelled, 'That way to Palermo,' were we able to break through the crowd and head toward our objective."

At the bottom of the hill, the column came to a broad avenue leading directly into Palermo. All the vehicles were ordered to halt. But the commanding officer said that he would not object to Belden and Knickerbocker, with their driver Whitey Beckman, driving into the city unescorted. "So I drove the jeep and Whitey sat in the back with his rifle and the three of us set out to capture Palermo by ourselves."

Belden said that, when they arrived in Palermo on the morning of July 22, the city was eerily empty of civilians. "There were no crowds as in Monreale," he wrote. "Only a few people were here and there." Passing through a stone arch, however, they ran into an advance patrol of the 3rd Division led by Lieutenant Colonel John Heintges, which, Belden said, had entered the city from the opposite direction.

Early that afternoon, a delegation of civilians offered to surrender the city to Brig. Gen. William W. Eagles, the 3d Division's assistant commander. But the offer was turned down since the division commander, Major General Truscott, had ordered that only Major General Geoffrey

Keyes, Patton's deputy, would be allowed to accept the Italians' surrender of the city.

Coming from his command post at Corleone, 30 miles to the south, Keyes arrived in Palermo around 7 p.m. on July 22 surrounded by aides and swarms of MPs and, according to Capa, demanded that the celebrating Italian gendarmes produce the general in command of Palermo.

"The gendarmes nodded and said 'Yes, yes,' but did not move," recalled Capa, who was Hungarian by birth. "The exasperated Keyes asked for an interpreter and I offered my services. I got the point over to the gendarmes somehow. I explained that the general wanted to avoid any unnecessary bloodshed and wanted the Italian general to announce the terms of surrender to the populace. The gendarmes nodded, 'Si, si,' climbed into a jeep with a couple of MP's, and took off toward the center of town."

Fifteen minutes later, the jeep reappeared, and what followed was a scene that AP correspondent Don Whitehead would later call "one of those comedies which frequently relieve the grimness of war." [9]

Seated in the back of the jeep, between to smiling Italian gendarmes, was an obviously unhappy General Giuseppe Molinero, who was ordered by Keyes into his command car. "Interpreter, come along," said Keyes, directing his order at a stunned Capa. [10]

Capa said that they drove to the Royal Palace and together exited the car in the courtyard, where Keyes demanded the immediate and unconditional surrender of the town and the military district of Palermo.

"I translated [Keyes's remarks] into French, the language I knew best, and hoped the Italian would understand me," Capa recalled. "He replied in perfect French and said that he would be only too glad to so so, but it was really impossible. He had already surrendered four hours earlier to an American infantry division that had entered the city from the opposite direction."

Keyes quickly became impatient with the delay. "Stop the jabbering, soldier!" he said. "I want unconditional surrender and I want it immediately!"

Capa said he explained to the Italian general that it may be easier, in fact, to surrender the second time and that besides Keyes had the authority to allow him to keep his personal belongings in prison. The general consented and promptly surrendered in French, Italian and Sicilian and asked whethere he could keep his wife as well.

"My translator's job was done," Capa wrote, "and I went back to taking pictures. Later, when the surrender ceremony was over, I saw the Italian general being led away to prison – empty-handed and alone."

The pictures that Capa captured on that extraordinary day appeared in the August 23, 1943, issue of *LIFE* under the headline, "The Surrender of Palermo: LIFE Photographer Robert Capa Enters City With the American Troops."

Following the fall of Palermo, Belden and Whitehead, along with Capa, decided to hook up with the 1st Infantry Division as it pursued the retreating Germans eastward across the island as far as Troina, where its main fighting force, the 15th Panzer Grenadier Division, abruptly halted its withdrawal and took a stand.

Several attempts by units of the 1st Division to take the city were rebuffed by vicious counterattacks by German artillery, and by August 2 – the fifth day of the battle – its commander, Major General Allen, had had enough and decided to launch an all-out attack against Troina across the entire front now held by the division. [11]

The main thrust of the attack was assigned to the division's 16th Regiment, and at dusk on August 2 Belden and Whitehead joined the 3rd Battalion under Major Charles T. Horner Jr., who would later be awarded a Distinguished Service Cross for his bravery in fighting the Germans near Troina on July 29, for the final drive on the rugged, hilltop city.

With the battalion initially pinned down by enemy artillery, Horner ordered a mortar barrage by Second Lieutenant John E. McCarthy, who, according to Horner, was "the best damned mortar man in this man's army," [12] and within minutes Belden and Whitehead saw a dozen or so German soldiers running down the hill toward them. "They've got their hands up," Whitehead yelled. Later, at the top of the hill, the Americans came across a German machine-gun post and in it a dead soldier on his knees.

"[H]is body [was] hunched forward in a tense position, as he had been in the act of firing when he was hit," Belden later reported. "He was headless, and there was a bloody stump sticking up from his shoulders that was his neck." [13]

Toward nightfall on August 5, Belden and Whitehead watched from a ridge about a mile from Troina as a formation of American B-25s unloaded their lethal weaponry on the town, which vanished behind a curtain of black smoke. Another aerial assault – this one by a series of dive-bombers – came just after dawn on August 6 even as Major Horner was ordering the 3rd Battalion to move toward the city en masse.

Whitehead wondered if Troina would be like all the other shell-pocked towns that they had passed through – "dead, stinking and depressing."

"I wondered if there would be old women sitting in doorways and peering out of dark rooms," he later recalled. "Always it seems the first living things you see in any wrecked city are old women. Old women and cats. They either are very brave...or forgotten." [14]

After the last wave of dive-bombers had left, the 3rd Battalion soldiers crawled out from the ditches they had dug and headed once more toward Troina, according to Belden's account of the battle, which ran in the August 23 issue of *Time*, passing along the way "a ghostly old woman lying amid crumbling plaster and shattered timber, who stretched out her hands to us, stared out of sightless eyes, and moaned like the wind whining through pine trees."

Arriving in the city, which had been abandoned by the Germans and was basically destroyed, Horner and several of his men found a girl of about 10 years old lying on a bench, with her black hair streaked with gray powder plaster. One of her legs was wrapped in bandages, and in her hands she clutched a cracker a soldier had given her. "She didn't move," Belden recalled, "but only stared at the ceiling."

On another bench was a boy of about 13 naked except for his underwear. "Over his body were red scars where he'd been burned," Belden wrote. "Our medics had no salve for burns with them, so the boy sat there, shivering from head to foot and in great pain. For a long while he remained silent, but finally his lips began to tremble, and his body shock with great sobs."

A little girl, no more than eight years old, sat down on the bench next to the boy and pulled his head down into her lap and stroked her hair. Little bird chirps came from her lips as if she were saying: "Don't cry, don't cry."

Belden said that, at that moment, Horner stood by the door with a decidedly grim expression on his face. "I never wanted to capture a town more than this in my life," he said. "But now ...."

It would take another 10 days of heavy fighting and many more civilian casualties, however, before the Allies would be able to drive the Germans out of Sicily and on to the Italian mainland. Just as the 1st Infantry Division was battling for possession of Troina, in fact, the 3rd Infantry Division, under Major General Truscott, was facing equally stiff resistance at San Fratello as it moved east from Palermo toward Messina along the northern coast of the island.

Audie Murphy, now a corporal in the division's 15th Infantry Regiment, described the area as heavily mined, with the enemy "entrenched and determined." [15]

"On our approach to the [Furiano River on August 3], we are caught in a concentration of artillery and motar fire," Murphy later recalled. "The earth shudders; and the screaming of shells intermingles with the screaming of men. We fall back, reorganize, and again storm forward. For a second time the barrage hits us. Again we withdraw."

To break the impasse, Patton ordered Truscott to conduct a flanking maneuver from the sea aimed at threatening the Germans from the rear, forcing them, as II Corps Commander Omar Bradley put it, to either abandon their frontal position and fall back or hold that position at the risk of encirclement and capture. [16]

But after an initial amphibious success on August 8, when a reinforced 2nd Battalion led by Lt. Col. Lyle A. Bernard landed without opposition at St. Agata, enabling the 3rd Infantry Division to advance 12 miles closer to Messina, a second amphibious landing – near Brolo – proved to be extremely costly for the Americans.

Patton had ordered the second attack to take place on August 11. But after checking with Truscott, who favored moving the operation to the next day to allow more time to position his forces to link up with the sea-borne operation, Bradley proposed the delay in a face-to-face meeting with Patton, who turned it down and insisted that the attack proceed as planned on August 11.

"George was anxious to get to Messina [ahead of Montgomery]," Bradley later wrote, noting that when he left the meeting with Patton, where he had argued that the amphibious assault would "mean nothing" unless it tied in directly with Truscott's forces by land, "I was more exasperated than I have ever been. As a subordinate commander of Patton's I had no alternative but to comply with his orders." [17]

In fact, Belden and Whitehead, who were covering the operation along with Tom Treanor, of the *Los Angeles Times*, and Homer Bigart, of the *New York Herald Tribune*, reported that it had gone badly from the start, noting that just after the 650-strong force had landed, the sound of rifles and machine-gun fire ripped through the air.

"The night was upside down with shouts, bullets and moving figures," Belden later recalled. "We could not know what was happening. A private clapped his hand on somebody's shoulder and said: 'What unit you from, Buddy?' A voice answered: 'Mein Gott.' A pistol shot rang out; someone howled and then gurgled gutturally." [18]

Daybreak on August 11 brought more fighting. In one incident alone, fifteen U.S. soldiers were killed while attempting to lay phone lines up a hill, while the Americans were successful in killing or wounding an estimated 100 attacking German soldiers over a one-hour period in the early daylight hours of August 11.

The assault commander, Lt. Col. Bernard, who had also led the amphibious landing at St. Agata three days earlier, ordered Company E to hold the beachhead if possible while Companies F and G – to which Belden and Whitehead were attached – made their way up Mount Cipolla, which overlooked the seaside town of Brolo.

At around 8 a.m., after the two companies had scaled the 750-foot-high hill and set up a command post, U.S. observers spotted German troops being unloaded from trucks east of Brolo and forming into units for an attack on Company E. By mid-afternoon, the situation had become extremely grave for the Americans as Germans launched one attack after another on the flats around Brolo and on the slopes of Mount Cipolla.

Belden reported that drinking water was also running low and was urgently needed for the wounded, "for as the fighting grew heavier, they were staggering up the hill, bloody and gasping and turning our command post into a hospital. The medics bandaged them swiftly with professional quietness and then lay them in foxholes where they broiled in the sun and once in a while cried for water, but otherwise remained silent." [19]

By late afternoon, enemy artillery and snipers had knocked out the U.S. beach-to-ship radio and the wireless link with the regiment and the division. All that was left were runners who were able with some difficulty to work their way up and down the mountain through enemy gunfire and the flames of burning brush. Several heavy German tanks broke through the U.S. infantry's thin line and crushed its beach defenses.

"What we had feared all day had at last happened," Belden later wrote. "We were cut off and trapped on the hill." [20]

Belden and Whitehead, for their part, were huddled with a wounded U.S. soldier from Indiana in a slit trench that they had dug as German guns slammed 88 mm shells against the hill and shrapnel buzzed over their heads. "Nobody will believe this," Whitehead recalled thinking at the time. "A lost battalion fighting for it life behind enemy lines, the hillsides blazing with fire. A colonel who acted like something out of a novel, no water, ammunition running low and a wounded soldier who mumbled about the corn crop in Indiana. I suppressed a crazy desire to laugh." [21]

Almost desperate, and anxiously awaiting the promised arrival of Truscott's 3rd Division from the west, Bernard ordered the American soldiers who remained on the beach and the flats to abandon their positions and to make their way up Mount Cipolla. Some chose to escape by swimming westward. [22]

But in the confusion, several American A-36 dive bombers were seen to appear suddenly in the sky heading inland. "Our hearts leaped with joy," Whitehead wrote. "They strafed and bombed the beach and hurtled toward [Mount Cipolla], where some troops stood beside their slit trenches cheering and waving." [23]

Belden said that he watched as they came closer – "nearer and louder, louder and faster, now buzzing and grinding, how in a high, shrill, nerve-consuming whine, they came toward the top of the hill." And suddenly he heard a voice: "Christ!" it said. "They're diving right for us." [24]

Two bombs were dropped squarely on Bernard's command post, killing and wounding nineteen men. An ear-splitting crash, Whitehead wrote, had made the earth shudder, and the screams of wounded men could be heard all around. [25] Belden wrote that smoke was choking him and the smell of gas was nauseating. Bits of trees and flying fragments were falling on him, he wrote, and "everything was a red black roaring. But I was not dead." [26] Other misplaced bombs landed on U.S. gunners below, destroying the four remaining howitzers. [27]

After the onslaught, Belden saw several dead or wounded American soldiers sprawled near foxholes that they had just missed before the bombs fell.

The next morning, a runner came sprinting to Bernard's command post and said that he had seen troops and vehicles on the coastal road below. The vehicles, he said, looked like jeeps. "Tell the men not to fire," Bernard said. "I'm going down to see." [28]

What he saw were troops and vehicles from Truscott's 30th Infantry Regiment, which had crossed the Naso River to the west overnight in pursuit of the Germans, who by now had fallen back to Cape Calava, some five miles to the east.

A total of 177 men had been lost in the operation. "I am certainly glad to see you," Truscott told Bernard. "General, you just don't know how glad I am to see you." [29]

Whitehead said that a short time later Patton rode up in his command car, along with Senator Henry Cabot Lodge Jr., of Massachusetts.

"His varnished helmet shone in the sun and the famous pearl-handled revolver glinted at his side," Whitehead wrote. "The command car stopped at the base of the hill where the tired, filthy infantrymen were filing down from fire-blackened [Mount Cipallo], dragging their feet like gaunt zombies. Along the roadway and on the sides of the mountain lay the bodies of scores of Americans cut down in the bloody twenty-four-hour battle. There were more bodies in the lemon grove below the road but we couldn't see them." [30]

Standing tall and straight in his command car, Patton spoke briefly to the troops. "The American soldier is the greatest soldier in all the world," he said. "Only American soldiers can climb mountains like those."

Whitehead said he suddenly felt ill. "All at once the whole little tableau sickened me," he wrote. "I wanted to get away from the voices of the general and the senator. The dead scattered on the hillside and in the lemon grove spoke eloquently enough."

14

SALERNO AND A DUMB GUY

The hundreds of reporters who were assigned to cover World War II for American newspapers, magazines and radio stations, including Belden, were accredited by the U.S. military, wore military uniforms and were cared for by the military – as long, of course, as they played by the military's rules.

Belden's press badge, issued in early 1943, identified him as an American civilian "attached to and under the authority of the United States Army." He was authorized, it said, to accompany the "Armies of The United States in the field."

But being part of the military did not mean they surrendered their right to have opinions, and even to express them. One of Belden's friends and colleagues in North Africa and Italy – Quentin Reynolds, who worked for *Collier's* magazine – was a case in point.

In mid-August 1943, after the U.S. Seventh Army and the British Eighth Army had driven the Germans out of Sicily, Reynolds and several other American reporters, including Demaree Bess, of *The Saturday Evening Post*, and Merrill Mueller, of NBC, got wind of an incident involving Patton that could cost him his career.

On the morning of August 17, Patton had entered Messina – "dazzling in his smart gabardines" [1] – as a conquering hero just hours after the last German troops had left the island, escaping across the Messina Strait to the Italian mainland. Driving the Germans and their Italian supporters from Sicily represented a major victory for the Allies, particularly following on their success in North Africa, and Patton praised his troops in an inspirational "Order of the Day" issued on August 22.

"[I]n the course of thirty-eight days of incessant battle and unceasing labor," it read, "you have added a glorious chapter to the history of war. Pitted against the best the Germans and Italians could offer, you have been unfailingly successful....But your victory has a significance above and beyond its physical aspect – you have destroyed the prestige of the enemy." [2]

Twelve days earlier, however, as the Seventh Army's 3rd Infantry Division was moving toward Brolo and beginning its race up the island's northern coast toward Messina, Patton visited the 93rd Evacuation Hospital at San Stephano, where his own prestige as an American military officer would be seriously tested.

Patton wrote in his diary on August 10 that, at the hospital, he had encountered an "alleged nervous patient – really a coward," and he had told the doctor to return him to his company, at which point the soldier began to cry, "so I cursed him well and he shut up." [3]

But independent and first-hand accounts of what later became known as the "slapping incident" were less generous toward Patton and more elaborate concerning the facts.

Several accounts spoke of Patton entering the hospital's receiving ward and talking to three soldiers in succession about their injuries and offering them encouragement. But then he encountered a fourth patient – Paul G. Bennet, a 21-year-old artilleryman with the 13th Field Artillery Brigade, who, when asked by Patton what his problem was, replied, "It's my nerves."

Patton was appalled. "What did you say?" he shouted. The soldier replied, sobbing, "It's my nerves. I can't stand the shelling any more." Patton went into a rage. "Your nerves, Hell, you are just a goddamned coward, you yellow son of a bitch. Shut up that goddamned crying. I won't have these brave men here who have been shot seeing a yellow bastard sitting here crying."

The general's loud voice caused the commander of the hospital, Colonel Donald E. Currier, to come running. "I want you to get that man out of here right away," Patton told Currier. "I won't have these brave boys seeing such a bastard babied." He then slapped Bennett across the face as he continued to curse him, then hit him a second time, knocking his helmet liner to the ground. [4]

Learning of the incident, several correspondents, including Reynolds, decided not to file stories about it, at least not immediately, but to bring their concerns directly to the attention of General Eisenhower, the commander of the Allied forces, who had been given a detailed account of the incident by Brigadier General Frederick A. Blesse, the headquarters' surgeon general.

Reynolds, Bess and Mueller flew to Algiers and on August 19 – two days after Patton had triumphantly entered Messina – Bess presented a report to Eisenhower's naval aide, Harry C. Butcher, in which he argued that "if I am correctly informed," Patton had subjected himself to punishment by general court-martial "by striking an enlisted man under his command." [5]

Later, Butcher recalled that the three reporters had said that they would refrain from writing stories about the incident but insisted that it would be impossible to keep "such a colorful scene out of the press" for long. Reynolds, he said, had told him that at least 50,000 American soldiers would shoot Patton if they had the slightest chance to do so. [6]

Eisenhower would later write frankly about the incident, appearing to defend Patton by saying he had been under "a terrific strain for a period of many days" and, moreover, sincerely believed that there is no such thing as battle fatigue. But he said that Patton's offense was serious. "To assault and abuse an enlisted man in a hospital is nothing less than brutal," he wrote.

Still, Eisenhower would to continue to praise Patton as a great leader. "His emotional tenseness and his impulsiveness were the very qualities that made him, in open situations, such a remarkable leader of an army," he wrote. "In pursuit and exploitation there is need for a commander who sees nothing but the necessity of getting ahead; the more he drives his men the more he will save their lives. He must be indifferent to fatigue and ruthless in demanding the last atom of physical energy."

Eisenhower also said that, in his view, it was important to "save" Patton for the battles that still facing the Allies in Europe. "As a result I determined to keep Patton," he said, adding that he had written him a sharp letter of reprimand and demanded that he apologize to the hospital personnel and appear before his divisions to assure them that he had given in to impulse and respected them as fighting soldiers. "Patton instantly complied," he said.

Shortly afterward, Eisenhower called the three reporters into his Algiers office and made the case for retaining Patton – despite their continuing insistence that he should be fired. He asked the reporters to, please, keep quiet about the incident, fearing that its disclosure would hurt morale back home. But he also made it clear that the reporters would not be punished if they chose to ignore him. "They were flatly told to use their own judgement," Eisenhower later recalled. [7]

Bess told Eisenhower that the three reporters had been discussing what would happen if they were to file stories on the incident. Their conclusion, he said, was that "we're Americans first and correspondents second. Every mother would figure her son is next." [8]

At the meeting, therefore, it was decided that the reporters would sit on the story and even deny that they knew anything about it, if asked. But word of the incident soon spread, and four months later the American columnist Drew Pearson devoted his entire syndicated radio show to it, causing a firestorm back in the United States. Several members of Congress called for Patton's resignation. But in the end, Eisenhower – supported by Army Chief of Staff George C. Marshall and Secretary of War Henry L. Stimson – was able to resist the pressure to send Patton back to civilian life and would give him command of the Third Army in Europe the next year. [9]

A couple of weeks later, Reynolds and the other reporters who had covered the Sicily campaign, including Belden, shipped out to Algiers to prepare for the upcoming invasion of the Italian peninsula at Salerno, scheduled for September 9.

In Algiers, of course, life was decidedly less tense than it had been during the 38 days of combat in Sicily – although the city did occasionally come under heavy Axis bombing. On August 26, for instance, thirty to forty twin-engine Ju 88s dropped flares in and around the city, then unloaded ten or so "500-pounders," mainly targeted at civilian property and personnel. [10]

But for the most part, Belden and the other correspondents – now numbering roughly 60 – were able to relax and enjoy themselves as best they could. Their base: the elegant, harbor-view Hotel Aletti, also home to visiting generals from the front and traveling diplomats, as well as, according to *LIFE* photographer Robert Capa, "very high-class ladies of dubious occupation." [11]

Only ten rooms had been set aside for the press, so finding a place to sleep was a challenge, even for the most experienced among them.

By the time Belden arrived, Reynolds had already finagled his way into a room already occupied by five AP and UP reporters. But he was soon able to improve on his accommodation when he ran into an old acquaintance, Al Schacht, as he was registering at the front desk. [12]

Schacht had once played major league baseball, pitching for the Washington Senators from 1919 to 1921, and was now, at 50 years old, a professional comedian entertaining the GIs with corny baseball jokes. He was called the "Clown Prince of Baseball."

Later that day, after Reynolds had convinced Schacht to let him have the extra bed in his room, four weary correspondents flew into the city from Sicily: Belden, Knickerbocker, Clark Lee (of International Newspaper Syndicate), and John Steinbeck (who four years earlier had won a Pulitzer Prize for *The Grapes of Wrath* and was now reporting on the war for the *New York Herald Tribune*). And after Schacht returned to the hotel that night – after his show for the GIs – he found his room filled with men, bedrolls, typewriters and various trophies from the Sicily campaign.

Reynolds said that Schacht did not mind the chaos as long as he could keep his bed. [13]

Steinbeck later wrote that the correspondents, including "Dour Jack Belden," who, he said, was endowed with a "basic pessimism" and has "seen everything and is difficult to impress," also shared a room with a "small, innocent, well-mannered" British consul who liked to think of the British and Americans as allies. He said it was generally agreed that the consul should have his own bed but if he went to the bathroom in the middle of the night, he might return to find Knickerbocker or Lee or Belden, or all three, fast asleep in it. [14]

But something else also bothered the British diplomat, Steinbeck wrote.

"Correspondents don't sleep much at night," Steinbeck observed. "They talked and argued and sang so that the poor consul didn't get much rest. There was too much going on in his room. He had to work in the daytime, and he got very little sleep at night. Toward the end of the week he took to creeping back in the middle of the afternoon for a nap. He couldn't get his bed then. Someone always had it. But at three in the afternoon it was usually quiet enough so that he could curl up on the floor and get a little rest."

For his part, Capa said that Belden – the "sweetest and also sourest tempered of the correspondents" – came into the room one night and unrolled his bedroll without saying a word, prompting the others to feel the need to offer their host an explanation. "[We] offered that Jack had been with Stilwell in the retreat from Burma," Capa said. Apparently, that was enough said.

Capa also wrote that one afternoon – as the reporters were sitting around "a bit bored, just a bit scared" waiting for a call from headquarters telling them where they were headed next – Steinbeck and Knickerbocker returned to the room with three bottles of Algerian schnapps, saying they thought it would help ease Lee's headache. [15]

The stuff tasted like hell," Capa said, "but we couldn't see Clark drink it by himself. So we pitched in and helped empty the bottles before the awful stuff could kill him."

Soon, Room 140 at the Aletti became home to a grand total of nine correspondents, whose numbers would also include Ernie Pyle, of the Scripps Howard newspaper chain; *LIFE* photographer Eliot Elisofon; and A.J. Liebling, of *The New Yorker*. On some nights, as many as eighteen reporters and photographers would have pitched tent in the room. Many slept on the balcony. Some slept in the bathroom, or even in the hall outside the room. [16]

From the balcony, they could easily see the Algiers harbor and would watch anxiously as more and more Allied ships were being loaded with troops, weaponry and other war-making materiel. As the room continued to fill to capacity, and beyond, one day – in late August – they received a call from headquarters telling them to report to Lieutenant Colonel Joe Phillips, the head of public relations. Quickly, they packed up their helmets and bedrolls and headed to his office, bidding farewell to the generous British consul and leaving him sad and alone in an empty room. [17]

Phillips told them nothing about the upcoming military operation – although most, if not all, of them knew that the destination would be the Gulf of Salerno. But he did tell them that from now on they would be "isolated," and one by one they were assigned to their divisions – some to airborne units such as the 504th Parachute Infantry Regiment, including Capa; Richard Tregaskis, of INS; and Seymour Korman, of the *Chicago Tribune*. But most, including Belden, were assigned to infantry units of the U.S. Fifth Army, led by Lieutenant General Mark W. Clark.

From Algiers, Belden was shipped 250 miles east to Oran, where he would board the USS Barnett with troops from the 36th Infantry Division. It was the same ship that had taken him to the Sicily beaches two months earlier.

On September 5, as Allied commander Dwight D. Eisenhower was hosting a bridge party at his estate in Algiers which included Clark and Butcher, the Barnett steamed out of the harbor at Oran at 12:15 p.m. on a northeast heading toward the Italian coast.

Butcher said later that Clark "did not seem to have his mind on the [bridge] game." Later that night, drove to the port, accompanied by

Eisenhower, where he boarded the new flagship, the USS Ancon, followed by thirty staff officers of the Fifth Army. [18]

While Clark understandably may have had other things on his mind during the bridge game with his friend of some 30 years, like the war, Belden was also apprehensive about what lie ahead, noting that the Germans were well aware that the Allies were coming and waited well-prepared, with machine guns and mortars at the ready.

"All they had to do was study the map and see that the obvious place for us to strike was south of Naples," he wrote. "Even correspondents who were not briefed before the operation and possessed no special information guessed on the basis of logic that that was where we would land."

On September 7, moreover, as the Barnett and the Ancon, along with dozens of other ships, were steaming toward their beachhead objective, Swiss radio announced that an Allied invasion fleet was carrying the Fifth Army toward Naples.

"The enemy knew not only approximately where we were going to land but when," Belden wrote.

Among those who were also concerned, as the nearly 700 Allied ships made their way toward Salerno, was novelist Steinbeck, who would land on the Italian coast near Paestum, along with Belden, as part of the 36th Infantry Division on the morning of September 9.

"In the moonlight on the iron deck," Steinbeck wrote, "they look at each other strangely. Men they have known well and soldiered with are strange and every man is cut off from every one, and in their minds they search the faces of their friends for the dead. Who will be alive tomorrow?" [19]

Up ahead the enemy is waiting, Steinbeck wrote. "Is he lying low with his machine guns ready and his mortars set on the beaches, and his artillery in the hills? What is he thinking now? Is he afraid or confident?" One American GI began to whistle softly, "just to be sure he is there."

Also among the non-combatants heading for the Italian shoreline that moonlit night in September was the British photojournalist George

Rodger, who would take a series of pictures to accompany Belden's report on the operation, which appeared in the September 27 issue of *LIFE* magazine.

He and Belden had also worked together a year earlier in Burma, covering Chennault's "Flying Tigers." His main claim to fame, however, would come in 1945 when he became the first photographer to enter the Bergen-Belsen concentration camp. That experience, which resulted in horrific pictures of a few survivors and piles of corpses that were published in *LIFE* and *Time* magazines and shocked the world, would so traumatize him that he was no longer able to work as a war correspondent again.

After leaving his job at *LIFE*, Rodger became a founding member, in 1947, of the photo collective Magnum Photos, along with Capa, Henri Cartier-Bresson, David "Chim" Seymour, and William Vandivert, and over the next 30 years he worked as a freelance photographer, taking pictures for *National Geographic* and other magazines and newspapers, mainly of the landscape and people of sub-Saharan Africa.

For his part, as the Allied armada continued toward the Italian coast in September 1943, Belden was concerned that Eisenhower's announcement on the evening prior to the planned invasion that Italy had surrendered to the Allies would have an unfortunate calming effect on the troops.

"Too many officers and men thought it was all over but the shouting," he wrote,[20] noting that there was no "tenseness" among the soldiers. "Lack of fear is the mark of well-trained and disciplined troops but it is also the mark of inexperience. These men were not scared and I didn't like it."[21]

Belden also had personal reasons for being less than enthusiastic about the upcoming invasion, writing in his diary as the U.S.S. Barnett made its way across the Mediterranean Sea that he had come down with malaria. "I feel no enthusiasm for this venture," he wrote, "and feel [that] Germans will be in vicinity where we land." To keep his mind off his own thoughts and physical misery, he buried himself in Clifton Fadiman's *Reading I've Liked: A Personal Selection Drawn from Two Decades of Reading and Reviewing Presented with an Informal Prologue and Various Commentaries.* It included selections from Steinbeck's *The Grapes of Wrath*.

Newsweek correspondent Al Newman, who was also onboard the Barnett, later told the editors at *Time* in New York that Belden should be cited for "bravery and gallantry above and beyond the call of duty."

"[Belden] had a bad cold when we started out [from Oran], then aboard the ship he suffered a recurrence of the malaria he contracted in Burma," Newman said. "Nevertheless he went in with the attack...." [22]

Belden later said the landing was the most difficult that he had ever participated in, noting that the Germans were so certain of where the Americans would land they had brought their defenses right up to and on the beach. At the water's edge, he said, machine guns threatened death to anyone who would attempt to come ashore. Mortars were positioned just behind them, and 200 yards inland from the beach German 88 mm anti-tank and anti-aircraft guns had been employed.

Just before midnight on September 8, the Barnett dropped anchor about ten miles offshore and began unloading troops into the small assault landing craft at 11:53 p.m.

Thirty-four rockets were fired onto the beach to soften up the enemy defenses. But German machine guns positioned at Torre di Paestum – a stone tower behind the beach – were preparing to welcome the U.S. troops as they came ashore. Several German tanks near the tower were also in position to open fire on the U.S. soldiers. [23]

Machine-gun fire from the Torre di Paestum sliced through the first two waves of soldiers from the landing craft but they did manage to reach the shore. Then it was Belden's turn.

"As we came abreast of the Navy patrol vessel marking our line of departure," Belden reported, "the assault waves bunched up and shells fell in among them. We need no order [to move toward shore]. We broke column, went into skirmish position and throbbed toward shore like so many racing boats, close together, with motors roaring and spray flying." [24]

Shells were exploding all around them, Belden said, and bullets slapped into his boat. "They snapped over our heads, rattled against the boat sides like hail and beat at the ramp door," said said, "seeming to say: 'When you open the door, I'll get you, get you, get you.'"

As they approached the beach, the boat's coxswain shouted at Belden and the soldiers to get ready. "The boat shuddered and the ramp creaked open," he said. "A man leaped into the void and his legs flailed the sea, which was babbling and breaking in a white froth on the white sandy beach. I stepped down. My legs sank to their knees and my feet touched the sandy soil of Italy."

Stumbling, Belden fell on his face, got up again and crawled to the beach panting with dozens of soldiers before they plowed through the sand dunes and came to a halt at a line of barbed wire. No one had wire cutters, so they lifted the wire for each other and crawled through. Just before dawn they broke through their eighth barbed-wire barrier and came out on a macadam highway.

The battalion commander ordered his soldiers to proceed to take a high hill in front of them – although Belden believed that plenty of German soldiers were already there looking down on them. Then the commander turned off to the right and proceeded down the highway. "There's no one there but Germans," Belden said. But the colonel continued, accompanied only by his walkie-talkie operator ... and Belden. [25]

"Any man who has been through numerous battles has a kind of instinct that enables him to sense a dangerous situation – a sort of smelling of the enemy, as it were," Belden wrote. "I was gripped by that indefinable sense of danger now and I followed the colonel cautiously and kept twenty or thirty yards behind him."

Then the colonel abruptly turned around and walked back toward Belden, who wanted to run back to the troops but stayed with the officer. "I thought I saw vehicles," the colonel said. Suddenly, they heard the sound of a truck and it was soon on top of them. They called for the driver to stop and to get out of the vehicle. When he did not, the American colonel fired a shot into one of the back tires. But there was no sound or movement from the truck. The walkie-talkie operator then fired his rifle, and Belden suddenly noticed a pair of legs on the other side of the truck.

Armed with nothing more than a short bayonet, Belden climbed over a low stone wall and inched his way toward the front of the truck hoping to see the enemy and to tell the colonel, who could only see the back end of the vehicle, where he was. Opposite the truck door and still behind the wall, he saw a man slumped down. The door on the opposite side of truck was open, and beneath it he saw a man on his back with his arms flung over his head – stiff and quiet as if he were dead.

Then, in an instant – "I don't know what made me do it, perhaps the malarial daze I've been working in ever since Sicily" – he threw one leg on top of the wall, then the other. Without warning, he felt something like a baseball bat hammer his leg. At the same time he heard gunfire and saw a burst of flame across the road, and he saw a figure.

He fell off the wall, and his right leg began to swell up. No one else was around. "I've been wounded," he yelled before he became so angry at himself for what he had done that he began to cry. "Damn fool! Damn fool!" he said. "China, Burma, Egypt, Tunisia, Sicily and goddam you, you expose yourself like a soldier seeing his first battle." [26]

With the pain growing ever sharper, and thinking that he could die there, he took a tin of sulfanilamide pills from his first-aid kit. But they had been soaked in water and had turned into a kind of floury paste, which he tried to swallow only to have most of it run down his neck.

Soon the colonel returned and said he would send for immediate medical help for Belden, and a few minutes later a soldier returned accompanied by a medic with a red cross on his arm. "I grinned inside," Belden later wrote. [27]

To ease the pain, he closed his eyes, and when he opened them again, he saw four medics standing in front of him. "Morphine," he said. One medic stuck a needle in his arm, and another slid a splint under his leg. Then they piled him on a stretcher and carried him out to the road and toward the German truck, where they left him and walked away saying that an ambulance would come soon and pick him up.

But Belden was scared, recalling a Chinese saying, "Fear a devil and there is a devil." Suddenly, he heard a car approaching. It stopped twenty yards away. It was a Volkswagen, with six men in it. One man got out and looked at the body of the German soldier on the road. Apparently without seeing Belden, he got back into the car and drove off.

Then the medics ran up from the other direction, out of breath. "We better get you out of here," one said, picking up the stretcher with the other medics and running with it to a two-story stone building twenty-five yards away. "Put me down there for shelter," Belden said, pointing to a spot behind the building. They put a rock under his head and left.

Heavy machine-gun fire erupted on the other side of the house. "Clearing the road," Belden thought. "But of whom?" Propping himself up, he then saw "with popping eyes" a column of tanks moving down the road, which "weren't ours."

"It's a strange thing to be wounded and watch the enemy's tanks go by and not be able to take cover or get up and run away or help yourself in any manner," Belden later recalled. "I think if I had been in the same position but not wounded, I would have been more frightened than I was then. As it was, I couldn't influence matters – I had no will and no responsibility. Anything that happened was just up to fate." [28]

After an hour or so, the medics returned, and Belden asked them to take him down to the beach. But they said that it was too far and none of their vehicles had gotten ashore yet.

"This isn't a training maneuver," Belden told them. "Get me near the beach. Somebody will put me on a boat....Let's get away from this road. This is no place for a wounded war correspondent and unarmed medics."

But they left, and for two hours Belden lay there alone. Four or five soldiers would occasionally pass by and look at him. One group put a pack of cigarettes on his chest. "Tough going," one of them said. Others would look at him as well, but they all always turned away – even one time when he shouted, "Hey, come over here, will you? I'm wounded."

After six hours, a young medic – no more than 18 years old, Belden thought – found him shaking from the cold and summoned a higher-rank medic, who said that no one could be spared to take him down to the beach. He said that they would put him near the road where an ambulance would pick him up, and the medic gave him another shot of morphine.

The medic also mixed a bottle of plasma and and stuck a needle full of it into him, and as the plasma dripped into his vein a line of German tanks suddenly appeared and began lobbing shells as they approached. An American heavy gun then came up the road, so, according to Belden, "this gun and the tanks were about to duel with each other at close range and we were right in the middle." [29]

Belden had been vomiting on and off for about an hour, and he did so again as two Italian officers happened to wander by and looked at him sympathetically. He asked them, through gestures, to take him down to the beach and they agreed. With the medic's permission, and with about two-thirds of the plasma bottle now gone, he was carried by the Italians toward the sea – although German shells were now raining down with increasing frequency on the beach.

The Italians were soon relieved by a four Americans who they had encountered along the way, and an ambulance eventually passed by and took him – as he threw up every five minutes or so – to a first-aid station by the beach, where a several doctors were in attendance.

Around the makeshift tent stood, sat or lay bloodstained men, and around the wounded men all along the beach were guns, trucks, tanks, bulldozers, DUKWs and jeeps. Down the beach "with their mouths hanging in the water," Belden wrote, were landing craft of all sizes and shapes. [30]

Casualties were brought to the beach by whatever means were available at the time, including ambulances, jeeps, trucks and hand-carried stretchers.

But it was not possible to set up a proper evacuation hospital to formally receive casualties until September 12 – nearly three days after Belden was hit – because battlefield priorities had delayed the arrival of tents and equipment.

The director of the hospital, Lt. Col. Paul K. Sauer, had landed with the troops and his staff at Salerno Bay at 2 p.m on September 9. But they would spend the next forty-eight hours doing little but poking their heads occasionally out of slit trenches as the Germans shelled the beach and enemy planes bombed and strafed the area. "We got a warm reception," Sauer said. "When we got ashore we found the enemy was only 800 yards ahead of us.

It was an exciting introduction to war." It took the night of September 11-12 to set up a working hospital, with dozens of canvas-walled wards. [31]

A medical officer who saw Belden on September 9 ordered him to be transferred to the hospital ship immediately after reading a card that had been attached to him by medics earlier in the day. "Broken femur, hit in two places," it read. "Patient has malaria; allergic to tetanus toxin." In his diary that day Belden could manage only six words: "Wounded. Brought aboard boat in splint." The next day, the ship sailed for North Africa.

Among Belden's wounded shipmates was a soldier he identified only as Joe, from Texas, who had taken a bullet in the stomach and could not eat. He and Belden could not see each other but they talked frequently. When Joe wasn't talking, Belden said, he was moaning. Another patient, Jack, who had lost a finger and suffered a broken hand and leg and had been wounded in his chest, never made a sound. He tried to sleep, and when he was not sleeping he just looked straight ahead, motionless.

"[W]hen I see Jack and Joe and sense the deathly stillness of the fellow with the spinal wound below me," Belden later wrote, "I think I'm lucky....I haven't been out of a war zone for seven years, but I don't think I ever really felt how the soldier felt until I was wounded and had to lie on the battlefield alone and in pain, as so many have done before me."

After three days, as the ship neared the North African port of Oran, one wounded soldier approached Belden's bunk and said he was so mad that he was never going to believe another radio announcer or newspaperman again.

"What have I done now?" Belden asked.

"Oh, not you, you're just a dumb guy who gets himself wounded," the soldier replied. "But I just heard the radio say that correspondents report that the Italian lit up the beach for us and we stormed ashore under cover of a heavy bombardment against the Germans, and everything looked like Coney Island."

Belden said that he, too, became angry and even felt like crying. "When people conspire to make a show out of war, when they try to conceal the suffering of war," he wrote later, "then that's what makes the soldier suffer most of all."

15

AN ARMY HOSPITAL IN ORAN

The week before Belden went ashore at Salerno with first wave of soldiers from the U.S. Fifth Army, in early September 1943, an Army hospital ship, the USAHS Shamrock, began easing out of the Port of New York, heading east.

Onboard the ship – in addition to the 202nd Hospital Ship Complement, which numbered 318, and her crew – were 29 newly minted members of the Army Nurse Corps. Only one of the nurses had ever been on a ship before, and only a handful had even seen an ocean, including a pretty 22-year-old blonde named Beatrice Weber, from landlocked Oshkosh, Wisconsin.

Weber had recently graduated from the Mercy Hospital School of Nursing in Oshkosh, run by the Sisters of the Sorrowful Mother. "They taught me to care for all patients as you would Jesus Christ himself," she later recalled. "My German Lutheran upbringing led me to dedicate my life to God the only way I could, and that was through nursing....For me, it was always a joy to go to work – in a spiritual way." [1]

Inducted into the Nurse Corps in May 1943, Weber was assigned to a platoon made up of one doctor, two nurses and nine enlisted men. She and the other members of the platoon were sent immediately to Camp Kilmer, New Jersey, to prepare for deployment overseas. But it was not until mid-August that they would board the Shamrock with the other doctors and nurses, along with the soldiers and crew.

At Camp Kilmer, the nurses were given several weeks of training for the long ocean voyage that lie ahead, including swimming lessons and drills on abandoning ship.

But Weber would say later that the time she had spent at Camp Kilmer had been wasted since she was passionate about nursing and wanted to get on with the job. "I dedicated my entire life to nursing and relieving suffering, both physical and spiritual," she said toward the end of her life, recalling that when she was only four years old her dolls and small pets became "patients."

Finally, on September 4, 1943, the Shamrock was on its way, headed for Italy. But fter only two days at sea, one of its engines sprung an oil leak and for another two days it sat dead in the middle of the ocean as its crew worked to stop the leak.

A week later, when it arrived off the Gulf of Salerno – with its crew expecting to quickly fill its 543 beds with wounded Allied soldiers – U.S. forces were still engaged in heavy fighting for control of the beachhead at Paestum. So the ship was ordered to stand by and wait offshore. It was not until September 25, in fact, that the first evacuees were welcomed on board; in many cases, their uniforms were still covered in blood and their boots caked with mud. [2]

In early October, Weber was transferred from the Shamrock to the 7th Station Hospital in Oran – a 750-bed facility set up to handle some of the casualties from the widening Italian campaign.

The city of Oran, as the American journalist A.J. Liebling described it at the time, appeared to be a cross between Miami Beach and the New York City neighborhood of Washington Heights, although "dirtier than either." It was built, he said, on the slopes and crests of a continuous ridge of hills rising behind its crescent-shaped harbor.

"Along the boulevards that offer good sea views there are 'style-moderne' apartment houses with rounded corners, lots of glass, and balconies in the European manner of 1929," Liebling recalled. "The older buildings are dingy but equally un-Oriental, and the climate is so cold in winter that the scattered palm trees look like a real-estate man's importation....The French say that Oran is the least French city in Africa, but it is at the same time the least African." [3]

Belden was admitted to the 7th Station Hospital on September 13 – four days after having been disabled by two German bullets and about three weeks before Weber would take up her post there as an Army nurse.

As the first casualty to arrive at the hospital from the fighting at Salerno, he was greeted with respectful silence by the men who were already there as the orderlies brought him in and paused briefly in the doorway to let everyone look him over.

The orderlies then carried him down to the end of Ward 161, which Belden described as "a large sunny ward ...bursting with the sound of many voices," where they wrestled him onto a bed with a wooden frame overhead that was used to hoist his splinted right leg in traction.

Soon, Belden settled into the routine of hospital life – lights out at 9 p.m.; lights on the next morning at 5:30 a.m. followed by temperature-taking, face-washing and tooth-brushing; breakfast at 7:30 a.m.; lunch at 11:30 a.m.; more temperature-taking at 3 p.m.; a back rub ("if you were lucky – and I wasn't – by a nurse") at 4 p.m.; dinner at 5 p.m.; sleeping pills at 8 p.m.; lights out again at 9 p.m.

"These sacred daily rituals, I and the other ward inmates soon discovered, were a blessing in disguise," Belden later recalled, "for, all combined together, they formed a time-slaughtering process that made the even monotony of the days somewhat bearable."

Among the patients at the hospital, Belden knew he was one of the lucky ones. There was Joe, an ensign who was with him on the USS Barnett. At Salerno, a shell fragment had knocked out one of his eyes. One day, he came over to see Belden and lifted the bandage over his eye so that he could see it. All Belden saw was a red mass. The next time he saw him he had black patch over the eye, and when he raised it all Belden saw was a white celluloid-looking substance that was now reposed in the hole in his head.

"It's very handsome, Joe," Belden said. A few days later, he left the hospital in what Belden sensed was a cheerful state of mind because he was about to get a glass eye. "I knew that Joe would be okay wherever he was," he wrote.

Belden later learned that Joe, whose last name Zaceck, had been transferred to St. Albans Naval Hospital in New York for further surgery. The last Belden heard, Joe was awaiting what the doctors called a "small plastic job" on his eye socket.

At the 7th Station Hospital in Oran, when not consumed by what Belden called the "daily sacred rituals," the patients would make their own entertainment, which included forming a pool to bet on the World Series and making an officer at the other end of the ward turn up his radio so they could hear a play-by-play rundown of the games.

Books were also made available to the inmates, he said, such as Thornton Wilder's Pulizer-Prize-winning novel, *The Bridge of San Luis Rey*, which Belden thought did not at all merit his attention. Instead, he managed to persuade the head Red Cross worker – a Miss Scott – to find some Shakespeare, Dostoevsky and Thomas Wolfe.

But for Belden, the never-ending parade of what he called "professional cheerer-uppers" that passed through the ward on a daily basis had just the opposite effect of what was intended.

"In my early days in the hospital," he recalled, "doctors, nurses, chaplains, visiting doctors, high-ranking officers on a tour of inspection and many people with vague occupations made of the ward a perpetual parade ground, sounding off the bugles of their good cheer with utter indifference to the likes or dislikes of us poor animals in the cage. From bed to bed they would gaily pass, and it made no difference who they were, their conversation was always the same. 'Well, how are you today? Getting used to it here? That's it, smile. You have no idea how lucky you are.'"

In one three-day period, Belden and a naval warrant officer named Slim, suffering from a painful case of sciatica, counted no fewer than 51 such groups. And eventually they rebelled, asking the inquisitors sarcastically, "Well, how are you today? Getting used to the patients? That's the stuff, smile."

The nurses were only marginally more comforting. The main difficulty, Belden said, was finding the Woman in the Nurse, although he did begin to notice some idiosyncrasies that would give them interesting and individual personalities over time. There was Miss Sterilized Smile, he said, and Miss Cross the Street, who would run around the ward so frantically that she always seemed to be crossing the street in heavy traffic. There was also Miss Granite Face, with her school-mistress glare.

But down deep, it was the loneliness of the hospital experience – exacerbated in his case by six years of basically uninterrupted exposure to the horrors of war in China, Burma, North Africa, Sicily and Italy – that haunted him the most. He wished, he said, that the nurses could be "more human."

Weber's arrival at the hospital, then, was what he would later describe as "the biggest news event in weeks" – not only because she was pretty but because she was "more human" than the others. She was also an equally welcome breath of fresh air for the other patients as well.

Belden wrote in what would become a career-altering article for *LIFE* magazine, published in its March 20, 1944, issue, that the hospital patients who would normally fall back to sleep after breakfast now remained wide awake, "vying with each other in saintly cheerfulness, all in the hopes that [Weber] would come and make their beds."

"They would practice their little dodges to gain her attention, such as dropping a pack of cigarettes on the floor when she was going by so that she would have to stop and pick it up," he wrote. "And whenever they thought they could get away with it, they would pass up a back-rub by a ward boy and later on innocently tell her that their backs had not yet been rubbed."

Years later, Belden said that he indeed was attracted to Weber and flirted with her the best he could from his hospital bed "in a rather sentimental, self-pitying fashion." But he denied that he had fallen in love with her, noting that the only memory he had had of her after being discharged from the hospital was of the few conversations they had had there.

"My own feelings probably interested me more than she herself did," Belden said years later. [4]

He did admit at the time, however, to having had an unusually strong attraction to the blond nurse from Wisconsin, saying that his feelings reminded him of a story he once read by the American novelist, playwright, screenwriter, journalist, and photographer Laurence Stallings, in which a wounded lieutenant in World War I fell in love with his nurse. But he also recalled that the story had ended poorly, with the nurse eventually marrying the lieutenant's doctor.

Belden wrote that, as he was being released from the hospital in early November, he saw Weber attending to another patient and let out a sad sigh, "blinking back," as he did, "a sentimental tear...." [5]

"Then they picked me off the floor – she did not say good-bye – and bore me down muted corridors and there was no pain," he wrote. "They carried me out under a palm tree and slid me in an ambulance and I thought of all the wrong things I'd said and all the right things I'd left unsaid...."

The ambulance then carried him slowly down to a dock in the Oran harbor, where he was bound to a litter with ropes and hoisted to the waiting USS Chase for the trip back to the United States and further hospitalization and care.

He said that seeing the blue Mediterranean Sea once again, exploring the "unaccustomed vastness of the sky" and feeling the rain falling "like teardrops on my face" prompted him to suddenly exult in having burst his prison walls, "in feeling the largeness of the world again and in knowing that America was waiting for me."

But the America waiting for him after 10 years abroad was not the America he had imagined.

"Many times during the blot and blur of battle and the pain of war," he wrote several months later, "I had thought of [America] with intense longing, as men in an alien land always long for the memory-haunted scenes of home. Many times I had conjured up dreams of the jungle streets of Brooklyn, of the luring lights of Broadway, Ebbets Field on a Sunday afternoon, and well-dressed women flashing down Fifth Avenue. Then at last came the day when I lay on deck in my stretcher and gazed on the sky line of New York, rising like Camelot through the mists. It was November, and I breathed in the smoke and sharp air and felt, like Odysseus, that I had conquered fate and it was fine, but wondrous strange, to be home again." [6]

On leaving the ship, to his surprise, he was interviewed by FBI agents who apparently were suspicious of his activities abroad. According to a memo prepared by agent D.M. Ladd for FBI Director J. Edgar Hoover, dated October 26, 1949, he was questioned by FBI agents "at the time of arrival in New York City aboard the USS Chase, November 21, 1943."

A more detailed FBI memo, dated June 12, 1951, when a full-scale investigation of Belden by the agency was under way, said he had stated on arriving in New York that his name was Jack Alfred Goodwin Belden and that he had presented a U.S. passport issued by the U.S. Consul General in Calcutta, India, on October 26, 1942.

He told the FBI agents at the time, according to the memo, that he was employed by TIME-LIFE Inc., and that he was returning to the United States as a result of having had his right leg badly shattered by gunfire while with the U.S. Fifth Army during the invasion of Italy.

On the voyage back to the United States on the USS Chase, meanwhile, the ship's carpenter had built a table over his bed so that he could write. "I wrote 70 pages of copy on hospitals, wounded soldiers, war neurosis etc.," he said in a letter to a *LIFE* reader in early 1944. But he said he was kept on board the ship until everyone else was off, and that "this material was taken away from me, and I never got it back...." [7]

From his bed at Doctors Hospital in New York, he wrote that – after what he called the "long and tormented years of war," and with the need to give some rest to "my exhausted soul" – it was like a dream fulfilled to surrender himself to "coddling and care" by the attending doctors and nurses.

"For days there was the wonderful thrill of reexploring unforgotten but long untasted foods and filling up on such simple things as eggs, milk and fruit," he wrote. "There was the excitement of the free press, with its bold and violent criticisms, the glorious sense of reading something that could not be suppressed, the moving experience of talking in a loud, unguarded tone, without peering through the window to see if anyone was listening there, and simple quiet and the knowledge of being temporarily free from the murderous suppression and slamming racket of war – all of these were mine and for a few days I was wealthy in the possession of them." [8]

But that would not last, and little by little, he said, the "other world of America" slowly made its way into his hospital room. It came first with the newspapers, in the few words written by a columnist or in some editorial comment. Then it came like a flood. He did not know why he had never noticed it before – unless, he said, his wish for an "unadulterated, happy land" had blotted it out.

"This thing – the thing that I abhorred – it was in this country, too," Belden wrote in his hospital bed. He knew the American people did not care about the war, or that they were seeking "surcease in a whirlpool of pleasure." But to see that "other thing" – so bold, loud, repellant and wide-spread – "for that I was not quite prepared." And he sensed it was every-where.

It was the nurse, he wrote, who raged against the Jews and the met-ropolitan press baiting the labor movement – "the one organized force in America that had opposed Fascism before Pearl Harbor." It was also the discrimination of blacks in the South; the "hysterical demagoguery" of Congress; editorial writers "screaming in tones of insane monkeys" that the Japanese were not members of the human race; and Undersecretary of State Joseph C. Grew, "with his country-club democracy," insinuating that the United States should keep the emperor in power in Japan.

"When I heard and read these things, my heart was torn asunder," Belden wrote, using a phrase from Thomas Wolfe's *You Can't Go Home Again*. After 10 years of "wandering and war," he said, he now had proof that the United States, "like all the rest [of the world], was sick with 'dread world-sickness of the soul'" – again seizing on the words of Wolfe. [9]

Belden wrote that, in his view, the United States was "getting her Fas-cism late." The reason: it was a wealthy country. "I believe this country is pregnant with reaction," he said, noting that there were men in business, government and the army who "do not give two cents for the people." [10]

He did not believe in good people ruling the country, he said, "but only in the mass of the people ruling themselves." [11]

One day, while in the hospital, the dynamic publishing duo of Alfred A. and Blanche Knopf had visited him and expressed an interest in publishing the manuscript he was working on, based on the success of his first book, *Retreat With Stilwell*, which they had published to solid reviews earlier in the year. He said that when he turned in the completed manuscript, however, they refused to publish it, adding that the decision was probably somehow related to unfounded rumors that had begun to spread suggesting he was temperamental and difficult – a result of his having been seriously wounded in Italy.

Belden said that, in his opinion, the rumors were clearly a reflection of the political climate in the country at the time, and of the fact that he was being increasingly seen by some in the political establishment as too leftist. His writings from China, in particular, were being viewed by some as decidedly pro-Communist.

Yet members of the armed forces were continuing to praise his work.

Lt. Henry I. Tragle, for instance, applauded his piece in the August 2, 1943, issue of *Time* magazine entitled "The Taking of White House Hill," which recounted a key battle in the war in Sicily in July 1943. He called it a welcome relief from the work of other war correspondents who, he said, had suggested that battlefield operations were a combination of chess and football.

"Milk-fed citizens will view with alarm your rashness in reporting the actual manner in which a soldier speaks when he is working," Tragle, who went on to win a Bronze Star for singlehandedly capturing a German general and his staff, said in a letter to the editors of *Time*, published in the August 30 issue. "Continue to give us Belden, verbatim."

At Doctors Hospital, Belden also received a letter from Lt. Karl F. Amalia, an instructor at the Army Air Forces Officer Candidate School in Miami Beach, Florida, saying that many men at the school had read his article in the September 27 issue of LIFE entitled "Hey, Soldier, I'm Wounded."

"We considered this one of the best stories to come from the front," Amalia said in the letter, dated December 7. "We thought your description of what a man thinks, feels and sees under [the] stress of battle [was] unusually well described....We would like to congratulate you on your fine reporting of warfare in the combat zones. All of us are glad to hear that you are well on the way to recovery. You have certainly earned a bit of peace and quiet."

Belden replied to the letter, saying it had cheered him up. "The fact that you are in the Armed Services and an instructor makes your comments that much more appreciated," he wrote. "I am rapidly getting better and hope I will be well enough to go back to the front in time for the offensive in Western Europe."

His doctor at the 7th Station Hospital in Oran – Capt. Allan B. Hirschtick – wrote to him at Doctors Hospital in late December saying he was happy to hear he had arrived safely back in the United States.

Hirschtick said that "business" at the Oran facility had slowed down considerably since he left and that boredom was beginning to set in. "[I]f it should continue in this fashion," he joked, "I don't see how we will be able to pay the rent."

All of Belden's ex-bedfellows, Hirschtick said, had been moved to other hospitals or had been sent back to duty. "Occasionally," he wrote, "we do return a patient to duty." He wished Belden well. "We all hope you will up and running around as soon as possible," he said.

16

BACK INTO BATTLE

On Christmas Eve 1943, as Belden was continuing to recover from his Nazi-inflicted gunshot wound at Doctors Hospital in New York, President Roosevelt was announcing from his home in Hyde Park about 100 miles to the north that Gen. Dwight D. Eisenhower had been chosen to lead the Allied invasion of Europe, set for the following spring.

But Belden's doctors had told him that the cast on his right leg would have to remain in place for at least another 12 months, meaning he would miss the invasion. So he rebelled, insisting that they remove the cast and release him from the hospital in time for the Allied operation. His argument was simple: he had been covering war for nearly a decade and was not about to quit just yet.

"I was scarcely well enough to make the D-Day invasion," he said, "but I was determined." [1] On March 21, in a meeting with John Shaw Billings, managing editor of LIFE magazine, he made his case. But Billings was skeptical, telling his diary that Belden was "still quite lame but wants to be in on the coming invasion." [2]

By early May, then, and still limping, he was on his way back to Europe again, this time on board a Norwegian freighter bound for England, where the Allies were preparing for the Eisenhower-led invasion of France. [3]

"Time is flowing by now and I am going back into battle," he wrote. "I am drugged with danger and excitement and I cannot move. And I hear, far off, the buzz-saw roar of the planes and feel the quick shiver of the earth and the obliterating crash of shells. I sense my power wasting drop by drop from me while the battle rages, and all my life is one violent blot again. Yet, while the youthful fires die, the old avowals stand – and we who were defeated are victorious and we who retreated advance again." [4]

But finding a place at the front this time would not be easy. A mini-firestorm had broken out over an article he had written for *LIFE* magazine, "Sequel to Salerno," published in the March 20 issue, as well as over a raft of allegedly anti-American opinions he had aired in his latest book, *Still Time to Die*, written while was still recovering in New York.

The *LIFE* magazine article, which focused on his feelings for an American nurse in an Army hospital in North Africa, was greeted with enthusiasm by the magazine's editors at corporate headquarters in New York.

Managing Editor Billings told his diary on March 2 that he had spent the day editing the piece. "Lunch alone," he wrote. "Reading Belden's 'Sequel to Salerno' – his hospital experiences in North Africa – fine stuff as usual." But on publication, it drew widespread criticism and ribbing from some of his colleagues at TIME-LIFE, who found it to be excessively maudlin and self-serving. Some readers also criticized the piece – although many said it accurately reflected their own experience.

An Army nurse from Knoxville, Tennessee, wrote to Belden saying that she and a patient of hers, Cpl. Jack Weiner, had fallen in love at an Army hospital in 1941.

"The rounds at night and the small chats you so able described [in the *LIFE* article] were a part of our lives – a great part I should say," she wrote, adding that they soon found ourselves becoming more and more in love. They were married in April 1942, and on May 19, 1943, their first child, Linda, was born.

"I wanted to tell you this since our stories were so nearly the same except that ours had a beautiful ending," she wrote. "You see these things aren't always just dreams of a sick soldier and his nurse."

Yet Belden was clearly hurt, and even offended, by the comments made by other readers, such as Edwin Hunt, who found the article to be objectionable on several counts.

In a 5-1/2-page reply to Hunt's letter, Belden strongly defended the form and substance of the article. But he did concede that it was "a bit on the sentimental side." He said if he had the chance to rewrite it, however, he would make it even broader and deeper in terms of sentiment and emotion. "I should lay myself open even more than I have done."

He said the article, in particular, did not adequately express the loneliness that soldiers feel, particularly for a woman. He said that he had written about those feelings and tried to analyze them in *Still Time to Die*. But he added: "[The book is] not good so save your money."

"Do you think it is easy to write that truthfully about yourself?" he asked Hunt. "To lay your feelings bare for every stray razzberry, stupid and bromidic comment? The reward for trying to give tongue to this loneliness which many soldiers feel is to receive a good kick in the teeth. Of course, while people say what I write is sentimental rot, some poor bastard of a soldier may be beating his head out on a hillside in Italy wondering where, before he dies, he can know again the sweet excitement of a woman."

He also defended having called one nurse Miss Granite Face and another Miss Sterilized Smile, noting that one depressed young reader had written him saying the article had made her laugh. "It cheered her up to know that other patients can be depressed," he said.

Another woman, he said, wrote to say that the article had persuaded her and several friends to become Army nurses themselves.

"I believe what General Stilwell once told me: 'If you can't tell the truth, keep your mouth shut'," Belden said. "So I am confined to write what I can write truthfully about – what I see and experience."

On board the Norwegian freighter, meanwhile, were four other passengers in addition to Belden, including two fellow correspondents: Rosette Hargrove, of the NEA feature syndicate, who wrote about fashion and other issues from Paris after the war; and Ned Nordness, of the Associated Press.

From the ship, Belden wrote to his mother apologizing for having left so abruptly. "But that is what you have to expect in this job," he said, adding that finding an airplane to take him to Europe had become too difficult, so he decided to take the slowest but surest means of transportation.

"The first two days were foggy and we had to proceed at half speed as ships in the convoy might collide," he wrote, "but after that it cleared, and since we have been in the Gulf Stream we have had several sunny days with all of us getting a sunburn. It has done me good to get some rest. Just now we are in the most dangerous area for submarines and the ship is constantly zigzagging so it's not comfortable, as we roll from side to side ...."

Belden told his mother that he had asked his publisher to send copies of *Still Time to Die* to her and his sister, Kathleen. Payment for the book, he said, had been transferred to TIME-LIFE for deposit in a government-guaranteed "savings society" and the National City Bank of New York. He had also purchased $5000 worth of war bonds with the money. But he said he did not like putting all his money in instruments or institutions that depend purely on what he called the "financial structure," preferring instead "something definite like land or a house."

"This is a poor letter," he wrote, "but as you will probably agree, it is better than my usual habit of none at all. I do not know whether we will land in Liverpool, Manchester or any one of a dozen spots, but at any rate we shall have to take a train to London. Until then – Love, Jack."

Before departing New York, Belden had been assured by the editors at TIME-LIFE that he would be accredited in London to cover D-Day, set for June 5, as its "number one" correspondent – or so he claimed. But it would not work out that way.

He arrived in London in late May, and *Time* magazine said in its June 19 issue that Belden had been assigned to cover the American landing near Carentan, noting that he was one of 20 or so TIME-LIFE reporters who would be accompanying the American and British troops.

But according to a brief biographical note he wrote at the time, he was still in England in early July – presumably waiting for his press credentials.

He later called D-Day "a day to which I had been looking forward for many years....Not to have made it has been very bitter for me...." [5]

It was becoming apparent, however, except perhaps to Belden himself, that the TIME-LIFE organization, under Henry R. Luce, was beginning to have second thoughts about his position as one of its lead war reporters. Unlike Teddy White, for instance, he had not been groomed and nurtured by the company and was, therefore, being seen increasingly as an outsider – a role that he himself, ironically, had cultivated with some enthusiasm since becoming a journalist in 1937.

His quiet relegation to the second tier of TIME-LIFE reporters who had been assigned to cover the expanding war in Europe – behind, among others, Charles Wertenbaker, chief military correspondent; William Lang; William "Bill" Walton; and William W. White – did not, of course, sit well with him.

"He's not happy about it," fellow journalist and friend Annalee Jacoby, who had been in touch with him, said in a letter to Teddy White in August 1944. [6]

But eventually – toward the middle of July – he would succeed in obtaining his press credentials, cross the English Channel to France, and head for the Cherbourg Peninsula, where heavy fighting was still taking place a month and a half after the landings at Normandy.

For the Allies, the initial objective of the Normandy campaign – securing a beachhead with adequate avenues of supply between Cherbourg and the mouth of the Orne River near Caen – had been achieved by the end of June. By early July, about a million men had been put ashore, along with more than 170,000 vehicles and 560,000 tons of supplies. [7] And now they were seeking to achieve a "breakout" through the German defenses near St.-Lo.

But advancing south from the port city of Cherbourg, which was captured on June 26 after three weeks of fighting, proved to be difficult.

Belden's friend and colleague from their days together in North Africa, Sicily, and Salerno, Don Whitehead, of the AP, who had come ashore with the American forces in Normandy on June 6, accompanied troops of the

U.S. First Infantry Division as they moved south from Cherbourg during the first week of July through towns and villages including St.-Saveur-le-Vicomte, Balleroy and Bolleville.

Some of the heaviest fighting of the Normandy campaign, Whitehead said, occurred near the crossroads town of La-Haye-du-Puits, which the American GIs called Hooey da Pooey. But in a dispatch filed on July 10 – about the time that Belden arrived in the region – Whitehead said that the Americans had broken and were headed for Saint.-Lo.

Over the next two days, Belden and Whitehead witnessed the fighting as the American infantry slugged their way through the German defenses until they were within two miles of St.-Lo, to the east.

"Fields and hedgerows on the ridges before St.-Lo were littered with enemy dead," Whitehead wrote in a dispatch dated July 12. "From a ridge-top could be seen gruesome evidence of the price the enemy paid trying to stem the drive of the Americans who came through the hedgerows behind the crash of [artillery] shells. Bodies lay stiff, grotesque positions in ditches and along the thick, green hedges torn by shrapnel and clipped by machine gun bullets." [8]

It would take another two weeks, however, for the Americans to break through the German line of defense, even after they had captured the city of St.-Lo on the evening of July 18 after the Germans, in Whitehead's words, "fought fanatically to stem the tide closing in on them." [9]

Belden's colleague, the American journalist A.J. Liebling, of *The New Yorker*, said that the American troops, after fighting through the Normandy hedgerows, had rushed into the town of St.-Lo "with all the joy of a band of claustrophobes released from a maze." But the Germans had immediately opened fire with heavy artillery on the troops as they came into the town, forcing the infantrymen to lie face down in the streets at the foot of the buildings for cover.

"The correspondents, flat on their faces like the rest, wondered whether the Pulitzer Prize was worth all this trouble," Liebling wrote. "They were further depressed by the magnificent aplomb of [Brigadier General Norman D. Cota, of the 29th Infantry Division] who walked erect down the center of the street, directing troops with his cane. When a sniper's bullet went through his right arm, he transferred the cane to his left hand. That gesture will be hard for us to match in our autobiographies." [10]

For his part, Belden said in a letter to his mother that he written a "long story" on the campaign for *LIFE* but that it had not appeared in print because "it became mixed up in transmission." But he also suspected that something more sinister may have been at play, noting that he had not heard from the editors at *Time* or LIFE in weeks.

"I am about as angry with the whole organization as I have ever been," he wrote.

The night of July 12 also brought some more discouraging news. His friend Brigadier General Teddy Roosevelt Jr. had died suddenly of a heart attack, at the age of 56, just over a month after he had come ashore at Utah Beach as assistant commander of the Fourth Infantry Division – the only American general to land on D-Day with the first wave of troops.

Belden had known Roosevelt since his time in North Africa, where the son of the former president had served as assistant commander of the 1st Infantry Division under Major General Terry Allen. Since then, he had spent many hours with Roosevelt and grew to like him personally and respect him professionally, particularly during the Sicily campaign when the two men discussed military strategy for hours in Roosevelt's cabin on the USS Barnett as it made its way toward Gela in July 1943. [11]

At a cemetery near Ste Mere Eglise, Roosevelt was buried on July 14 – Bastille Day – in the presence of, among others, several American war correspondents, including Liebling, who wrote later that Roosevelt had survived more "front-line perils" than any other general in the European theatre but in the end had succumbed to a lowly heart attack. [12]

For his "gallantry and intrepidity" at Utah Beach, Roosevelt was posthumously awarded the Medal of Honor – the highest decoration awarded by the U.S. government to members of the military.

"He repeatedly led groups from the beach, over the seawall and established them inland," the medal citation said. "His valor, courage, and presence in the very front of the attack and his complete unconcern at being under heavy fire inspired the troops to heights of enthusiasm and self-sacrifice.... Brig. Gen. Roosevelt moved from one locality to another, rallying men around him, directed and personally led them against the enemy. Under his seasoned, precise, calm, and unfaltering leadership, assault troops reduced beach strong points and rapidly moved inland with minimum casualties. He thus contributed substantially to the successful establishment of the beachhead in France."

No doubt, Roosevelt would have participated in the follow-up Allied incursion into northwestern France, which continued on the morning of July 26 with the Allied bombing of the German line along the road from St.-Lo to Periers – "the greatest attack ever launched by the American army," according to Belden, who reported from the scene, "on foreign soil."

Belden said in a cable to *Time* in New York that, for an hour and forty minutes, 1800 heavy bombers and a lesser number of light bombers – in armadas of fifty and a hundred aircraft – had covered the entire sky with black dots barely visible from the ground.

"A ceaseless roll as of gigantic kettledrums shook the earth and a cloud of smoke and dust two miles high hid both the American and German lines," he wrote. "It seemed as if nothing could remain alive under such an assault."

Killed in the attack, however, were more than one hundred American infantrymen, including Lieutenant General Lesley J. McNair – the highest-ranking U.S. soldier to be killed in action in the European Theater of Operations – who had gone into an observation post to watch the beginning of the attack. [13]

At 11 a.m., following the aerial bombardment, the infantry jumped off under cover of artillery fire but quickly ran into trouble as the Germans rose from their foxholes and countered with heavy small-arms fire. According to Belden, the attack slowed, faltered and progressed only a few hundred yards at a time. But on the second and third day, the infantry opened up a gap in the German lines and the armored units started pouring through.

Belden said in a cable to *Time* that, on the left flank of the breakthrough, the 2nd Armored Division – known as "Hell on Wheels" – shot past the towns of St. Gilles and Canisy, knocking out sporadic tank opposition and taking 2500 German soldiers prisoners in the process. One prisoner in a chateau outside Canisy told Belden that he and fifty men were captured without a struggle.

On the right flank, meanwhile, the 3rd Armored Division – engaged in an enveloping movement toward Coutances – was slowed by a German infantry unit that had set up a defensive position on a ridge overlooking the town. "In a column...on a road which we had supposedly captured," Belden wrote, "I and my companions were fired on by thick volleys of machine gun fire from positions...only a few hundred yards away. Under such circumstances, with fire from ahead, the rear and the flanks, it is hard to keep one's nerve, but our troops continued pushing forward despite the pockets of enemy resistance left behind."

From Coutances, the U.S. forces drove east and west and gradually worked south toward the burning town of Gavray, where they were met by machine gun fire, prompting the pilots of U.S. fighter aircraft, according to Belden, to open up on the German troops in a "steep, swooping dive within a hundred feet of the ground."

"There right below us," he wrote, "was a double column of German vehicles, bumper to bumper, stretching in and out of the town of Gavray at least a mile long, almost every vehicle in flames or shattered, charred hulks. Around and about us our fight planes were sweeping and diving, ruthlessly pummeling and strafing everything in sight."

By July 30, the coastal town of Avranches – south of Gavray – was firmly in U.S. hands. But on the road to Villebaudon, near La Denisiere, U.S. forces encountered stiff resistance and vicious combat ensued before the Americans eventually gained the upper hand.

"Having achieved a breakthrough," Belden wrote, "we have exploited it with energy and dispatch to make sensational gains in ground. These gains materially threaten the existence of the whole German army in southern and central France ...."

At Villebaudon, in a tent set aside for war correspondents, Belden ran into Ernest Hemingway, who was now on assignment for *Collier's*, three years after he and Belden had met for the first time in Chungking, China. Still married to fellow reporter Martha Gellhorn, Hemingway asked Belden for the address of the TIME-LIFE office in London, where his latest love interest, Mary Welsh, was working as a reporter for the Luce-run organization, and Belden obliged.

In a letter to Welsh, dated July 31-August 1, Hemingway said that, in Villebaudon, he was attached to an infantry unit – the 22nd Infantry Regiment – that had been on the attack for eight straight days. "Have been with very good guys," he wrote. "They have so much worse time than flyers do.... Anyway been very happy here and had good time with infantry again." [14]

Hemingway said that he and a few colleagues had just captured a German motorcycle with a sidecar, as well as a large German Mercedes-Benz staff car. "It is a convertible and had a bullet hole through the steering column and wiring shot up but we got it going OK...." Many Germans have been killed, he said, but perhaps as importantly to the heavy-drinking Hemingway, he also said that "we have gotten excellent cognac from the armored [German] vehicles."

Among the correspondents at Villebaudon, he said, were his favorites: Walton, of TIME-LIFE, and Kenneth G. Crawford, of *Newsweek*, who was widely reported to have been the first American journalist to land at Normandy on D-Day. "I do not know Bill Walton well," Hemingway said, but he is "kind and loving." He also expressed some admiration and respect for Walton for having parachuted into Normandy on D-Day with the 82nd Airborne Division.

"France is fun now," Hemingway wrote to Welsh. "We have liberated great areas without destruction due to using infantry, air, and armor intelligently."

Hemingway later suggested he had participated in the D-Day landings, saying in a July 22 *Collier's* article, for instance, that "the day we took Fox Green beach" was June 6. But, in fact, he had returned to England on an assault transport, the USS Dorothea L. Dix, the same day after a troop landing craft had brought him close to – but not onto – the beach. [15]

Back in London, where was assigned to write about the Royal Air Force, he set up shop comfortably at the Dorchester Hotel – still not having set foot in Normandy after having been in Europe for more than a month.

But his chance to hit the Normandy beaches, as it were, would come in the first week of July when he flew to Cherbourg in a small plane used to ferry war correspondents across the British Channel to spend a few days with Walton and Charles Collingwood, of CBS, who had set themselves up in a roomy, white stone house with a butler and a cook. [16]

Collingwood, who was only 26 years old and had landed at Utah Beach with an underwater U.S. demolition team on D-Day, said later that a "memorable bash" had been held at the villa in honor of Hemingway's arrival. Each morning, he said, they would leave the villa to cover the war down the road and return at nightfall to continue their alcohol-filled festivities.

Several other correspondents, writers and photographers also made the Walton-Collingwood house a temporary home-away-from home (and from the war), including Wertenbaker, Capa and the American playwright Robert E. Sherwood, a longtime admirer of Hemingway who, in a review in the November 1940 edition of the Atlantic, had called *For Whom the Bell Tolls* a "rare and beautiful piece of work."

Hemingway returned to England after about a week in Brittany to continue his pursuit of Welsh. He would return to France on July 18, assigned to Patton's Third Army at Nehou in Normandy – well behind the front lines at the time. A week later, he was transferred to the U.S. First Army, under Lt. General Omar N. Bradley, just as it was breaking through the German defenses at St.-Lo.

Patton, who had been sidelined by Eisenhower over the "slapping incident" he had been involved in in Sicily in August 1943, had been cooling his heels in England and itching for a chance to again show his stuff in battle, which came on August 1 when he was given formal command of the Third Army.

Several years later, Eisenhower wrote that in Patton – despite their long-standing personal differences – "we had a great leader for exploiting a mobile situation." [17]

Under Patton, the Third Army raced south to the town of Laval and then north and east toward Argentan and Le Mans, respectively, while the First Army took Mortain in preparation for an enveloping maneuver at Falaise, in cooperation with the Third Army, as well as the Canadian First Army and the British Second Army, which were pushing south from Caen.

Belden reported from Le Mans on August 11-12 that, with the Allied encirclement of the Germans at Falaise close at hand, the German army was on the verge of suffering its greatest defeat of the war outside of Russia. "The Reichswehr High Command will have to show its hands within the next few days," he wrote, "or run the risk of suffering the dissolution of a large part of the German army in France." On August 14, he wrote that almost the entire German army appeared to be convinced that it was beaten and that the war would be over soon.

"The American army in France tonight is putting the finishing touches on the most daring grand-scale maneuver in the history of the United States foreign wars," Belden wrote from the scene of battle. "General Bradley and his subordinates have thrown a great loop around a major part of the German army in France, crumpled up its left wing, smashed into its rear echelons, and as I write are approaching a junction with the Canadian forces around Falaise, threatening an estimated ten German divisions with complete encirclement....[W]e will have liquidated the strongest part of the German army in France and brought the war very near to a close."

The ensuring battle, which lasted until August 21, was the most decisive of the Normandy campaign, clearing the way for the Allies to continue to press on toward Paris and eventually the German border.

Eisenhower later said that the battlefield at the so-called Falaise Pocket, where an estimated 50,000 German soldiers were trapped by Allied forces, was one of the most horrific "killing grounds" of the European theater.

"Roads, highways and fields were so choked with destroyed equipment and with dead men and animals that passage through the area was extremely difficult," Eisenhower wrote after the war. "Forty-eight hours after the closing of the gap I was conducted through it on foot, to encounter scenes that could be described only by Dante. It was literally possible to walk for hundreds of yards at a time, stepping on nothing but dead and decaying flesh." [18]

By August 16, meanwhile, Patton's XX Corps had already moved to within striking distance of Chartres, only 50 miles from Paris.

That afternoon, at the command post of the Corps' 7th Armored Division, Patton inquired as to when it would be in a position to capture Chartres and was told, to his astonishment, that it might take some time since the Germans were putting up a tough fight.

"There are no Germans," he replied, angrily. "It is now three o'clock. I want Chartres at five or there will be a new commander." [19] It was not until the following day, however, that the Americans, who would run up against stiff opposition from the Germans, were able to capture the city made famous for its stunning, 13th-century cathedral.

On entering Chartres with the XX Corps on August 17, Belden, not surprisingly, was drawn to the women who remained and had survived – and, in some cases, participated in – the five-day battle for control of the city.

He said that the women fell into three groups: the "wretches" who were having their heads shaved by an angry crowd because they had consorted with the Germans; the "respectable" women who had never slept with a German and applauded the head-shaving "with just the right measure of gaiety and self-indignation"; and a large group of women who flirted with the Americans.

But then there was another young woman, he said, who did not seem to belong to any of the groups. She neither applauded the head-shaving nor flirted with the huge number of American correspondents who had descended on the city. She wore a light brown jacket and a flowered skirt with a revolver stuffed in the waistband. A ribband around her arm bore the legend FTPF, which stood for "Francs-Tireurs et Partisans Francais."

The next morning, as Belden was walking toward the cathedral, he saw the young woman – probably no more than 17 years old – herding a group of 25 German prisoners toward the U.S. MPs. Later, she told him that she and two male comrades had captured the German soldiers the night before in a wood outside the city.

Her name was Nicole, and she had been recruited into the French resistance earlier that year by a young man who went by the name of Lieut. Roland.

"I studied her for a while to see what were her feelings," he told Belden. "I told her little by little about the work I was doing. I asked her if she would be scared to do such work. She said, 'No. It would please me to kill Boche.'"

Belden said that Roland taught Nicole how to use a submarine gun and gradually introduced her to other members of his group of resistance fighters.

One night, she was entrusted to participate in a railway bridge-blowing operation, and on the night of July 14, with her submachine gun, she killed her first German.

"Nothing please Nicole so much as the killing of the Germans," Belden wrote in an article, "The Girl Partisan of Chartres," published in the September 4, 1944, issue of *LIFE* magazine. "I could find no traces of what is conventionally called toughness in Nicole. After routine farm life, she finds her present job thrilling and exhilarating. Now that the war is passing beyond her own home district she does not think of going back to the farm. She wants to go with the Partisans and help free the rest of France."

Also covering the battle for Chartres, along with Belden and the other American war reporters, was Tom Treanor, of the *Los Angeles Times*, whose last story – "Cathedral Battle Viewed By Treanor," datelined Chartres – was published on August 18, the day before he was fatally injured when his jeep was crushed accidentally by an American tank near the village of Ermont.

AP reporter Don Whitehead said that Treanor – a veteran foreign correspondent who had reported from the Middle East, Sicily, Italy and northern Europe – was one of the most courageous, enterprising and colorful figures among the men who report on wars. His story on the D-Day invasion, Whitehead said, was one of the best ever written. "News of Tom's death spread gloom among the correspondents who knew him," Whitehead wrote at the time. [20]

The *Los Angeles Times* said in reporting on his death that Treanor had told the doctor attending to his wounds, Capt. William Werner, of Los Angeles, that he was sad he would not be able to cover the liberation of Paris. He was buried several days later at a U.S. Army cemetery near Le Mans.

17

FROM PARIS TO AACHEN TO MALMEDY

The liberation of Paris on August 25, 1944, while obviously an event of mammoth historic proportions, would also signal, not surprisingly, the long-awaited liberation of the American soldier – and of the American war correspondents who had accompanied them for two months as they fought their way through the hedgerows, towns, cities, villages and countryside of northwestern France.

The reporters, including Belden, would write extensively of the French girls in their "multicolored summer dresses," as he put it, who showered them with hugs and kisses as they rode along the wide boulevards of the French capital on that sunny Friday in late August.

"On the day we arrived, Paris was the most beautiful city I ever saw," Belden exuded in a letter to his mother. "I thought the Parisian women were marvelous." A.J. Liebling, who covered the event for *The New Yorker*, would take the issue a tantalizing step further.

"These girls show legs of a length and slimness and firmness and brownness never associated with French womanhood," Liebling wrote. "Food restrictions and the amount of bicycling that is necessary in getting around in a big city without any other means of transportation have endowed these girls with the best figures in the world...." [1]

For his part, Belden's long-time reporting companion, Don White-head, of the AP, wrote that when his jeep rolled through the gates of Paris on the morning of August 25 he was "smothered, but pleasantly, with soft arms and lips giving the usual French double kiss." [2]

Ernie Pyle said that, on entering Paris by way of rue Aristide Briand and rue d'Orleans, he and his traveling companion, Henry Gorrell, also of the AP, were "kissed and hauled and mauled by friendly mobs until we hardly knew where we were....Paris seemed to have all the beautiful girls we always heard it had." [3]

But it would not be long before those friendly hugs and kisses would turn into other forms of endearment.

As the historian Antony Beevor has explained, the Parisiennes welcomed the Allies with "unstinted generosity in their tents and armored vehicles." The U.S. 4th Infantry Division, in particular, which was bivouacked in the Bois de Vincennes on the eastern edge of the city and on the Ile de la Cite behind the Notre-Dame cathedral, "enjoyed the generosity of young Frenchwomen," he said. [4]

Forrest C. Pogue, an official Army historian, reported that a sign outside the door of the American-occupied Petit Palais announced that condoms were available inside to all U.S. soldiers. Prostitutes in Pigalle (known by the GIs as "Pig Alley") and Montmartre, he said, were servicing more than 10,000 GIs a day. [5]

It is unclear whether Belden also chose to indulge in the carnal pleasures of the day along with the other Americans. But it would be surprising, given the times and his own inclinations, if he did not.

Home for him, as well as for the other war reporters in the days and weeks following the liberation, was the Hotel Scribe – except for Hemingway, who chose to "liberate" the five-star Hotel Ritz for himself and his entourage.

Set aside for the 200 or so American reporters who, like Belden, had been assigned to cover post-liberation Paris, the Scribe was quickly turned into what French writer Simone de Beauvoir – describing the hotel restaurant – called an "American enclave in the heart of Paris," with white bread, fresh eggs, jam, sugar and Spam. [6]

Belden and the other TIME-LIFE reporters and photographers were put up initially in a large, beautifully furnished room in the Scribe that had been set up as a temporary office by the organization's European bureau chief, Charles Wertenbaker. There, on the night of August 25, they unrolled their bedrolls and slept on the floor awaiting more comfortable quarters.

In the room next door, the American writers Irwin Shaw and William Saroyan, along with the director and producer George Stevens, were housed as distinguished members of the U.S. Army Signal Corps. [7]

Throughout the war, the film unit that Stevens headed shot hundreds, if not thousands, of rolls of footage documenting, for instance, the Allied landing at Normandy; the liberation of Paris; and the meeting of American and Soviet forces at the Elbe River south of Berlin on April 25, 1945, as well as scenes from the Duben labor camp and the Dachau concentration camp.

Life at the Scribe, however, was particularly strange given that most of the reporters and photographers had been in the field for so long. Ernie Pyle said his room was a corner suite with easy chairs, a soft bed, a bathroom, a maid and hall-porter service. There was no electricity at the hotel during the day and no hot water at all. But otherwise, Pyle could only assume, it was exactly like it had been in peacetime.

"Sitting there writing within safe walls and looking out the window occasionally at the street thronged with happy people," Pyle wrote in a dispatch from Paris dated August 28, "it was already hard to believe there ever had been a war; even harder to realize there still was a war." [8]

In the evening, the press corps, including Hemingway, who would occasionally wander over from the Ritz, gathered in the hotel's basement bar to exchange stories and partake of a seemingly inexhaustible supply of champagne. [9]

Pogue, the Army historian, said that the bar was one of the few in Paris that was open at night. An enlisted man could get a table in the private room of the bar, he said, and drink champagne – Mumm's Cordon Rouge at 235 francs a bottle ($4.70) or Veuve Clicquot at 350 francs ($7.00).

"It was amazing," Pogue wrote in his diary on September 1, "to be sitting in this rather swank bar, only steps from the opera and the Cafe de la Paix, being served champagne in fragile glasses by white-coated waiters." [10]

LIFE photographer Robert Capa, whose pictures accompanied several of Belden's articles for the magazine, including "The Girl Partisan of Chartres" (in the September 4, 1944, issue), said he spent the eighth day after the liberation at the bar of the Scribe ("the Army's grand gesture to the newspapermen") teaching the bartender, Gaston, how to make what he called the "most potent of pick-me-ups," the "Suffering Bastard," made with tomato juice, vodka and Worcestershire sauce – known today as a Bloody Mary.

"The liberation of Paris was the most unforgettable day in the world," Capa wrote. "The most unforgettable day plus seven was the bluest. The food was gone, the champagne was gone, and the girls had returned to their homes to explain the facts of the liberation. The shops were closed, the streets were empty, and suddenly we realized that the war was not over....Gaston poured the mixture....I finished the drink. I felt much better all around." [11]

Back in the United States, meanwhile, Belden's second book, *Still Time to Die* was published to rave reviews. His first book, *Retreat With Stilwell* had come out the previous year, also to widespread applause.

His latest book – a series of essays on the battles had witnessed during his career as a reporter in China, North Africa and Italy from 1937 to 1943 – was mainly about, as he put it, the "essence of war." It was also to some extent about strategy and tactics. "But mostly," he said, "it is about myself in the midst of battle." [12]

Its title – taken from the 19th-century Prussian military theorist Karl von Clausewitz – reflected von Clausewitz's belief that no country's eventual fate can hinge solely on the outcome of one battle, no matter how decisive it had been, because fortunes can always change. "There is always still time to die," he wrote.

Belden dedicated the book to the soldiers who, in 1944, were then lying on the "once good but now mangled and bloody earth, striving to get at each other's throats, who stare up at the stars at night recalling their lost youth and the forgotten days of peace, who are consumed not so much with mutual hatred for each other as with their united hatred of war."

A *Time* magazine reviewer said that the book was "often frankly bitter, often overemotional," but in the end it "carries the conviction of a man whose spirit has been tried by seven years' intimacy with war's 'dumb, bestial, suffering, weariness, and utter and devastating exhaustion.'"

"It rises a notch above other able war reporting," the reviewer wrote, "through Correspondent Belden's provocative summing up of what he has learned in his seven war-filled years."

Orville Prescott, in *The New York Times*, said that Belden brought a unique perspective to the work. "Probably no correspondent of our time," he wrote, "has seen so much of war for so many years, so continuously, so intimately as has this young reporter from Brooklyn."

Still only 34 years old, Belden remained in Paris for about a week after the liberation, before heading out again with the U.S. infantry in early September, this time in pursuit of the Germans northeast along the Marne River through Chateau-Thierry and Reims.

Capturing the sentiment of the moment, Ernie Pyle said that, for the hard-bitten corps of American war reporters, the gaiety and "big-cityness" of Paris had, in a strange way, worn them down, and they were now eager to return to the field.

"In Paris we had slept in beds and walked on carpeted floors for the first time in three months," Pyle wrote. "It was a beautiful experience, and yet for some perverse reason a great feeling of calm and relief came over us when we once again set up our cots in a tent, with apple trees for our draperies and only the green grass for a rug." [13]

For Belden, his first opportunity to see the American GI in action again was near Mons, Belgium, just across the French border, where, according to the editors of *Time*, the Americans were quickly victorious over an "outgeneraled and defeated German army."

"The Battle of Mons will rank as one of the most decisive actions in our campaign in Europe," Belden wrote in an article published in *Time* on September 18, noting that 20,000-30,000 Germans were "slaughtered, decimated or dispersed" in the Maubeuge-Mons area within a few hours after U.S. and German forces – both marching to the north on parallel roads – collided early on the morning of September 3.

Eisenhower wrote in *Crusade in Europe*, published in 1948, that the battle, "in ordinary times," would have been acclaimed as a great victory for the Allies. But the times were far from ordinary, he said, and the incident passed almost unnoticed in the American press. [14]

Traveling with Belden was Ira Wolfert, of the North American Newspaper Alliance, who also wrote for *Collier's* and *Reader's Digest*. A fellow New Yorker, Wolfert, then 36 years old, had already won a Pulitzer Prize for his reporting from the Pacific in November 1942. He had also written the much-acclaimed best-selling novel *Tucker's People*, published in 1943, which was later turned into the 1948 cult film "Force of Evil." His second novel, *An Act of Love*, was also a best-seller.

By 1951, however, Wolfert had become a victim of the McCarthy era when, on April 1, the House Un-American Activities Committee (HUAC) issued a report accusing him of being Communist. Its evidence: he was listed as a "sponsor" of the anti-anticommunist Scientific and Cultural Conference for World Peace, held in March 1949 at New York's Waldorf Hotel.

Wolfert was also cited by the HUAC– mistakenly, he later noted – for having been a "panel speaker" at the conference, along with W.E.B. DuBois, Howard Fast, Shirley Graham, I.F. Stone, Louis Untermeyer, F.O. Matthiessen, Sam Wanamaker and others. It also listed him as "affiliated with from five to ten Communist-front organizations" and put him among only twelve writers and artists who had been "supported by Soviet Agencies, press or radio." [15]

Belden, who later in life would also be suspected of harboring Communist sympathies, said in a letter to his mother from Belgium dated September 18, 1944, that he admired Wolfert for having won a Pulitzer Prize and for having written an "excellent" novel (i.e., *Tucker's People*).

He said that, since leaving Paris, he and Wolfert had tracked U.S. armored units through northern France – "a rather trying business" and "very tiring."

Belden also expressed frustration with his inability to cover the story the way he wanted to. The story – the freeing of France and Belgium and the collapse of the German army in those two countries – had become "so big," he said, "that it is impossible swallow it all....."

"It's all been continual rush and go and everything we have seen has been more or less spectacle and froth and I am afraid I have had little time to see what has really been going on beneath the surface," he wrote. "Spectacle becomes rather repetitious after a while and you can't write about it any more and not feel it much any more either."

What he and Wolfert did feel, however, was the continuing affection of the local population. As the first reporters to enter Liege, Belgium, after it was captured by the Americans on September 8, for instance, they were overwhelmed by the reception they received.

"It was very wild," Belden told his mother, noting that the cafes lining the main street of the town stayed open all night to welcome the Americans. "People were cheering and yelling and standing on the tables singing 'A Long Way to Tipperary' and dancing to Victrolas and snaking up and down the cafes and strange people would buy you bottles of champagne and girls would be all over your neck kissing and hugging you."

The kissing and hugging, however, would be short-lived. From Liege, the U.S. 1st Army was once again ordered to move out and to begin its push into Germany itself, with Belden and Wolfert dutifully accompanying it.

"It has begun to get cold now," he told his mother. "All my clothing save what I was wearing was stolen in Paris and I have no overcoat at the present time."

Ill-clothed but eager, Belden crossed into Germany with the U.S. 1st Army near Aachen on September 14 – the first time the Americans had taken the fight to German soil. Each morning, he and Wolfert would travel to the front to cover the movement of U.S. troops, then return to their hotel in Liege at night to write their stories.

Belden said there was plenty of hot water for a bath at the hotel. " But this is not much use as we still have to put on the same dirty clothing," he wrote. "I am afraid that all of us are weary with everything and at the moment only wish the war would end."

But, of course, the war did not end, and in Europe another eight months of fighting lay ahead.

By far the bitterest fighting in the European theater, in fact, would come in October 1944 when the Americans launched a massive assault on the imperial city of Aachen, involving some of the most brutal street-by-street, house-by-house urban combat ever seen.

Stephen E. Ambrose, the American historian, has argued that the decision to attack Aachen was a mistake because it slowed the Allied advance eastward at a cost of some 5,000 casualties. But he has also said that the Americans had no choice, and so the commander of the U.S. First Army, Lt. General Courtney H. Hodges, who had succeeded Bradley in August, ordered his troops to prepare for an attack by moving toward the German border on September 12.

Belden reported from the scene that day, in fact, that half of the vehicles attached to an American reconnaissance unit had become stuck in the mud just short of the border but that no Germans had fired on them, confirming the prevailing American assumption that the Germans would fall back further to the Rhine River and mount a do-or-die defense from there.

"Now, however, there was no one but ourselves on the road, and all strangely silent as we came out of a small wood," Belden wrote. "A house loomed on our left. It was silent, grim and foreboding....Here was hostile land."

On September 14, the U.S. First Army crossed the Siegfried Line into Germany, encountering little opposition, and the Nazi commanders, according to Belden, quickly realized that the Americans had an "armed fist in the heart of their defenses" and counterattacked. But it was too late; the GIs were able to hold. [16]

Fort after fort – many of them manned by only two or three German soldiers – fell to the Americans, and most GIs figured that the war would now be over in a matter of days.

On September 22, reporting from outside Aachen, Belden said that German civilians were already turning over their weapons to the American GIs. "The people we have seen are all obedient [and] there has been no evidence of sabotage," he wrote.

But that in no way suggested that the German soldiers who had been assigned to defend Aachen on direct orders from Adolf Hitler – i.e., the German 246th Division under the command of Colonel Gerhard Wilck, consisting of about 5,000 men, five tanks, nine 105-mm howitzers and six 150-mm guns – would give up without a fight.

Belden told the story of the ensuing battle for Aachen, which began on October 11-12 with massive American air and artillery strikes following more than a week of attacks around the city, through the eyes of two American soldiers who led their units in what essentially became hand-to-hand combat with the enemy.

The two soldiers – Lt. Colonel Derrill M. Daniels and Lt. Colonel John T. Corley – had been specially trained in Weymouth, England, for street fighting prior to the Allied landing at Normandy on June 6.

Belden said that Daniels, who commanded the 2nd Battalion of the 1st Infantry Division's 26th Infantry Regiment, led his soldiers into Aachen "through the backdoor" from the east and methodically cleaned up every street block, while Corley, commander of the 3rd Battalion, went around the town, seized Observatory Hill and then thundered into the city from the north and swept up any final resistance that still existed.

"It was an answer to a commander's dream," Daniels told Belden. He was given a free rein, he said, to attack Aachen the way he wanted to, and he did, taking his time.

Daniels, a former state etymologist from Geneva, New York, said he was initially concerned about locating possible enemy snipers at the rear.

"Assaults on cities have always run into trouble because the rear was not properly cleaned out," he said. "So when we entered Aachen,

I determined we should not have this kind of trouble. I spread my companies out across the whole city and gave them certain definite blocks to take each day. Then each company assigned certain portions of blocks to each platoon, and the platoon leader in turn assigned houses to each squad. We never moved on until every house and every room and every cellar had been searched."

For the first time in the war, the fighting, in Aachen, was done exclusively during daylight hours because troops could easily become lost in buildings at night.

Daniels said his units rarely advanced straight down a street but instead broke into individual houses to root out the enemy with gunfire and grenades one by one or in groups. "You never can locate an enemy position [in street fighting] until you're on top of it," he said. "In the open you can look out at the terrain and figure out where the enemy will go. But you never know what block or house he will go into in a city."

Belden said in a cable to his editors at TIME-LIFE in New York that the Battle of Aachen, which ended just after noon on October 21 with the surrender of Col. Wilck – trapped with 400 of his men in an air raid shelter without food, water or ammunition – had shown that the German commanders continued to have the will and the means to turn every city into a fort, causing enormous destruction and suffering throughout the Third Reich and potentially turning the country into a land of homeless refugees.

"If the Germans continue to fight for every city in this manner," Belden wrote, "by the end of the war village, city and town life in Germany will no longer exist. There will only be fields of ruins and memories."

Historian Ambrose has said that the Battle of Aachen should never have happened because it benefited neither side. "This was war at its worst, wanton destruction for no purpose," he wrote. [17]

The war, meanwhile, was also taking its toll on Belden's long-time colleague, Ernie Pyle. After twenty-nine months overseas, including nearly a year on the front lines, the 44-year-old reporter was forced to return to the United States, conceding in his last column, written from France at the end of September, that he hated to leave but that "I have given out."

"My spirit is wobbly and my mind is confused," he wrote. "The hurt has finally become too great. All of a sudden it seemed to me that if I heard one more shot or saw one more dead man I would go off my nut. And if I had to write one more column I'd collapse...." [18]

Another American reporter, David Lardner, who wrote for *The New Yorker*, was also lost to the war in the fall of 1944 when his jeep was blown up by a land mine near Aachen. His driver was also killed, and Russell Hill, a correspondent for the *New York Herald Tribune*, was badly injured in the blast. [19]

Lardner, who was only 25 years old and less than a month into his tenure as a war reporter, was the son of the sports columnist and short story writer Ring Lardner. His brother, James, had died in 1938 while fighting on the side of the Loyalists in the Spanish Civil War as a volunteer in the International Brigades.

By mid-November, some U.S. First Army troops had managed to fight their way into the snow-mantled Hurtgen Forest. But their progress was slowed by a week of rain, sleet and snow that continued to fall from low-hanging clouds, which had prevented the Allied bombers based far from the front lines from engaging the enemy – until the weather cleared somewhat on November 16.

Belden said that at 10:30 a.m. on that Thursday morning the first sun in weeks on the German front shone like a dirty penny through the over-cast sky, "which broke apart in places like a gray ice floe, showing patches of a forgotten blue sky." A half an hour later, Allied fighter and medium bombers shot in and out of the grayness "like wraiths" to unload an esti-mated 10,000 tons of bombs on the German front facing the American First and Ninth Armies.

"The air howled and whined and then was racked by a deep, harsh throbbing as the first of 2,350 heavies joined the fighter and medium bombers," he wrote. "A minute later there was a hollow rumbling and pounding like a waterfall on rocks and the earth shock." Lt. Col. Robert Evans, he said, turned from his chess game to look at his watch. "Right on the dot," he said and moved his bishop to check his opponent's king as the greatest single daylight air attack in history, according to Belden, had begun.

With Belden, Don Whitehead, of AP, reported that after the bombers had passed the U.S. GIs emerged from their foxholes and began to assault enemy positions.

"For days the army had been preparing for this move," he wrote. "Convoys rolled over muddy roads to the front with food and ammunition and other battle supplies....Gen. Hodges was ready for the attack. The break in the weather turned his legions loose." [20]

Whitehead and the other correspondents, including Belden, stood on the edge of Mausbach, seven miles east of Aachen, watching the attack. "Planes dived at enemy positions and down the road a mortar squad was tossing shells at the enemy," he wrote. Yet a week later – on Thanksgiving Day – U.S. troops were still only inching their way forward in some of the bitterest fighting since the Normandy invasion.

"The enemy's resistance is stubborn," a staff officer told Whitehead, "and the going is slow and difficult." Still, he said, 3,530 Germans had been captured by the First Army since the offensive began on November 16. [21]

With the Germans making American gains as costly as possible, the bloody, drawn-out fighting in the Hurtgen Forest continued into early December. And Belden and Whitehead began to believe that, as the enemy dug in, there would be no early end to the war.

"A winter campaign seems inevitable," Whitehead wrote. "The Germans are showing no indications of cracking up either on the military or home fronts. That is not a cheerful pre-Christmas picture but it is the sober opinion of most of the observers with the fighting troops." [22]

After filing his last report from the German front, on December 4, Whitehead returned to the United States to visit his family. He had not seen them in nearly nine months, and a trusted military confidant had told him that "nothing much was going to happen" in the war while he was away. [23]

But that was not the case, as Belden and the other correspondents, including Hal Boyle, another AP reporter, would soon find out.

On December 18 – two days after the Battle of the Bulge had begun in Belgium's Ardennes Forest – Belden reported from Malmedy that a number of German soldiers had broken through the Allied lines and attempted to massacre 150 American prisoners.

"All the Americans were unarmed and had been prisoners for an hour when the Germans opened up on them with a Schmeisser pistol from a distance of fifty yards," Belden wrote in a cable to *Time* in New York head-lined MURDER. "Some of the prisoners were instantly killed, some were wounded, and many fell down unhit. The Germans then went among the bodies and shot those who groaned or moved. It was a clear attempt at murder."

Accounts differ over exactly what transpired in what became known as the Malmedy Massacre. But there is widespread agreement on a number of corroborated facts, including that troops of the Kampfgruppe Peiper, commanded by SS Lt. Col. Joachim Peiper, opened fire on December 17, 1944, on more than 100 American soldiers who had been disarmed and assembled in a field next to the Cafe Bodarwe, two miles southeast of Malmedy.

It was not until January 14, 1945, however, that U.S. Army engineers, using mine detectors, uncovered the snow-covered bodies of 71 victims of the massacre.

Belden said in a cable to *Time* in New York on December 18 that he and Boyle, of AP, had spoken with several of the survivors of the incident, who said that the majority of the men may have escaped by diving to the ground and lying still. But an hour after the attempted slaughter, he said, fewer than 15 survivors had escaped back to the U.S. line.

T/Sgt. William B. Summers told Belden: "Some of us who played dead got away later, but we had to lie there and listen to German noncoms [non-commissioned officers] kill with pistols anyone who showed signs of life."

Belden said that he and Boyle had ridden back with the first survivors to the medical clearing station less than two miles from the scene of the incident.

Private William F. Reem told them that the Germans had disarmed the U.S. soldiers and taken their wrist watches and anything else they wanted. "Then they stood us all together in an open field," he said. "I thought there was something wrong, the way they made us huddle together. Then a Heinie officer said something to a tankman and he shot at us with a pistol. We had our hands up at the time but as soon as that pistol went off some of us began dropping to the ground. Lucky we did, too, because one of them set up a Schmeisser pistol in an armored car and fired pointblank at us. There was nothing to do but play dead."

For an hour or so, the survivors lay in the field among their dead comrades, half frozen in the cold, listening to the sound of gunfire and the rumbling of tanks until the Germans had moved off. Then they made a dash for safety, with the unwounded helping the wounded through a barbed wire fence and through the woods and over a hill back to the U.S. line.

"One got a bullet in his leg," Belden wrote. "Another had his toes shot away. Blood was leaking from his galoshes. A third was shot in the head, the hand and the leg. The medics were digging at him when I last saw him. The Germans were still only a short distance away."

After the war – on May 16, 1946 – Peiper and 70 members of his Kampfgruppe, along with his army commander, chief of staff and corps commander, were arraigned before a U.S. military court, which found them guilty of war crimes at Malmedy. Forty-three of the defendants, including Peiper, were sentenced to death; 22 defendants were sentenced to life in prison; and the rest were sentenced to between 10 years and 20 years imprisonment. But none of them was ever put to death, and by 1956 all of them had been released from jail.

The AP story that Boyle wrote about the incident ran under the headline, "Nazis Turned Machine Guns on GI POWs." An American historian later wrote that if it had not been for Boyle's presence at the scene, it is unlikely that the incident would have achieved the international notoriety that it did. It is unclear why Belden's account of the massacre – sent to *Time* in New York on December 18 – was never published.

18

A BABY BOY AND THE FBI

It happened quickly and without warning, in January 1945, and suddenly he was without a job. His last story for Henry R. Luce's TIME-LIFE organization was published in the January 1 issue of *Time*. Then, he was fired.

The editors had introduced the piece, which told of the Allied retreat in the Belgium as German troops broke through, by saying that, after months of witnessing advance and victory by the Americans, Belden and the other correspondents had received word that the enemy was again on the move. His story, they said, was a first-hand account of the "muddle and mess of retreat."

"I noticed in myself a feeling that I had not had for some years," Belden wrote. "It was a feeling of guilt that seems to come over you whenever you retreat. You don't like to look anyone in the eyes. It seems as if you have done something wrong. I perceived this feeling in others too."

Shortly after his 35th birthday, in early February, he wrote to his mother in New Jersey saying he had been fired by TIME-LIFE. "Don't particularly know the reasons," he wrote, "and am not particularly interested." Perhaps, he said, it had something to do with his "views on China." Later, he told a friend it may also have been linked to the opinions he expressed in his book *Still Time to Die*, which had come out the previous September.

An internal TIME-LIFE memo dealing with personnel matters – from Editorial Director John Shaw Billings to Roy E. Larsen, president of TIME Inc., dated December 18, 1944 – said that Belden was being let go. "Price too high," Billings said of Belden, "production too low." He told his diary on December 29 that costs at the company overall were rising unacceptably and that "something must be done about it, we all agree."

"With rising costs, the more we take in the less we seem to make," Billings wrote. "I propose a cut across the board. Throwing out all frills." In a diary entry on January 5, 1945, he wrote, "We are all very budget conscious. there is even talk of cutting out drinks charged to *Time*." He said that the bill for liquor in 1944 had been $10,000. [1]

For his part, Belden, of course, had written extensively about China over the years, beginning in 1937 as a correspondent for United Press in Peking. His views, when expressed, were always and unequivocally pro-Chinese. He saw both good and bad in the policies and practices of the Nationalists under Chiang Kai-shek as well as the Communists under Mao Tse-tung. But he consistently sided with the Chinese in the defense of their nation against the Japanese. His "views on China," in short, were balanced – although some have argued that they bent toward the Communist cause, which, of course, would not have set well with the pro-Chiang powers-that-be at TIME-LIFE who put Chiang and his wife on the cover of the January 3, 1938, issue of *Time* magazine, calling them "Man and Wife of the Year."

At TIME-LIFE, Luce's staunchly anti-Communist views were well-known and clearly had an impact on the hiring and firing practices at the company. "The only way I can make myself understood is to try to imitate a drill sergeant," he said in one memo to Billings. "I do not want any Communist sympathizers working for TIME Inc. I hope that statement is plain for the record."

It was, however, Belden's broadly unconventional take on the prevailing social and political atmosphere in the United States, along with his worker-oriented world view and his indirect criticism of Luce, that probably did him in at TIME-LIFE .

Belden wrote in *Still Time to Die* – published in September 1944, when the United States was still at war in Europe and the Pacific – that he was appalled by the racism, anti-Semitism, and xenophobia that he had seen since returning to the United States in late 1943 to recover from the gunshot wound he had suffered while covering the U.S. landing at Salerno. People in business and government, he wrote, "do not give two cents for the people," and, moreover, he said, the United States was becoming Fascist.

"I believe in farmers and workers everywhere," he wrote. "I do not believe in the falsehoods, the shams and the deceits of the statesmen, the generals and the 'leaders'. I do not believe that if we only had a number of good people, the world would roll smoothly on its axis. I do not believe in good people ruling us, but only in the mass of the people ruling themselves."

The United States, he wrote, was pregnant with reaction. "I hope the birth of Fascism here will be abortive," he said. "I see no guarantee that it will be."

But even "more frightening," he said, was the talk of an "American Century" [2] – a reference to a phrase coined by Luce in a five-page essay in the Feb. 17, 1941, issue of *LIFE* magazine. It was his most famous work, and it set out a vision for what Luce called a "gloomy," "nervous" and "apathetic" America. It called the American people to join forces to spread the American vision worldwide.

"[T]he cure is this," Luce wrote, "to accept wholeheartedly our duty and our opportunity as the most powerful and vital nation in the world and in consequence to exert upon the world the full impact of our influence, for such purposes as we see fit and by such means as we see fit," Luce wrote. "As America enters dynamically upon the world scene, we need most of all to seek and bring forth a vision of America as a world power which is authentically American and which can inspire us to live and work and fight with vigor and enthusiasm....It now becomes our time to be the powerhouse from which the ideals spread throughout the world and do their mysterious work of lifting the life of mankind from the level of the beasts to what the Psalmists called a little lower than the angels....It is in this spirit that all of us are called...to create the first great American Century."

Belden said in a letter to his mother, dated February 26, 1945 that he was not upset that his relationship with TIME-LIFE had come to an end because it had become a "terrible outfit" to work for. But he conceded it was difficult not having a large news organization as an employer, with all expenses paid. "Living is very dear over here," he said. [3]

He later told an acquaintance he had become increasingly offended by the eagerness of TIME-LIFE editors to kill or heavily censor what he wrote, including an article about American soldiers fraternizing with their German "enemies," whose homes and villages were now being invaded. When it became clear that the article would not be published, he circulated a petition among his fellow war correspondents protesting the policy. It garnered widespread support. [4] But a short time later he was fired by TIME-LIFE.

Without work, Belden chose to stay in Paris. He was offered a job by *Newsweek* magazine, but he turned it down. He was also approached by the *New York Herald Tribune*, but nothing came of it. For six weeks, according to the letter to his mother dated February 26, he had done "absolutely nothing." He made a brief trip to London, he said, where he knew no one, so he returned to Paris "out of sheer loneliness."

His health was also a problem. A new bout with malaria, which he first contracted in Burma in 1942, had put him in bed for a few weeks. "Malaria comes back once in a while and doctors say I probably [will] have it for the rest of my life," he told his mother. He had also grown "terribly fat." But above all, while he had saved some money to live on, he had not written a word.

"I am thinking seriously of just working for myself and doing what I want to do," he said. "Trouble with this working for yourself is that the pressure is off and you don't have to work and so you get in the habit from day to day of doing nothing. A habit I've been in for some weeks now."

He continued to live with the other American correspondents at the Hotel Scribe – for only $3.00 a day. But he had just met a French girl by the name of Paula and was upset that outside guests were only allowed to enter the hotel twice a week. "This makes it difficult," he said, "[because] you have to go to...to her house and eat bread and spaghetti."

Belden thanked his mother for the box of food she had sent. He had received at the front, he said, but had saved it to bring back to Paris "as I knew [Paula] would enjoy it." Cigarettes and chocolate, he said, were always in demand.

He complained there was nothing to do in Paris except walk the streets. "Paula and I just walk along the Seine or in some of the narrow streets in [the district of St-Germain-des-Pres] looking at old curiosity shops or bookshops," he wrote. He said that Paula's English was improving.

Sales of *Still Time to Die,* meanwhile, appeared to be strong, he said, with about 12,000 copies sold to date and another 70,000 shipped to The Literary Guild Book Club. Another 10,000 copies had been printed in a special armed services edition for U.S. soldiers. "Guess I'll make about $10,000 on the book, which is very good, I think," he said.

But Belden ended the letter to his mother by saying he was deeply troubled by the news that his old friend and associate from China and Burma, Gen. Joseph W. Stilwell, had been recalled from China, where he had been serving as commander of U.S. forces.

"Stilwell had entirely too much integrity to hold such a political position without finally being stabbed in the back," Belden wrote, adding derisively of Stilwell's successor, Gen. Albert C. Wedemeyer, that he was "one of those generals who says, 'Just call me Al.' "

His old friend's recall had come after he had convinced U.S. Army Chief of Staff George C. Marshall to urge President Roosevelt to effectively order Chiang Kai-shek to put Stilwell in command of all Chinese armed forces. But Chiang refused, and instead he demanded that Roosevelt replace Stilwell immediately, which he eventually agreed to do, and on October 19, 1944, he was recalled back to Washington, D.C. On

January 23, 1945, he was named commander of Army Ground Forces in the United States and he served as commander of the U.S. Tenth Army during the closing days of the Battle of Okinawa in June 1945 and later as commander of the U.S. Sixth Army. He died of stomach cancer at his home near San Francisco on October 12, 1946, at the age of 63.

Fired by TIME-LIFE, Belden approached Harper & Brothers, publishers of *Harper's* magazine, whose president, Cass Canfield, was heading to Paris to take over the Office of War Information in Europe. On February 27, 1945, he and Canfield had dinner at a Paris restaurant, and the publisher agreed to help Belden obtain press credentials. But he did not agree to pay any of Belden's expenses or to publish anything he wrote.

Toward the end of March – bored with Paris – he headed out again to be with the troops, who were now preparing to cross the Rhine River at Wesel and attack the industrial heartland of the Third Reich.

Belden and the other reporters, operating out of a press camp set up in the castle in Mönchengladbach once occupied by Hitler's minister of propaganda, Joseph Goebbels, spent the night and day of March 23-24 witnessing the river-crossing at Wesel, which Eisenhower would later describe as the operation that had "sealed the fate of Germany." [5]

Thousands of Allied guns, according to CBS reporter Eric Sevareid, who observed the operation along with Belden from the eastern shore of the Rhine, had opened fire on Wesel, producing a "pounding clatter that made one feel his teeth were coming loose." Later that night, he and Belden moved to a small house to get some sleep. "Now and then mortar shells came in, and frequently their fragments banged against the thin walls that protected us," Sevareid wrote. "Belden began to snore at once, but I could not sleep. I lay in the rubbish...waiting for the next mortar explosion." [6]

Eisenhower also watched the assault from an old church tower across the river from Wesel, along with Lt. General William H. Simpson, commander of the Ninth Army. He said that he and Simpson had gone down to the water's edge to see the GIs who were preparing to get into the boats for a nighttime crossing of the river.

"We joined some of them and found the troops remarkably eager to finish the job," Eisenhower later recalled. "Nevertheless, as we walked along I fell in with one young soldier who seemed silent and depressed."

" 'How are you feeling, son?' I asked."

" 'General,' he said. 'I'm awful nervous....' "

" 'Well,' I said to him, 'you and I are a good pair then, because I'm nervous too. But we've planned this attack for a long time and we've got all the planes, the guns and airborne troops we can use to smash the Germans. Maybe if we just walk along together to the river we'll be good for each other.' "

" 'Oh,' he said, 'I meant I was nervous; I'm not anymore. I guess it's not so bad around here.' And I knew what he meant." [7]

The next morning, Belden and Sevareid awoke and rose stiffly to their feet, filthy and aching to the bone. The wet pastures outside were still smoking from the battle the night before, and the sky was blue and clear except for a gray haze that hung over the spot where Wesel had been. Three young officers were still asleep in the dining room, looking like exhausted children, and a picture of the Last Supper hung askew on the wall. [8]

At 10 a.m, on schedule, long lines of transport aircraft and gliders – 1572 and 1326, respectively – appeared in the sky to the west of Wesel, escorted by some 900 fighter planes, and thousands of Allied paratroopers and infantry soon landed on the eastern bank of the Rhine, placing "strong forces," as Eisenhower put it, "in a position to deny the enemy use of significant portions of that great [Ruhr] industrial area." [9]

The following day, British Prime Minister Winston S. Churchill met Eisenhower near Wesel. "My dear General," he said, "the German is whipped. We've got him. He is all through." [10]

The fate of the Germans may have already been sealed, but several weeks of heavy fighting would follow. On April 30, Hitler committed suicide in Berlin, and Goebbels became chancellor of Germany but only for one day before being shot dead on his orders by an SS officer, along with his wife Magda, who had earlier poisoned their six children. On May 8, the Germans surrendered unconditionally at a ceremony at Supreme Head-quarters Allied Expeditionary Force (SHAEF) in Rheims, France.

At the end of the European campaign, Belden returned to Paris and, still without a job, resumed "doing nothing," which included a "murderous" poker game in late May with several friends and colleagues – Collingwood; Capa; Morgan Beatty, of NBC; and Edgar Snow, who said later he had been relieved of $800. [11]

For his part, Belden told his mother he had always wanted to return to China for the end of the war. "But now," he said, "I don't know whether I will or not."

What he did know was that he was extremely fond of the "very lovely, mature" French girl, Paula. He had met and courted her during the Allies' victorious entry into Paris the previous August, and on August 23, 1945 – six days after the Japanese surrendered, ending World War II – he and Paula Allouard were married.

Later that month, the couple traveled to the United States where, according to the FBI, Belden immediately met his old friend and colleague from China, Agnes Smedley. Two agents who were assigned to cover Smedley's movements said in a report to FBI Director J. Edgar Hoover that she and Belden had had lunch at the Mayflower Hotel on Park Avenue in New York City on August 31.

The FBI had long been interested in Smedley because of her suspected association with the Communist Party. But in mid-1945 it stepped up its surveillance and investigation of her after Whittaker Chambers, a former member of the Communist Party who was then senior editor at TIME-LIFE, told FBI agents that she was definitely a Communist – "no question about it." [12]

Israel Epstein, the journalist, author and long-time Communist who had known Belden since the 1930s, said that, in fact, he had first become aware of the FBI's interest in Smedley in early 1945 when she had stayed overnight at an apartment that he and his wife were living in on Riverside Drive in New York.

"Within a half an hour, the doorbell rang," Epstein wrote. "A solidly built man said he had come to check on the refrigerator. From the manner in which his wandering eyes observed everything in the room on the way to the kitchen, we suspected a different aim." Thirty-five years later, he said, a declassified FBI report noted that Smedley had slept over that night at his flat. [13]

Smedley and Belden most likely first met in 1938 when they were both living and working in China, specifically Hankow, covering China's war with Japan. They had stayed in touch, and in March 1943 Smedley, who was living in the United States, wrote a review of Belden's *Retreat With Stilwell,* published in *The Progressive* magazine, in which she claimed that "someone" was attempting to prevent the book from being distributed to U.S. troops because it was critical of Chiang Kai-shek's armed forces. [14]

The FBI agents who were clandestinely monitoring Smedley's activities in August 1945, meanwhile, reported to Hoover on the occasion of Belden's luncheon engagement with Smedley ("who has a long record of Communist activity") they had interviewed the manager of the Mayflower Hotel, who told them that Belden was the author of *Retreat With Stilwell* and a correspondent with *Time* and *LIFE* magazines. He was also "connected" with the *New York Herald Tribune,* the manager said, according to the agents, who said that their report was based on their "surveillance" at the hotel.

Belden and his new wife spent the fall of 1945 in the United States shuttling between New York City and Summit, N.J., where his mother still lived. In mid-February 1946, they attended a party in New York for Stilwell and his wife hosted by Teddy White, where they caught up with number of old colleagues and acquaintances, including Smedley; Epstein and his wife Elsie; Eric Sevareid; Betty Graham, who was about to leave for India to be a freelance writer; and Annalee Jacoby. [15]

Smedley wrote to a friend after the party that Belden's "new French wife" was due to have a baby "any day now." A son, David, was born to the couple later that year.

But it would not be long before marriage and fatherhood would fall victim to Belden's wanderlust and his continuing fascination, even obsession, with China. He later wrote that, in 1946, when the civil war in China began, he was in the United States "trying like so many people to put in order a life that had been uprooted by many years of war." He had been away from China for four years, he said, and during that time great changes had taken place in that country. Yet one thing remained the same, he said, and that was that there was still no peace.

"For immediately after the conclusion of hostilities with Japan," Belden wrote, "the Chinese people had plunged into a civil war that was incomparably more vast, terrifyingly more impassioned and dangerously more important than any conflict they had ever waged in the four thousand years of their tortured history." [16]

Belden said that betting against Chiang in that internal conflict had seemed suicidal. He had an army four times larger than the Communists' Eighth Route Army, and he had an air force, railways, gunboats and motor-driven transportation, and the Communists had none of that. Letters that Belden received in the United States from American businessmen in Shanghai claimed that the generalissimo's army was much different than the corrupt one that Belden had known four years earlier. One businessman predicted that the war would be over in a matter of weeks.

Newspaper accounts seemed to confirm that view. With the aid of the U.S. military, Chiang appeared to be racking up victory after victory. "[I]t was hard to believe that the Communists had a chance to resist successfully, much less to win the war," Belden wrote. [17]

Yet in the middle of 1946, friends of Belden in China began to send him news of some interesting developments in the north of the country, notably, important gains by the Eighth Route Army and the gradual isolation of Chiang's Nationalist forces. As a result, Chiang's progress had been slowed and a long war now appeared to be a possibility. The Reds, according to Belden, had suddenly thrown a revolution at the head of the generalissimo "like a bomb." But not one word about the revolution, he said, had made its way into the newspapers back in the United States.

"I knew that the only way to learn anything about this revolution was to go there," Belden wrote, telling a friend many years later that his wife Paula had already moved to St. Tropez. "I thought about the thousands of lives that were being sacrificed in China's civil war...and about millions of starving farmers whom the Communists had hurled on to the bitter road to revolution. Could the comfort of one foreign life be better sacrificed than in trying to find out what this war and revolution was all about? In this somewhat solemn frame of mind I packed my suitcase, said good-bye to my wife and boarded a slow boat to China." [18]

19

CHINA (AGAIN) SHAKES HIS WORLD

The sudden death of Gen. Joseph W. Stilwell on October 12, 1946, left Belden stunned and saddened. He had known and admired the man since 1935 when the two first met, in Peking – Stilwell, as a military attache at the U.S. Embassy, and Belden, only 25 years old, a budding war reporter.

Belden was also the only reporter to accompany Stilwell on his tortuous "walkout" through the jungles of Burma in 1942, which Belden chronicled in the first of his three books, *Retreat With Stilwell*, published the following year.

It was not surprising, therefore, that before heading to China in early November, Belden chose to spend a few days with Stilwell's widow, Winnie, at the couple's home on Inspiration Way overlooking the Pacific Ocean in Carmel, California.

As they walked on the beach, the question of who would be responsible for compiling and publishing the general's papers undoubtedly came up. No other reporter had been as close to him as Belden had, and Winnie trusted him. But she later told Agnes Smedley she planned to write a book herself. [1]

In December 1946, however, Smedley, who doubted Winnie's resolve, said in a letter to a friend that Belden had tentatively agreed to write a book about Stilwell when he returned from China. "Only someone like Jack, very close to Stilwell, could write the book," she said, "and Mrs. Stilwell would never release papers to anyone who had not been close to him. Jack was the closest of all correspondents to him ...." [2]

But the task of arranging and editing Stilwell's papers for publication – with Belden still off in China – would eventually fall to Teddy White, who had recently resigned as a correspondent for TIME-LIFE over what Belden said was "Luce's penchant for untruths and his ignoring what his own correspondents in the field" reported.

Belden arrived in China in late December 1946 after what he described as a "miserable" 42-day trip across the Pacific. He had jumped ship in Hong Kong in 1933 without a passport, and while he had a passport this time, he never used it. Instead, when his ship anchored off of Tangku – the port of entry for Tientsin – a customs official boarded the vessel and announced that he would not allow the passengers to go ashore because it was against regulations. In the same breath, however, he let it be known that he was the father of many children and would not want to see them starve to death.

"We quickly grasped his point," Belden wrote later, adding that the customs official, without hesitation, demanded the leather jacket that Belden was wearing, which he did not get, along with $200 and a gold watch from another passenger, which he did acquire. Forgetting the regulations, the official then dumped the passengers ashore in an empty field "where neither we nor he would be inconvenienced by any customs or immigration formalities....[It] was the first indication I had that the officials of Chiang Kai-shek were still the same old masters of the art of the squeeze that they always had been." [3]

After stopping briefly in Tangku, where he encountered a group of American soldiers guarding a dump filled with ammunition destined for Chiang's Nationalists, he made his way to Tientsin and then on to Peking, which he had left in 1939 in the company of Stilwell and his family, on December 31, 1946.

Belden said that the city had changed little in outward appearance. But he said that an atmosphere of war and revolution clearly hung over the country, from Harbin to Shanghai and from the Yellow Sea to Inner Mongolia. He said that an American attempt to negotiate a truce between the Nationalists and the Communists, led by George C. Marshall, was doomed to fail, which it did, in fact, a year later.

"[N]o clairvoyance was needed to see that China's already full-fledged civil war would become an all-out conflict for control of the Asiatic continent," Belden later wrote. "Because the routes might be closed at any moment, I decided to go immediately into the Liberated Areas." [4]

But getting from Peking to the "Liberated Areas" – i.e., areas not controlled by Chiang's Nationalist troops – would not be easy, even for a relatively young man (he was about to turn 37) who spoke fluent Chinese.

Belden knew that the most decisive theatre of the civil war at the time was the North China Plain – a vast flat region lying between Chiang's capital in Nanking and his troops in Peking, Tientsin, North China and Manchuria – and that unless Chiang could beat his way across the plain to link up his capital with his troops in the north, which were now isolated, he would not be able to unify China and prevail in the war with the Communist insurgents. So he set his mind early on seeing and interviewing the Communist general who stood in the way of Chiang's necessary drive from the south northward: Liu Po-cheng.

Liu's headquarters, however, were located near Hantan, in the province of Hepei, some 300 miles south of Peking across the North China Plain; at least two-thirds of Belden's trip to see him would have to be made by mule-drawn cart.

Belden knew Liu as one of the most competent and colorful of the Communist commanders. He had been at the vanguard of the Red Army's Long March through China in 1934. A hand grenade in combat had blown out one of his eyes, so he was now known by various names including Blind Liu, the One-Eyed General and the One-Eyed Dragon.

Armed with a duffel bag, camera and typewriter, Belden left Peking in early January 1947, and after several days crossed into the Liberated

Areas at Potow. There, he prepared to begin his long journey across the North China Plain, having changed 4,000 of Chiang's dollars into 80,000 Communist dollars, and he left Potow on January 21 as an overnight snow storm continued to rage.

"[The snow] was still coming down," he wrote, "as a crowd of children followed me to the outskirts of Potow's walls. A mule harnessed to a Peking car waited for me beside the mud wall of a collapsing house. A small boy, carrying a whip, went from one side of the cart to the other, fastening the traces and adjusting the harness. The mule stamped his feet on the ground as if he knew cold and drew back his lip and whinnied. My duffel bag was tied on the back of the cart on the outside; my camera case and typewriter place under the roof of the cart on the inside." [5]

Belden spent the next several months – by cart and on foot – "wandering around" the Liberated Areas, as he put it several years later, interviewing dozens of local Communist Party officials, often for several days at a sitting, and gathering material for what would become his most well-known book, *China Shakes the World*, published in 1949.

He said years later that, as far as he knew, he was the only journalist traveling in the Chinese countryside at the time. [6]

Christopher Rand, an American journalist reporting from China for the *New York Herald-Tribune*, told a friend in the spring of 1947 that he was having the time of his life "wandering about China as my fancy dictates." But his son, Peter Rand, wrote years later that it was "all but impossible" for an American correspondent to cover the civil war from the Communist side because the U.S. government had alienated the Communists by airlifting Chiang's troops to North China. Only Belden, he said, was able to befriend the Communists and see through "the looking glass." [7]

Belden's insights, accordingly, were highly valued by U.S. officials posted in China whose primary mission was to cover the civil war and report their findings back to the State Department in Washington, D.C. One of those officials was a young diplomat, John F. Melby, who had arrived in China in 1945 after serving at the U.S. Embassy in Moscow.

Melby met Belden at the U.S. Embassy in Nanking on October 26, and the two men had a long conversation about what Belden had learned about the Communists' short- to medium- term intentions in their war with the Nationalists.

"[Belden] says the Communist plan is to have Generals Liu Po-cheng and Chen Yi consolidate their armies this winter in the Tapieh-shan, a rugged hilly area in central China north of the Yangtze [River]," Melby wrote in his diary the day after he met Belden – insights that he also undoubtedly sent along to his bosses in Washington, D.C. "And they are pouring in hundreds of workers there and to the south. The next spring they will strike at the Nanking-Shanghai area."

Melby said that Belden also expressed concern over a "growing mental rigidity" among the Communist leaders in Hopei, as well as over the "increasing use of terror against any form of opposition, and the extermination of large sections of the population."

He said that, according to Belden, the Communists in Hopei had largely put an end to their anti-American propaganda and were concentrating instead on the abuses of Chiang Kai-shek.

"The combined result is to create in the peasants a terror and furtiveness [Belden] has never before seen in Communist areas," Melby wrote, "and he has seen most of them." [8]

Later recalled to Washington, where he wrote "The China White Paper," published in August 1949, which sought, among other things, to explain why a Communist victory in China was imminent, Melby was ousted from the foreign service in 1953 during the McCarthy era – a dismissal he later attributed to his relationship with the American writer Lillian Hellman, who was reputed to be a former member of the Communist Party.

Belden said that when he emerged from the Liberated Areas in the fall of 1947 and went to Shanghai he was appalled at the ignorance of all foreigners, as well as the "generals and propagandists," about the growing strength of the Communists and the reasons behind the failure of Chiang Kai-shek to bring the war to an end.

"Officials rode around in cars bought up at seven thousand dollars American money from American importers who moaned in their Scotch and water at the American Club about the hard times that had come to China," he wrote. "Out in the country the peasants were eating millet husks. But here in Shanghai, officials and businessmen, their mouths full of food and curses for both the Communists and Chiang Kai-shek, were eating five bowls of rice at one sitting and complimenting one another on the tastiness of the Mandarin Fish, the Gold Coin Chicken, the fatted Peiping Duck, and the specially warmed yellow rice." [9]

Parties also continued unabated at the foreign correspondents club, located on the 18th floor of the Broadway Mansions in Shanghai, where White Russian mistresses mingled with American wives – while both cursed the Chinese. The war, he said, was not preventing American Army personnel from holding "homey gatherings...on China's supposedly sovereign soil...."

"The ignorance of people about events that were transpiring in Communist areas surprised me," Belden wrote, adding that when he told foreign officials that a Communist offensive had begun, one high-ranking Army officer said, "Forget it. The Communists have no weapons and will never be able to launch an offensive."

Belden said that, as far as American diplomats in China were concerned, they were deathly afraid of becoming tainted with what he called a "politically pink tinge." The fact that some congressmen in the United States were sounding off about "Reds" in the State Department, he said, made the diplomats reluctant to report back home on the revolution taking place in the Communist-held countryside, even as they were keen to report openly on the corruption in the Chiang government and the incompetency of his generals. "I'm not sticking my neck out," one American official told Belden.

Noting the existence of a burgeoning "Communist witch hunt" in the United States, Belden was particularly critical of his former employer, Henry Luce, of TIME-LIFE, who, he said, had often expressed sympathy for Chiang and was undoubtedly moved by his own anti-Communist feelings.

Belden said that Luce had sent William C. Bullitt, a former U.S. ambassador to Moscow and Paris and now an important foreign policy spokesman for the Republican Party, to China to report for *LIFE* magazine, and when he returned to the United States, he wrote an article for the magazine calling for direct and open U.S. military intervention in support of Chiang so that China would be kept out of the hands of Stalin.

The article said that, in mid-1947, Chiang held all of the territory north of the Yangtze River and "small bands of bandits, some of which call themselves Communists, hold remote areas" south of the river.

Bullitt said that the United States should begin immediately to develop in cooperation with Chiang a plan to win the war, including through military means.

"[T]he essence of the problem is the ejection of every armed Communist from the soil of China," he wrote, adding that American military experts believe that it would take three years to meet that objective. "If China falls into the hands of Stalin, all Asia, including Japan, sooner or later will fall into his hands. The manpower and resources of Asia will be mobilized against us. The independence of the U.S. will not live a generation longer than the independence of China."

Bullitt said that the key was Manchuria – "the finest piece of territory in Asia" as large as France and Germany combined – where, he said, Communists troops were already in control of the north and troops from the Soviet Union held Darien and Port Arthur in the south. "If Manchuria should be abandoned to the Communists or should fall into their hands by conquest," he wrote, "a course of events fatal to China would follow....The urgent need of the [Chiang] government armies in Manchuria for ammunition and spare parts...is one which cannot be filled in a leisurely manner. It requires immediate action....President Truman can legally take this action at once....He can act in time to keep Manchuria out of the hands of the Soviet Union." [10]

Having read the article, Belden decided to travel there "to see for myself." What he found, he said, was little or no evidence to support Bullitt's claim that the Russians were interfering in the Chinese civil war. On the contrary, he said, since the beginning of 1947, Chiang had been on the defensive there, and the Communists controlled 90 percent of Manchuria, two-thirds of the railways and much more. He said that Chiang, therefore, was at pains to explain his "colossal failure outside the Great Wall," and he had found a convenient villain in Stalin.

But Belden did concede that some of the Japanese weapons that had been captured by the Russians as they withdrew from Manchuria may have fallen into the hands of the Eighth Route Army, although Chiang clearly had captured far more arms from the surrendering Japanese in September 1945 than the Communists ever did. It was also probably true, he said, that the Russians turned over to the Communist troops some trucks in exchange for Manchurian products.

Belden said, moreover, that "it seems obvious" that the Chinese Communists will be "closely linked" to the Soviet Union down the road. But he said that pouring billions of U.S. dollars into Manchuria to help Chiang win the war would only offend the common sense of the Chinese people and backfire. [11]

"In short," Belden wrote, "Bullitt was advocating a program that was based on wrong assumptions to begin with and on questionable conclusions to end with." [12]

Belden's views were echoed, oddly, by none other than Mao Tse-tung in a major radio broadcast delivered on Christmas Day 1947, in which he said that the civil war, at its core, was a struggle of the armed Chinese people against feudalism and dictatorship and toward independence and democracy.

"Under these conditions," Mao said, "Chiang Kai-shek's military superiority and American aid are factors that can only play temporary roles. The unpopular nature of the Chiang regime and the support or opposition of the people, however, will play constant roles." [13]

But for Belden, convincing those in the U.S. news media to hear out his views would not be easy.

On returning to the United States in the fall of 1947, he immediately began drafting two articles for publication – one on the probable downfall of the Chiang regime and the other on life as lived in the Communist-controlled areas of China. Both were initially accepted by *Collier's* magazine. But they were later rejected, according to Belden, under pressure from the "China Lobby."

Success in pitching the articles would not be any easier at *The Saturday Evening Post*, where he was respected and admired by Martin Sommers, the foreign editor, a good friend of Edgar Snow and former fellow reporter. [14] But in the end, the editor of the magazine, Ben Hibbs, had reservations, saying in a memo to Sommers in early January 1948 that he was "more undecided than I have been on any project for a long time." He agreed with Sommers, however, that "we shouldn't kiss it off without trying to see if something can be worked out."

Hibbs told Sommers that his concerns centered on what he felt was Belden's continuing and strong support of the Chinese Communists, which made it unlikely, he said, that the Post could ever get some "usable copy" from him.

"I am afraid...that he is so interested in the Commie cause that he will be quite unyielding," Hibbs wrote. "And I, in turn, refuse to publish any more articles that are strongly slanted for the Chinese Communists. I agree with Belden's estimate of Chiang and his regime, but I simply can't believe that the Commies are as fine, high-minded folks as he seems to think."

Hibbs said that he agreed with Sommers that the magazine could get something unusual, "perhaps even sensational," from Belden. But he said that, in his view, this would not justify publishing "strongly slanted Leftie articles." He then directed Sommers to tell Belden "frankly how we feel... and if he doesn't want to go along on that basis we'll just have to pitch the whole thing out."

In a letter to Belden dated January 18, 1948, Sommers explained the situation and told him that the magazine would be willing to pay $3000 each for the two articles "if [they] are acceptable" under the terms outlined by Hibbs.

Sommers told Belden, who was recovering from a bout of strep throat at St. Luke's Hospital in New York City, that he could "forget about us" if he thought that their "fair and reasonable" attitudes were unfair.

"At the same time," Sommers continued, "having been where you've been and seen what you've seen for so long, I can understand how you feel so sympathetic to the people who have been your companions, and so indebted to them, that you would produce articles which we would consider unreasonably pro-Chinese Communist. This is not to say that I for a moment doubt your integrity as a reporter or your very great capacities as a writer. If I did, I wouldn't be writing this....Whatever happens, it seems to me you surely should have a successful book out of your trip...."

Enraged, Belden scribbled a note on the letter saying "You Prick," and the project was dropped.

Years later, Belden also revealed that after returning to the United States from his trip to China he had been asked to write a series of articles for the *New York Herald-Tribune*. But Joseph Barnes, the foreign editor, had later withdrawn the offer, saying "shamefacedly," according to Belden, that "this is a Republican paper."

As Sommers, of *The Saturday Evening Post*, had said, however, the trip to China had generated plenty of material for a book. He spent most of 1948 working on it, producing in the end what has since been called a neglected masterpiece: *China Shakes the World*.

It was during this period that Belden also had other things on his mind – a passionate love affair, by all accounts, with a screenwriter and author from California by the name of Nel King. In one letter to him – addressed to "my friend, my lover, my plush-head, my grouchy angel"– she said that, being "thousands of miles from you," she missed him.

"I think of you driving along all alone in our car," she wrote, "and it's raining and cold, and you're wearing your camel's hair coat and your hair is standing on end, and you have to read the maps yourself, and you take wrong turns and get lost and get all mad, and when night comes you take your little mashed suitcase out of the back of the car, and brush your teeth, and sleep all alone in one twin bed. And you get cold in the night – there aren't enough covers – and you wake up and get mad again and smoke cigarettes and read the chess book. Oh, I miss you, I miss you."

Another letter – dated December 10 and sent from Laguna, California, to Belden in New York – said it had been comforting to hear his "cross little voice" in a telephone conversation that they had had the previous night.

"Sorry you're in such a turmoil getting the book finished," King wrote, "but one foot before the other plod plod and before you know it it'll be in galley proofs and you'll be off to something new."

But the relationship, which began when Belden stopped in California on his way to China in the fall of 1947, would end peacefully without an exchange of marriage vows. He was still married to Paula Allouard, who remained in France, and King was destined to marry – albeit briefly – the American painter and writer Douglas W. Gorsline.

With *China Shakes the World* finally finished, Belden could be pleased. It was promoted initially with much fanfare by Harper & Brothers, which released the book in 1949 saying it was bound to be controversial because U.S. policy toward China had bitterly divided Americans both within and without the government. "But no matter what your political views," it said, "*China Shakes the World* is worth reading solely on its merits as a book– for its mass of instructive facts, its fascinating story and its contemplative originality."

The publisher described the book as a kind of "laboratory exposition of the technique of insurrection," with Belden taking the reader into the caves and huts of Chinese peasants – "all of them protagonists in one way or another of the revolutionary struggle." For the first time, it said, Belden had told the story of the reasons behind Chiang's failure and the Communists' success.

"The tale he weaves," the publisher said in promoting the book, "is a tangled one of war and politics, strategy and dialectics, of murder, poison and seduction, all taking place in the midst of a struggle for survival between between three different types of civilization: feudalism, capitalism and nascent socialism."

Reviews of the book were positive, with Orville Prescott, of *The New York Times*, for instance, calling it "wonderfully readable, dramatic, terrible and highly informative" and "certainly provocative."

The *Saturday Review of Literature* said that it was one of the best books ever written about the Chinese people, "crammed with sufficient atmosphere and intrigue for half a dozen novels...."

Belden's friend and colleague Edgar Snow wrote that the book was filled with "enthralling pages" that told the story of thousands of peasants fighting for existence: "real men and women – in suffering, in degradation, exulting and in sorrow, battling, provoking, avenging, loving, murdering, dying for petty or exalted aims...."

Yet, in the wake of the Communist takeover of the Chinese mainland in October 1949, some political commentators began to suggest that Belden and the book may have played an unhealthy role in pumping up the image of the Chinese Communists in the United States.

John T. Flynn, for instance, wrote in a book published in 1951 entitled *While You Slept: Our Tragedy in Asia and Who Made It* that *China Shakes the World* was "pro-Communist." He called it "a glorified account of Communist China and the achievements of the Reds." [15]

Belden wrote Snow a decade later saying he thought that the book had come out at an opportune time, just as China was falling to the Communists. But he said that, in his view, McCarthyism had killed it.

As for Belden, after finishing *China Shakes the World*, he remained on the East Coast, receiving mail variously at his mother's home in Summit, N.J.; the Algonquin Hotel in New York City; the White Face Inn in Lake Placid, N.Y.; and the office of Nate Bienstock, a life insurance agent in New York City – and later a literary agent – whose clients included several of

Belden's former war-time colleagues: Charles Collingwood, Eric Sevareid and John Steinbeck.

Belden's presence in the United States, however, would also enable the FBI to more closely monitor his activities, which it did with a vengeance. The fact that he had just returned from a reporting trip to China, where he spent his time exclusively in Communist-held areas, heightened the agency's interest in him.

His continuing association with Agnes Smedley, moreover, did not help his cause. In early 1948, as the anti-Communist rhetoric continued to rise across the country, the FBI's investigation and surveillance of Smedley intensified, due in large part to a report it had received the previous fall from Major Gen. Charles A. Willoughby, head of intelligence for General Douglas MacArthur, claiming that Smedley was connected with a Soviet spy ring in Tokyo prior to the outbreak of World War II. [16]

In *China Shakes the World*, Belden blasted the Willoughby report, saying that the charges against Smedley were "so fantastic" that the Army had to back down. "[B]ut the bared fangs were clear enough to anyone who tended to scare easily," he said. What was happening, he said, was a "kind of long-distance and indirect bulldozing of American writers" – an attempt to frighten observers of the China scene, he said, with the specter of an "American gestapo." [17]

Also living in the United States at the time, along with Belden and Smedley, was Edgar Snow, who, as the author of "Red Star Over China," published in 1937, and other works, was known in right-wing circles as the Communists' most prominent apologist.

Snow had recently returned from India where he had been on assignment for *The Saturday Evening Post* covering, among other things, the assassination of Mahatma Gandhi on January 30, 1948.

Since the spring of 1946, Snow had been courting a politically sophisticated, 26-year-old actress by the name of Lois Wheeler, who had read *Red Star Over China* as a teenager in her native California. They had met at an after-theatre party at the Waldorf Hotel in New York where Wheeler was appearing in the Moss Hart comedy on Broadway, "Dear Ruth."

A co-founder of The Actors Studio, Wheeler went on to star in Arthur Miller's "All My Sons," winner of the New York Drama Critics' Circle Award in 1947. On opening night, Snow sent her a dozen roses, and when her contract expired, she went to Europe to meet him. That summer they traveled through France, Italy in a Renault "quatre chevaux" until Snow was hospitalized in Bern, Switzerland with a serious kidney infection.

Wheeler said later that, in Bern, they had lived for a while in a high-ceilinged apartment overlooking the river. "I boned upon high school shorthand to take notes during the news interviews Ed handled with ease and depth," she said. "He was good, and hard, at work." [18]

After their marriage in May 1949 – at Snedens Landing on the Hudson River north of New York City – the Snows entertained visiting actors, journalists, scientists and poets, including Belden and Smedley, at their home in Rockleigh, New Jersey. Calls from "twin-clad" FBI agents, she said, came with increasing frequency.

Wheeler said that Smedley was a close friend whose books on China – *Battle Hymn of China* and *The Great Road: The Life and Times of Chu Teh* – had contributed greatly to her understanding of that country. It was from Snedens Landing, she said, that Smedley was spirited away to escape FBI surveillance, covered by a rug in the back seat of the car. [19]

As for Belden, according to Wheeler, he could be playful and funny. His books, particularly *China Shakes the World*, had made a significant impression on her. In her book, *China on Stage: An American Actress in the People's Republic*, she noted favorably that Belden had praised the Communists' ability to stage plays for the peasants, quoting him as saying that their whole theatrical effort was "extremely impressive" and could not have been more democratic. [20] But he could also be sad and melancholy. He was, she said, "clearly in need of a few happy times." [21]

Following the publication of *China Shakes the World*, Belden decided to give up writing – at least about China – because he thought that his book was not appreciated, despite high praise from many reviewers. "I had expressed in writing what I felt and knew to be true," he told a friend years later, "but my own country denied me that."

He was also "well-tarred with the Chinese brush," he said, which meant that he could not find work. "I was forced out of writing, so I decided to literally resign from the rat race for good....One needs spiritual inspiration to write. I now had none and was never to find any again. I was badly hurt, bitter, cynical and disenchanted with the world." [22]

To help revive his reputation and good name, however, Belden was urged to contact Harold L. Ickes, who had served as interior secretary during the Roosevelt administration from 1933 to 1945 and was now a syndicated columnist defending liberal causes in the *New York Post*.

Smedley said that she had been in touch with Ickes on his behalf and that he had promised to see Belden and "not to bite [his] head off, as his often his custom with people...." But nothing came of the initiative in the end.

Contacting Ickes, however, did have some positive impact in Smedley's own case. She and Ickes had been exchanging correspondence about the situation in China since late 1947, and in February and March of 1949, she fed him disparaging information about Gen. Willoughby, who had been the source of the slanderous report about her to the FBI in October 1947. In two columns published in the *New York Post* in mid-March, Ickes called Willoughby a racist and near-Fascist, which put him and the China lobby on the defensive – at least temporarily. [23]

But by August 1949, Smedley's savings had run out, and the political harassment she had been subjected to since mid-July 1946, when the FBI put her on its special Security Watch List, became unbearable So she decided to leave the United States as soon as possible. In mid-November, she was seen off at a New York pier by the Snows and other friends and boarded an American liner for Le Havre, France, where she crossed the English Channel and was greeted by friends in London. [24]

Her life in London, however, would soon take a turn for the worse. She wrote to friends back in the United States, including Belden, saying that she was convinced that if and when she returned "home," she would be in a terrible fix since "the bastards have not let up on me and do not intend to....My spirit is wilted – really wilted."

Smedley also said that her health had deteriorated, and on April 28, 1950, she wrote to her friend, Margaret Watson Sloss, who was living in Oxford, England, saying that she was about to undergo an operation for a stomach ulcer. She said that she did not expect to die but that, in case she did not recover, she wanted Sloss to, among other things, send the manuscript of the book that she was working on to Belden at his mother's home in Summit, New Jersey. "Mr. Belden and Edgar Snow are to have charge of my manuscripts," she wrote.

On May 2, she wrote a letter to Ickes in New York saying that she expected to survive the operation, adding, however, "I prefer death to returning to the U.S.A." The operation was performed on the afternoon of May 5, and the next day she died from, according to her death certificate, pneumonia, acute circulatory failure and the effects of the operation. [25]

20

MCCARTHY WANTS TO KNOW

The American playwright Arthur Miller, who knew Belden and was, with him, a fellow traveler in the fight against McCarthyism, said that in the late 1940s and early 1950s expressing any opinion remotely considered to be "left or even liberal" was cause for rebuke.

Miller said that, during that period, he and Belden were among a dozen or so other "stars" who came together to discuss what they could do to help stem the tide of anti-Communist hysteria sweeping the country.

Every Tuesday evening, in the ground-floor Greenwich Village living room of Jack Goodman, a senior editor at Simon & Schuster, the group met to develop what Miller called a "counter-tide in the media to the overwhelming propaganda of the right." But the initiative, he said, came to naught.

"After many months, many proposals, many actual attempts to publish one or another reply to the prevailing paranoia," Miller recalled, "not a single line from any of us had seen print anywhere." He said that frightened editors across the country simply shut them out. "The shock, if not dramatic, was noticeable: whatever our reputations, we were little more than easily disposable hired hands." [1]

Others, however, recalled things differently, saying that the group, which also included Edgar Snow, John Hersey, William L. Shirer, Joseph

Barnes, Robert Capa, Ira Wolfert, Millard Lampell (the screenwriter, novelist and songwriter) and John G. Morris (the renowned journalist and photo editor), did in fact succeed in placing a full-page ad in *The New York Times* protesting the blacklisting of writers, entertainers and others.

It also contributed to a column in *The New Republic* and putting up money to investigate the witch-hunting newsletter *Counterattack*.

For his part, Morris said that just attending the Goodman-sponsored gatherings put their reputations at risk. "But we made no effort to hide our activity," he said. "On the contrary, the group sought, through newspaper and magazine pieces and radio broadcasts, to reestablish the American tradition of free speech and the right of dissent. Despite distinguished bylines, we got almost nothing published." [2]

Yet, what their well-meaning effort to "reestablish" the right of free speech and dissent would lead to was stepped-up targeting by the government and the FBI.

Goodman, for instance, was called before the House Un-American Activities Committee to explain why the meetings were held at all and how, as a non-Communist, he could have sponsored, as Miller recalled the situation, "such an anti-American campaign involving so many first-class authors and editors."

Miller said that "within our hard-drinking band," there obviously had been an informer because the House committee knew the names of every participant. [3]

Informers, in fact, were plentiful in those days and always eager to offer their opinions on the innermost beliefs of their long-ago friends. One of them was Freda Utley, who said in her 1951 best-seller, *The China Story*, that Belden, as a TIME-LIFE correspondent, was "instrumental" in convincing the American public that the Communists – both in Asia and Europe – were America's best allies.

"In his book *China Shakes the World*," Utley wrote, "he sings the praises of the tough, intrepid and cruel Communists, and seems almost to enjoy recalling tortures they inflicted upon their enemies, and upon the innocent or neutral victims of civil war."

Utley said, moreover, that Belden and a number of other American reporters who, like her, were posted in Hankow, China, in 1938, notably Snow and Smedley, were part of a "pro-Chinese Communist group." [4]

Years later, Belden said he indeed had known Utley in Hankow, where they were members together of the so-called Last Ditchers club, but that he was never as "anti-Communist" as she was. [5]

For its part, Belden's former employer, TIME, Inc., aggressively promoted Utley's book, calling it a "tellingly documented account of the errors and confusion which lost the U.S. its last chance to save free China." It said in an article in the May 21, 1951, issue of *Time* under the headline "The Mistake of the Century" that Utley – a "seasoned, firsthand observer of China events" – had rightly pointed to the "pro-Communist...coterie" of writers, professors and lecturers who had reviewed books in the 1940s, including Snow, Owen Lattimore and Teddy White.

By the time Utley's book appeared in print, the FBI had already been monitoring Belden's activities for several years. FBI Director J. Edgar Hoover had issued a "request for information" on Belden in October 1949. But the agency had taken note of him as early the summer of 1945, when two FBI agents had staked out a luncheon engagement that he and Smedley had had at the Mayfair Hotel in New York. A brief FBI report on the meeting said simply that it had taken place, and that Belden reportedly was a close friend of Smedley, "who has a long record of Communist activity."

In May 1950 – in a move most likely unrelated to the FBI's surveillance of his activities – Belden obtained a U.S. passport for proposed travel to France to visit his wife and child, according to his application, "and to travel." He said on the application that he planned to leave the United States by boat or plane sometime between May 15 and June 15 for an indefinite stay abroad. It is unclear, however, whether the trip actually took place. [6]

A year later, on June 12, 1951, FBI agent V.P. Keay sent a memo to A.H. Belmont, head of the bureau's domestic intelligence division, noting that a decision had recently been taken to review the FBI's files "relative to persons mentioned by Utley [in 'The China Story'] as pro-Communist," including Belden, in order to determine "necessary action."

The memo included some basic biographical information about Belden, drawn from the 1950-1951 edition of "Who's Who in America," then listed a series of "Contacts With the Bureau" that Belden had had over the years, beginning with an interview conducted by FBI agents with him in November 1943 on his arrival in the United States from North Africa.

But more significantly, the memo cited what it called Belden's "activities" in connection with the so-called Hollywood Ten, including a report in *Counterattack* on April 14, 1950, which said that Belden had been among the writers, entertainers and publishers who had signed a brief on behalf of the group filed with the U.S. Supreme Court on February 25, 1950.

The memo said, moreover, that Belden was one of a number of writers and artists who had signed a petition dated April 27, 1950, calling on the Supreme Court to hear the appeal of the group, which had been convicted of contempt of Congress for failing to appear before the House Un-American Activities Committee. Finally, it said that the *Daily Worker* – the newspaper of the Communist Party USA – reported in its May 12, 1950, edition that Belden had jointed a number of others in petitioning the Supreme Court to review the Hollywood Ten case.

It said that Belden had had some "association" with "pro-Soviet individuals," notably Smedley, citing their luncheon engagement in August 1945 and their continuing friendship, along with the fact that Smedley, in her will, had named Edgar Snow as her executor and literary trustee and directed that Snow and Belden be given the right to edit her last manuscript for publication.

Belden's name had also appeared on an invitation list for a dinner held on February 14, 1950, by the China Welfare Appeal in New York City, the memo said, adding that the FBI had obtained the list through "trash cover" – an agency euphemism for searching through garbage.

The memo said that the China Welfare Appeal – a subsidiary of the China Welfare Fund, founded in Shanghai in 1945 by Soong Ch'ing-ling, the widow of Sun Yat-sen and vice chairman of the People's Republic of China from 1959 to 1975 – had been established to raise funds and supplies for Chinese Communists. It was listed as a subversive organization by the office of the U.S. Attorney General in 1948 and classified as "Soviet communist controlled."

The memo ended with a recommendation that the FBI's Espionage Section decide on the "advisability of opening an investigation concerning Belden." And in July 1951, Hoover ordered the bureau's Newark, New Jersey, office to initiate a "security investigation" to determine if Belden's background and activities justified his inclusion in the FBI Security Index. [7]

A memo from Hoover to the Newark Special Agent in Charge dated July 2, 1951, also ordered the New York office to verify Belden's employment and to furnish the Newark office with any other "pertinent" information. [8]

Compiling the Security Index, in fact, dated back to the fall of 1939 when Hoover ordered all of the bureau's Special Agents in Charge to prepare a list of individuals "on whom there is information available to indicate that their presence at liberty in this country in the time of war or national emergency would be dangerous to the public peace and the safety of the United States government."

The initiative's initial objective, as the war in Europe was heating up, was to target persons of German and Italian "sympathies." But Hoover's directive was also concerned about those individuals – U.S. citizens or aliens – who might harbor Communist sympathies, and in October 1939 the FBI began an investigation of the Communist Party and the German American Bund, employing tactics such as hiring paid informants and attending of mass meetings and public demonstrations. [9]

By November 1939, the FBI had begun preparing a list of individuals with strong Nazi and Communist "tendencies." The citizenship status of each individual was determined, and cards were prepared summarizing the reasons for placing them on the list.

The scope of the information obtained through the initiative was reflected in an estimate put out by the FBI in 1944 saying that nearly one million people "knowingly or unknowingly had been drawn into Communist-front activity." [10] In early 1946, Hoover informed Attorney General

Tom C. Clark that the FBI had found it necessary to intensify its investigation of Communist activities even further. [11]

Concerning Belden, meanwhile, for about six months beginning in 1951, the FBI's Newark office followed through on Hoover's earlier order to conduct a formal "security investigation" of him, and on January 10, 1952, it sent the FBI director a report saying that it ascertained that he lived at 96 New England Ave. in Summit, N.J., where his mother also lived. But the report contained no new information beyond what it had not been previously reported, except that informants "with known reliability" and familiarity with Communist Party's activities in New Jersey had said that Belden was "unknown to them." [12]

A month later, the FBI's New York office said that it had spoken with an informant who knew Smedley and who said that she was "elated and proud" of her friendship with Belden and had, to a certain extent, "sponsored" him. But the informant, according to an internal FBI memo dated February 7, 1952, had never heard Smedley say that Belden was pro-Communist, although she had made it very clear that the two definitely held the same political convictions.

"It is [the informant's] belief," the memo said, "that Belden was pro-Communist because of his associations with Agnes Smedley." [13]

Later that month, the FBI's Albany, N.Y., office reported that it had been in touch with a confidential informant at the Yadoo artists' colony in Saratoga Springs, N.Y., who had known Smedley well during her time there from July 1943 until March 1948.

"[The informant] described Agnes Smedley as being an outright Communist whose Communistic convictions were firm and ever prevalent," the Albany office wrote. "She advised that Agnes Smedley exhibited no discretion in expressing her convictions and that she was straight forward and direct in delineating her Communistic philosophies." [14]

The FBI, in fact, had been monitoring Smedley's activities at Yadoo, where she had been writing and lecturing, since the fall of 1944.

Earlier that year, Rep. John S. Gibson (D-Ga.) had urged the FBI to open an investigation into Smedley's background and activities on the basis of references to her in a report by the House Un-American Activities Committee. The FBI quickly took up his suggestion, enlisting Mary Townsend, the secretary to Yadoo's director, Elizabeth Ames, to keep track of Smedley's movements and to provide it with copies of any notes or correspondence that she might have occasion to type up for her. [15]

In June 1952, the FBI's Newark office reported that it had not been able to come up with any specific information regarding Belden's possible involvement with the Communist Party. But it said that it had interviewed two respected residents of the Summit, N.J., who knew Belden personally: Sgt. John Sayer, a police officer, and Albert Bartholomew, principal of the local high school.

Sayer said that Belden maintained a permanent residence at his mother's home on New England Ave. but that he had spent little time in the Summit area since graduating from high school. While attending Colgate University, he returned home on holidays and spent his summer vacations in Summit. But since then, he had only come home periodically for short periods of time. To the best of Sayer's knowledge, the Newark office reported, "he maintains no other permanent residence but travels from city to city or from country to country in his profession as a free lance writer and usually stays in one place only as long as the opportunity to practice his profession exists in that area."

Perhaps sealing the argument against any FBI plans that may have had to put Belden's name on the Security Index, Sayer told the agents that he had known Belden well since grade school and high school, and that he had never heard any derogatory information about him or his family.

"[N]o family has a better reputation in Summit than the subject and his family," the Newark office quoted Sayer as saying. He and his family, the office said in a memo dated June 26, are well-known to everyone in the community because he is "one of the local boys" who made a reputation for himself and "attained prominence throughout the world."

Bartholomew also stood up for Belden, saying that he had known him since he had started high school and had followed his career closely since then. While in high school, he said, Belden had had an excellent reputation, and since that time, Bartholomew had heard nothing derogatory about him or his family.

"The townspeople of Summit, N.J., feel quite proud of [the] subject inasmuch as he has gained wide acceptance as a writer," the Newark office reported Bartholomew as saying. "He and his family are one of the most respected in the community." [16]

Later that day, in fact, the Newark office sent a memo to Hoover saying that the Belden case was being closed.

"[I]t is believed that [the] subject's activity does not appear to warrant a recommendation for listing as a SI [Security Index]," the memo said, "and inasmuch as the subject is a writer, it is believed it would be inadvisable to request permission to interview him." But the memo cautioned that the Newark office could not know for sure whether Belden was "actually active" or had been active in the Communist Party because "due to [his] continual travel status it is difficult to determine...." [17]

While the FBI's interest in him may have eased, his financial difficulties continued to worsen. He did not have a job, and sales of *China Shakes the World* were poor – hit by what John M. Hamilton, the former dean of the school of communication and now executive vice chancellor and provost at Louisiana State University, has called in his latest book, *Journalism's Roaming Eye*, "a political climate that froze out anything positive about Communism." [18]

One royalty check for six months of sales, in fact, came to only $28.07, which angered Belden, who refused to cash it. "I do not believe the sum is correct," he wrote Cass Canfield, the president of the book's publisher, Harper & Brothers. But even if it were correct, he said, "I find it not acceptable. I have thought of framing it as a reminder of the folly of writing books. But then I hardly need a tangible reminder."

Belden raised the issue again in another letter to Canfield, saying that he had received only $3,500 on sales of nearly 8,000 copies when, under a previous agreement, he should have received at least $6,000. But he also touched on a broader point, which went to the heart of the debate raging in the country over the McCarthy-inspired Communist witch-hunt.

Canfield had made it clear in an earlier telephone conversation, Belden said, that he was opposed to promoting *China Shakes the World* any more since "it might be unpopular." He also said, according to Belden, that Canfield did not want to publicize the book "for political reasons."

But Belden said that, in his view, recent events had made the book even more timely and pertinent than it had been when it was first published. "Is the staff of Harper's really so qualified to tell what is politically popular?" he asked. "And what is meant by unpopular? Unpopular with whom? Joe McCarthy?"

Writing another book – a war novel, as Canfield had suggested – was out of the question, Belden said. In fact, he said, he had been considering writing such a book, covering a span of 15 years or more and set in China, Europe and the United States. But in light of the publisher's "present attitude toward my present book...I am in grave doubt about the wisdom of undertaking any such project." [19]

An editor at *Harper's* at the time, Michael Bessie, said years later that Belden, in fact, had written the opening chapters of a novel set in China but that the rest of the book never came through. [20]

On June 16, 1953, meanwhile, according to an FBI review of the passport files of the U.S. State Department, Belden saw fit to renew the passport he had been issued in May 1950 – for the purpose, he said, of traveling to France to see his wife. He said he planned to New York on TWA Airlines on or about June 21 and to stay in France for two or three months. But in fact it stayed for nearly a year – until April 1954, when again, in Paris, he renewed his passport – this time to remain abroad "on personal business." He listed his permanent address as 109 Bellevue Avenue, Summit, N.J., and his current residence in France as rue Saint-Pierre in St. Tropez. [21]

But with his marriage effectively over, Belden returned to the United States in the summer of 1954 – without his wife and son – and headed to Nevada to obtain a divorce. There, he drove a taxi until his divorce came through later that year. He also gambled, and he plunged headlong into what he would later call the "madness of poetry" despite conceding in the end that he was really "no poet." [22]

His interest in China, however, remained strong – as evidenced in a letter to his friend Edgar Snow in November 1962, in which he said he was looking forward to reading Snow's new book, *The Other Side of the River: Red China Today*, drawn from material that Snow had gathered during a five-month reporting trip to China two years earlier.

It was a propitious time for the book to come out, Belden said, because people were starved for news about China.

Belden also told Snow he was concerned about his 16-year-old son David, who had not been able to come to the United States from France to visit him the previous summer. He asked Snow, who was living in neighboring Switzerland with his wife Lois and their two children, if he could give his son Snow's address "in case he's in your vicinity."

It was also clear from the letter that Belden, who had long admired Snow for his discipline as a reporter and writer, was envious, even jealous, of Snow's having been the first American reporter to return to China since the Communists assumed power in 1949.

"By the way," Belden wrote, "if you're ever down in Geneva or see some Chinese could you ask if I would be let in. If they have any doubts about me just reassure them I'm a forthright reactionary. I am a little serious."

But Snow clearly was a special case, and his visit to China would not be setting any precedent anytime soon for visits by other American reporters – a point that was made clear to Snow in long interviews he had with both Chou En-lai and Mao Tse-tung while he was in the country. [23]

Snow and his family, meanwhile, were spending much of their time in Switzerland, moving from one place to another in the early and mid-1960s, and in 1968 they finally purchased an old farm house near the village of Eysins, north of Geneva, which they restored. His wife Lois wrote after he died from pancreatic cancer there in February 1972 that, in fact, they had not moved to Switzerland specifically because of blacklisting and harassment but because her husband's earning capacity had been negatively affected by the political climate prevailing in the United States at the time.

"Actually we drifted away [from the United States]...almost by accident," she wrote, "seeking to earn a living, and the freedom to work, that had been curtailed at home during that period of political irresponsibility....Ed found it possible to publish in the European press, to earn a living again, to return to China to pick up the metier cut short by the bullying of McCarthyites and those cold warriors who specialized in screaming 'Red.'" [24]

Without the financial means to move overseas, Belden remained in the United States. He also married again, this time to a high school teacher on Long Island by the name Eleanor Stuart, who already had two small children of her own. Another child – a boy – was born to the couple a year after they were married in August 1963. [25]

But this marriage, too, would not last, and in the spring of 1966 Belden applied for and was granted a new U.S. passport, valid for five years. In his application, he said he planned to travel to France to see his son and would be leaving New York between April 15 and May 1.

Friends said, however, that Belden fled the United States not to see his son but to escape his wife. There were domestic fights and court appearances, and there was alimony to be paid. Years later, he said that a U.S. "martial court" had ordered him to forfeit a sum that it knew he could not pay on his meager taxi-driver earnings. "So I left the U.S. not wishing to submit to such judicial tyranny," he said. [26]

Now in France, he spent his days writing poetry, gambling and passing time. He saw little of his son David, who lived near Chamonix. He enjoyed the regular Saturday night poker games organized by the American writer and expatriate James Jones. But being too serious, he did not really fit in with the fun-loving bunch. One night, gambling in Montparnasse, he managed to win $20,000. Other nights, however, he lost. [27] One friend said he clearly had become more dedicated to gambling than to writing. [28]

21

WITH NIXON IN CHINA, ALONE IN PARIS

The publication, in 1970, of a new edition of *China Shakes the World* buoyed Belden's sagging spirits, giving him at least temporarily the hope of new royalties and a measure of financial security.

It was the first time the book had reappeared in print since its initial publication in 1949, and it included an introduction that heaped praise on what it called this "neglected masterpiece."

Owen Lattimore, who wrote the introduction, also said that the book's author, although largely forgotten, was one of a kind and worth reading or re-reading. "In the late 1930s and the war years," he wrote, "Jack Belden was to me, and I think to quite a number of people who had been in China longer than he had, a legendary figure....Most of the rest of us, except for Edgar Snow and Agnes Smedley, were a prosaic lot....He was one of the great war correspondents...."

Lattimore said that one of Belden's strengths was that he distrusted the intelligentsia (a claim that Belden himself later dismissed as nonsense). He also possessed a "fellow-feeling" for the disinherited and the down-and-out, Lattimore wrote, knowing what "underemployed peasants, underpaid workers and sullen soldiery did about sex and drink and drugs." [1]

The two men most likely met for the first time in the early 1930s, when Lattimore was living in Peking and editing the journal *Pacific Affairs*, published by the Institute of Pacific Relations, and Belden was teaching English at Peking University.

But Belden, while he admired Lattimore, who was 10 years older, had little use for him as a book reviewer many years later. In 1982, for instance, he called Lattimore a "nice guy" but then snottily branded him a "scholar" who looks at events after they happen. "I portrayed...emotions in the midst of events while they were happening," he said.

He also dismissed Lattimore's review of *Still Time to Die*, in which Lattimore said that during his early years in China, Belden had reacted violently against "white man" attitudes – "so violently as to make himself a kind of Kipling in reverse; a Kipling of the left" – which prompted Belden to say that this was the kind of cliche he did not normally use. "Left and right meant nothing to me in the 1930s," he said, "except [as] useless slogans and labels and [they mean] even less to me today. Today's leftist is tomorrow's rightist." [2]

The re-publication of *China Shakes the World*, meanwhile, would have little positive impact on Belden's precarious financial situation. But it probably had something to do with an invitation he received the following year to return to China that fall on an all-expense-paid trip, which, he said, he only accepted "because no media would pay my way." [3]

Earlier that year, he had renewed his passport at the U.S. Embassy in Paris "for the purpose of remaining abroad indefinitely," according to an FBI memo dated November 16, 1971. It was valid for five years and for travel to all countries except Cuba, North Korea, North Vietnam...and mainland China. But in March, the restriction on travel to China was inexplicably lifted. [4]

The invitation to return to China, in fact, was not a fluke. It had come straight from the office of Premier Chou En-lai, who had probably seen the new edition of *China Shakes the World* and wanted Belden – a friend from the 1930s and 1940s – to be among the first wave of American reporters to visit the country since the Communist takeover in 1949.

Also included in the group was Belden's old friend, F. Tillman Durdin, of *The New York Times*, along with his wife Peggy, who over the years had become ardent supporters of Chiang Kai-shek. But to Chou that did not matter. He wanted them to be there. [5]

Arriving in China in early September 1971, Belden was greeted at the airport by representatives of the Chinese People's Association for Friendship with Foreign Countries, whose aim, it had claimed since its founding in 1954, was to promote "friendship and mutual understanding between the Chinese people and other peoples throughout the world."

But friendship and understanding were not on the minds of the FBI agents who were still on his tail, despite having formally closed their investigation of him in 1952. Before he left for China, the FBI's legal attache (Legat) in Paris, in June 1971, sent a message to the Bureau's headquarters in Washington, D.C., asking for information about him. But the only information it could come up with was nearly 20 years old.

That fall, however, the FBI's office in Hong Kong noted in an urgent telex to FBI Director Hoover that the New China News Agency had reported that Belden had arrived in Peking on September 21 and was welcomed as an "American Friendly Personage."

"Belden not identifiable in files this office," the Hong Kong Legat said in the telex, dated September 23, "but State Department contact advises he is author who was very active in anti-Vietnam war movement." [6]

Hoover said in a follow-up letter to the Washington, D.C., field office that Belden was "strongly procommunist, pro-Chicom and profoundly bitter against the United States." He also said that Belden had been a "Chinese communist apologist" since the 1940s and was a long-time friend of Agnes Smedley, "a well-known communist sympathizer in the 1940s."

The letter also said, incorrectly, that Freda Utley, in her book, *The China Story*, had called Belden a Communist, although it was quick to add that the charge had never been proven. It said that, nevertheless, copies of the letter were being sent to the FBI's Newark office and to the FBI Legats in Hong Kong and Paris "since investigation on subject might be requested of those offices on a future date."

In November, the Hong Kong office reported to Hoover that it had received "nothing additional relative to [Belden] since the initial data taken from New China News Agency." But the Paris office was not about to abandon the hunt, saying in a memo to Hoover in early February 1972 that "sources" in Paris were very much aware of "our continuing interest in the activities of the subject and will furnish any additional information upon receipt."

Belden's trip to China, in the meantime, was not going well. He was not happy with the arrangements that had been made to see the country since his schedule did not allow for any real interaction with the Chinese people, which had provided the basis for his reporting and writing on China since the 1930s.

He was also ill, suffering from a respiratory infection that had brought on a heavy and nagging cough, and he was frustrated with being confined for days to his room at the Peking Hotel waiting for instructions from his Chinese handlers. On the afternoon of October 4, for instance, he and a number of other Americans who were on a visit to China were instructed to stay in their rooms because they were about to get a telephone call. "Is this house arrest?" Belden asked one of the Americans.

But in the end the wait was rewarded with a call inviting the Americans to a dinner with Chou En-lai the next evening at the Great Hall of the People.

It was a lavish affair, with Chou receiving the 60 or so American guests, including Huey P. Newton, a co-founder of the Black Panther Party, and several of his associates, as they arrived. According to an internal FBI memo, Newton's visit was part of a trip to China by members of the Revolutionary Union, which the agency identified as a "pro-Chicom, Marxist-Leninist organization."

The FBI also linked Newton's visit to Belden's arrival in the country, saying in an October 28 memo devoted specifically to the Revolutionary Union that the Washington, D.C., field office was conducting an investigation "concerning Belden who is last known to have resided in the Newark territory." [7]

By early October, when the dinner with Chou took place, Belden had already been in China for about a month. He had seen some of the country outside of Peking, including the port city of Tientsin, which he had visited in the winter of 1934-1935 to escape from his job teaching English in Peking. His return trip to China in 1946 had also included a stop in Tientsin.

Belden wrote in his diary on September 24, 1971, that returning to Tientsin yet again – this time to visit a textile factory – was depressing.

"Went off with Yang and Wang in car with driver Ho to Tientsin," he wrote. "The idea was that I was a seaman and should see the port." But the streets of the city were "very dusty and the scene drab," and he was immediately deposited in the old Astor House Hotel in the British Concession. "Empty lobby, no life. Went up in old lift given room with bath and two beds....Put in a room alone to eat, which sort of annoyed me and felt lonely and isolated."

Belden said he tried to remember what Tientsin was like when he was there years ago but could only recall that, sometime in the mid-1930s, he went to a dance hall where "she held me close and said she wanted to go to hotel with me and when I asked why she said because .... And who would say that to me now and who would speak to me so freely....And now I was going to be taken to a wool textile factory." [8]

His trip, by all accounts, would not get better. A friend recalled seeing him at the airport in Peking in February 1972 – alone and in a sorry state, without an overcoat, watching as President Nixon and his entourage, including 87 members of the White House press corps, arrived for a ground-breaking visit to the country Belden knew so well. [9]

Nevertheless, he did manage to catch up with some old friends during the visit, including Sol Adler, who had moved to China in the 1950s after resigning from the U.S. Treasury Department in the wake of accusations by Whittaker Chambers and others that was a Soviet spy.

Belden had known Adler since the early 1940s when Adler, an economist, was posted as Treasury's attache in Chungking. As early as 1939, however, Chambers, a former member of the Communist Party who had gone to work for *Time* magazine, had identified Adler to then-Assistant Secretary of State Adolf A. Berle as a member of an underground Communist cell in Washington, D.C., known as the Ware Group. [10]

Another American – Elizabeth Bentley, who spied for the Soviet Union but then turned U.S. informer – had also identified Alder as a Treasury contact in Chungking for the so-called Silvermaster spy ring in 1945. He died in China in 1994.

Disappointed with his trip, Belden spent about a month with the Durdins in Hong Kong, where Tillman was serving as bureau chief for *The New York Times*, before returning to France.

Durdin later recalled that, while in Hong Kong, Belden had rambled on at length about his troubles with his wife, life as a taxi driver in New Jersey, quarrels with his publisher, and fights with the editors at *LIFE* and with Nate Bienstock, his agent for a time.

Back in France, Belden wrote a friend saying that "from a personal standpoint, [the trip] was a disaster, partly through sickness and partly through many other things." [11] He had spent about three months in a Peking hospital, but he had still come away from the trip with notebook filled with information and anecdotes. But he wrote nothing, even after Durdin suggested that he write something about the trip and send it to *LIFE* magazine. [12]

He was also homeless, living at the Hotel Saint-Michel in Paris, unable to afford it and "not too well." He wrote to Edgar Snow's widow Lois in Switzerland saying he had been offered a house for a month in the middle of France but that it was in an isolated village on top of a hill, with no food or cafe.

"My legs particularly bother me," he wrote, "and I am scared to go there alone."

Belden said he was sorry he had missed the Snows when they were in China in the fall of 1971 to participate in ceremonies marking the 22nd anniversary of the founding of the People's Republic.

"I repeatedly asked when you were coming," he wrote, "but could get no information. I was also hustled without any necessity out of Shanghai to Hangchow [100 miles southwest of Shanghai] on the weekend that you came."

Belden said that he envied Lois for her upcoming trip to China, "especially if you are with friends [which] was one of the banes of my experience there – poor little rich boy all alone in freezing hotels in Sian, Lanchow – hotels for 3-400 people."

As for what he was doing now, "I am just trying to keep alive." He said he had applied for a fellowship from the National Council of the Arts in Washington, D.C. But he had not heard back from them. "[I] fear [the application] may have been glommed onto by Customs," he said.

The world, he wrote, was depressing – "Greece, Chile, America, Russia – and the trend is definitely governments cooperating at the top to crush their own people below....If we're not yet at 1984, we're pretty close to 1983 3/4."

He told Lois Snow that her husband had lent him $400 before he went to China and that he could repay part of it but "can't send it all just now." [13]

Meanwhile, his writing, such as it was, had dwindled to nothing more than a few dozen sonnets, which he sent to Harper & Row for possible publication. Many concerned a young girl; six were about internal struggles in China; one was about the CIA; and one was about France. But nothing came of it. He also wrote an occasional letter to Lois Snow in Switzerland. "And that's about all," he said.

Turning 65 year old, in February 1975, he applied for Social Security benefits but was turned down. The reason: he had not contributed to the system long enough. Royalties from his books came to a meager $600-$700 a year – and to his astonishment, nothing had come from the Foreign Language Institute in Peking, which had published without his approval an "abridged and simplified" English-language edition of *China Shakes the World* that omitted chapters in which Belden had expressed serious misgivings about the future of liberty under the Communists.

"It appears," Belden said, "that 'abridged and simplified' means censored. They even added things I never said." [14]

In a letter to Lois Snow in August 1976, he said he was feeling "rather desperate" – financially, emotionally and spiritually – and that he wanted to leave Paris for "almost any place just to get out of this city...." But his poor health and shaky financial situation would not allow him to do so, he said.

That November, he spent time with Snow and her children at their farmhouse in Switzerland, just north of Geneva, where he was looked after by the Snow family physician, Dr. Robert Panchaud. After arriving back in Paris, he reported to her that he had arrived at the train station "well-bundled up in Chinese coat...with foot warmer, Chinese calendar and peanut butter intact...." He said he had been ill and had stayed in bed for two days at his one-room flat at 5 rue Commines. "I miss the cold but clearer Swiss air," he wrote. "Also miss the bathtub,the books, the chocolate cakes (for years never had anything like them), the apple pie a la mode, the fish chowder and the soups, to say nothing of the reminiscences as well as breakfast and lunch and dinner in bed."

It did not appear to help much that he now was enjoying the much-needed company of a female companion, Dominique. Together, they had given up smoking, and they shared the same dry sense of humor. But his financial situation was still dire and seemed to depend entirely on whether or not Harper's would agree to publish his sonnets. "If I don't hear from Harper's," he said, "I don't know what will happen to us."

But in the end, the publisher rejected the sonnets, with no reason given. "I don't know how I'm going to stay alive much longer," he told Lois Snow in a letter dated June 29, 1978, noting that he and Dominique were no longer seeing each other, "and I am beginning not to care much one way or the other."

But again, he would take advantage of Lois' generosity and travel to Switzerland to spend time with her at her house in Eysins. It was a "nice house," he told her after the visit, "[with] a family atmosphere [and] unaccustomed baths, good food, healthy air, personal care and kindness – all of which for a long time I have missed and needed."

He said his blood pressure had shot up again. He also had to have another tooth pulled, so "I ain't got much to chew with or on except the cud of old age at the moment." But he said he still hoped to realize his latest dream of publicly reciting his poetry for pay. "As there was a student underground and a counterculture," he said, "so there is a kind of poetry underground and many go around reciting and make a good living out of it....Near bums without much talent, I know, go around giving recitals (in English) in Europe at poetry festivals and give lectures at universities....If one knows how, a living can be made." [15]

But realistically, he concluded, his fortunes – such as they were – would depend much more on his writing than on his reciting. He later told Lois Snow he had tried to recite some poetry to himself but that, with all the missing teeth, all that came through was a "nice echoing whistle." Perhaps, he said, he should become a bird imitator. [16] So he fell back on his writing and sent (in 1978) a book-length poem he had written to a long-time admirer, George Wald, the Nobel-Prize winning biologist at Harvard University, who promised to see what he could do to get it published.

The poem, which took its title, "Send Down Thy Visible Spirits," from Shakespeare's King Lear, warned of the threat to evolution from nuclear radiation. It also angrily denounced government secrecy, which, he argued, endangered political, social and artistic liberty.

But Wald, according to Belden, found it more difficult to find a publisher than he had thought it would be. He had tried Houghton Mifflin Co. in Boston. Its poetry editor called the work admirable but "archaic" and advised against publishing it, and while the publisher told Belden that, in his opinion, it was a "remarkable achievement," he would have to accept his poetry editor's advice. "I would prefer to be unremarkable and marketable," Belden quipped.

Wald then offered to solicit contributions from four leftist foundations for a "Belden fund" to help see him through his financial difficulties. A small sum was collected. But when the check arrived, he was shocked to read in an accompanying letter that one of the contributors had demanded that he stop "bad-mouthing" China.

Belden was furious, and he immediately fired off a letter to Wald, dated March 28, 1979, saying that he could not in good conscience accept the check. "I do not know who had contributed to a 'Belden fund,'" he wrote. "You say people who love me....But anybody who loves me would not make such a request of me...." [17]

Later that year, he replied to a woman who had written to him after obtaining his address from Monthly Review Press – the publisher of the 1970 edition of *China Shakes the World* – saying that "if MR informs you I am alive and well, they are only half right, as I'm only half alive and half well."

He said he had been denied Social Security benefits by the "American state" and was finding it "nigh impossible merely to keep alive." His writing, he said, had been restricted to verse, and in addition to 70 or 80 "love-hate" sonnets, he had composed a long poem on dinosaurs – "a sort of moral, pseudo-scientific ironic tale of the fall of grandeur and the rise of little mammals."

"Thank you so much for your kind words," the letter concluded. "When one is a little hungry, they at times offer sustenance." [18]

But his living arrangements in Paris were becoming increasingly untenable. The French police had refused his request for a permanent residence card, which would have enabled him to receive financial assistance from the French government specifically targeted to the aged, on the grounds that he was not able to prove that he had lived in France for at least five years.

"This, of course, makes me question the sense of staying in France," he wrote in a letter to Lois Snow.

He was also under pressure from his landlady to move out of his one-room flat at 5 rue Commines because she ostensibly needed it for her daughter. He explored the possibility of moving to the cite d'artistes, just opposite Ile St.-Louis, where foreign artists and writers could live for little rent. But he was told that the waiting list for an apartment could be one or two years.

Day-to-day support continued to come from friends like Lois Snow, who provided money, food, cigarettes, clothes and even home-made cookies. "Cookies arrived Jan. 6," he said in a letter to Snow dated "Jan. 10 some year" (actually, 1979). And they had arrived just in time "for my water and electricity went off then and stores were closed for French reasons and I fed on cookies all by myself and consumed [them] in two days.

Very nice!" But in the same letter he also said he was only looking to keep alive. "For what reason god knows."

Snow also provided him with two much-needed coats – one a short Chinese jacket he used indoors and a long Chinese overcoat that made him look like a "rice bucket," which he used as a bathrobe and a street coat. [19]

He was beginning to suspect, meanwhile, that his failure to obtain a French residence card had something to do with politics. "Every week I'm told (fourth hand) that everything is okay," he said in a letter to Lois Snow dated October 11, 1981, "but now I'm told there are political factors...probably nasty gossip passed on from the Americans to the French."

Eventually, however, he was able to secure a residence card through the good offices of a friend who was close to the wife of then-President Francois Mitterrand, which enabled him to receive a small but regular French government stipend and to move into a government-run retirement home. [20]

His mother Mabel, meanwhile, who had been a source of strength throughout his life and of some financial support for many years, was threatening to outlive her son. At 93, and almost totally blind, she was tempted by a marriage proposal from a man who suggested that they leave the old people's home and move to Florida.

"The human spirit," Belden wrote to Lois Snow on receiving the news about his mother from his niece, "is an awesome thing."

Now 76 years old, ailing and living in a retirement home, Belden made one last visit to the United States in 1986 to celebrate his mother's 100th birthday. After a short visit, he returned to France, and his health took a turn for the worse.

But his interest in China – and in crossword puzzles – did not wane. His reading material included *The New Yorker* ("I'd forgotten what good reporting *New Yorker* non-fiction articles could be."); the *International Herald Tribune*; and Nien Cheng's autobiography *Life and Death in Shanghai*, published in November 1987, which detailed her persecution, torture and six-year imprisonment during the Cultural Revolution.

"Outside of all her pain and suffering," Belden said, "her experience with socialist bureaucracy reminded me of my many years of experience with the French. Is this what 'socialism' produces?"

He said he was starved for English-language reading material. "I had to subscribe to the [*International Herald Tribune*] because I couldn't face the mornings without something to read," he wrote. "A wasted life abroad. My French is terrible but my English is going to hell too." [21]

22

"IT WASN'T A LOVE STORY"

For weeks, the doctors responsible for Belden's care at the Maison de Retrait Charcot retirement home in Paris had been evasive, despite repeated calls for answers. He had been experiencing severe pain in his back and legs for some time and wanted to know the reason. "I am in a lot of pain and just don't know what to say or do," he wrote to Lois Snow in early October 1988. [1]

Later that month, the doctors broke the news, informing him that he had metastatic lung cancer. Alone, and with few friends, he pondered the pain he would still have to endure, and he was scared.

A surprise visit in early December by Tillman Durdin, then living in California, cheered him up. He said he was touched and flattered by the gesture, which had been facilitated by Bob McCabe, an editor at the *International Herald Tribune*, who had befriended him several years earlier.

After the visit, McCabe wrote Durdin in California saying that Belden had just returned "home" from the hospital and was being taken care of by a nurse and a maid who came around for an hour or two each day. The stipend from the French government, McCabe said, was sufficient to cover his rent, utilities, food and household care. "Financially," he said, "he is not rich, but he is really in pretty fair shape." [2]

But the pain he was experiencing was constant and increasing – "pain pain pain," he wrote Lois Wheeler Snow in March 1989 – despite heavy doses of morphine that had been prescribed by a cancer specialist. [3]

"He gets around the building pretty well," McCabe wrote Durdin, "and gets out too, but only occasionally. I try to take him outside when I'm over there on the two or three days a week I can stop by. The other day, on his own, he forced himself to walk two blocks, to the grocery store. He made it all the way, leaning on parked cars along the way for support. In the doing of it, he caused himself more pain, but he will probably do it again. He is not short of courage." [4]

Another friend from his China days, Alex Buchman, who was also living in California, suggested moving Belden to a hospice or a nursing home in southern California. But after looking into it, he and Durdin concluded that, in his condition, it would be too costly and complicated, and in any event the facilities for elderly in the United States were not that nice. "I feel it would be better for Jack to stay where he is," Durdin wrote to McCabe in early February 1989. [5]

Shortly afterward, Belden wrote to McCabe thanking him for all he had done and was continuing to do for him. "Without you I would have had an insupportable existence," he said.

Echoing Belden's sentiments, Durdin wrote to McCabe in mid-March saying that he, too, appreciated what McCabe was doing for his old friend. "You are being a great guy and a great friend for him."

But Durdin also said that, as a result of some publicity he had generated through the Overseas Press Club, an offshoot of the club, The Correspondents Fund, which was created in 1943 to provide financial assistance to journalists in need, would be sending Belden a check for $3000. "I am sure he could find ways to use it that could ease his condition," Durdin said. [6]

On receiving the check, Belden sent it to Lois Wheeler Snow and asked her to open a savings account in Switzerland in his name. He also said that Beatrice Weber, his nurse at the 7th Station Hospital in Oran in

1943, had arrived from her home in Arizona and was "deluging" him with "religious sentiments." He called her "Miss Arizona."

Weber, who had married and divorced in the intervening years, spent about three weeks with Belden offering him comfort and spiritual support. One day, she read a letter to him from Durdin that had just arrived. "I was glad to get your letter with the report that you are holding your own against the cancer," the letter began. "I mentioned you the other day to Hugh Crumpler, who is in newspaper work here now but was UPI on the India-Burma front during the Japanese war. Don't know if you ever knew him. He is admirer of your book 'Retreat With Stilwell' and made the point that World War II books are now enjoying a new life in reprints. Did you ever think of having yours reissued?"

"Do keep in touch," Durdin concluded, "and let me know if there is anything I can do for you in this part of the world." [7]

But Belden's health was worsening. A few days before Weber arrived in Paris, he fell and broke his hip and was in greater pain and delirium than ever before. So their conversations – between intervals of rest that became longer and longer, as she watched him grow weaker – became ever-more serious.

Weber, who was now 68 years old, told Belden that after she graduated from the Mercy Hospital School of Nursing in Oshkosh, Wisconsin, she had dedicated her life to serving God in the only way she knew how – through nursing and caring for other people.

She later said that, despite his gruff exterior, Belden was a deeply spiritual person like her. She said she had told him on his death bed in Paris that his lifelong search for the truth was actually a search for God. You begin the search, she said, because God has already found you. [8]

Belden told Weber that he had once studied the Old Testament but that throughout his life he had found nothing more than hypocrisy in organized religion. Shortly after being diagnosed with cancer, he said, someone had visited him and left some sleeping pills and a book with directions on how to take one's own life entitled Dying With Dignity.

He asked Weber to count out 50 pills, which she did, and he put on his glasses and read the directions in the book. "First, take a shower," it said, "then get dressed in your best clothes. Groom your hair, face and nails, then lay down on your bed."

Weber told him she hated to see him do it. "Flush those damn things down the toilet!" he shouted. Closing his eyes, and holding her hand, he told her he felt weak – yet comfortable and at peace. "What I feel now is probably one of the greatest experiences of my life," he told her. "I feel weightless and free."

As he slept, heavily sedated with morphine, she left his room without saying good-bye and returned to the United States. A few days later, on June 3, after a friend had read him a farewell card she had left for him, he died.

On June 19, a small memorial service was held for him at the Père-Lachaise Cemetery (Cimetière du Père-Lachaise), where he was cremated.

"Nobody understands why I returned to see Jack in his final days," Weber said later. "It sounds like a love story. What it actually was, was a story about a lost soul searching for forgiveness from God and moving on. It certainly wasn't a love story." [9]

NOTES

CHAPTER 1

1. Letter from Belden to Lois Wheeler Snow, courtesy of Snow.
2. Ibid.
3. Note from Belden to Weber, courtesy of Weber.
4. Ibid.
5. Beatrice Weber, "Sequel to the Razz-Berry of Jack Belden, Foreign Correspondent (1910-1989)," courtesy of Weber.

CHAPTER 2

1. Note from Belden to his mother, undated, courtesy of Weber.
2. Letter from Christopher Swezey to Belden, dated August 2, 1931, courtesy of Weber.
3. Weber, "Sequel to the Razz-Berry of Jack Belden, Foreign Correspondent (1910-1989)."
4. Ibid.
5. Note from Belden to his mother, undated, courtesy of Weber.
6. Ibid.

CHAPTER 3

1. Jack Belden, *China Shakes the World* (New York: Harper and Brothers, 1949), p. 10.
2. Weber, "Sequel to the Razz-Berry of Jack Belden, Foreign Correspondent (1910-1989)."
3. Ibid.
4. Interview with author, 1979.
5. Israel Epstein, *My China Eye: Memoirs of a Jew and a Journalist* (San Francisco: Long Review Press, 2005), p. 61.
6. Barbara W. Tuchman, *Stilwell and the American Experience in China, 1911-45* (New York: Grove Press, 1970), p. 142.
7. Ibid., p. 182.
8. Jack Belden, *Still Time to Die* (Philadelphia: The Blakiston Co., 1944), p. 3.
9. Frank Dorn, *The Sino-Japanese War, 1937-1941: From Marco Polo Bridge to Pearl Harbor* (New York: MacMillan Publishing Co., 1974), p. 48.
10. Ibid., p. 50.
11. Ibid., p. 54.
12. Belden, *Still Time to Die*, p. 307.
13. "Butchery Marked Capture of Nanking," *The New York Times*, December 18, 1937.
14. Stephen R. MacKinnon and Oris Friesen, *China Reporting: An Oral History of American Journalism in the 1930s and 1940s* (Berkeley: University of California Press, 1987), p. 34.
15. Ibid., p. 32.
16. "Japanese Atrocities Marked Fall of Nanking After Chinese Command Fled," *The New York Times*, January 9, 1938.

CHAPTER 4

1. "Man & Wife of the Year," *Time*, January 3, 1938.
2. MacKinnon and Friesen, *China Reporting*, p. 38.
3. Ibid.
4. Ibid., p. 39
5. "Notes from a War Correspondent," *The Daily Standard* (Celina, Ohio), February 12, 1938.
6. "Notes from a War Correspondent," *The Middletown Press* (Middletown, Connecticut), February 5, 1938.
7. John P. Davies Jr., *Dragon by the Tail* (New York: W.W. Norton & Co. Inc., 1972), p. 195.
8. Ibid.
9. Belden, *China Shakes the World*, p. 368.
10. Freda Utley, *Odessey of a Liberal: Memoirs* (Washington, D.C.: Washington National Press Inc., 1970).
11. Letter to Stephen MacKinnon, courtesy of Charles W. Hayford.
12. Belden, *Still Time to Die*, p. 44.
13. Davies, *Dragon by the Tail*, p. 196.

CHAPTER 5

1. *Time*, November 10, 1941.
2. Robert M. Farnsworth, *From Vagabond to Journalist: Edgar Snow in Asia 1928-1941* (Columbia: University of Missouri Press, 1996), p. 344.
3. Edgar Snow, *The Battle for Asia* (New York: Random House, Inc., 1941), p. 155.
4. MacKinnon and Friesen, *China Reporting*, p. 194.
5. Ibid., p. 56ff.
6. Ibid., p. 57.

7. Theodore H. White, *In Search of History: A Personal Adventure* (New York: Harper & Row, Publishers, 1978), p. 54.

8. White and Annalee Jacoby, Thunder Out of China (New York: William Sloane Associates Inc., 1946), p. 10.

9. White, *In Search of History: A Personal Adventure*, p. 280.

10. Ibid., p. 70.

11. Ibid., p. 80.

12. Emily Hahn, *China to Me* (Philadelphia: The Blakiston Co.,1944), p. 118.

13. Ibid., p. 142.

14. Ibid., p. 113.

15. MacKinnon and Friesen, *China Reporting*, p. 105.

16. Epstein, *My China Eye: Memoirs of a Jew and a Journalist*, p. 132.

17. Martha Gellhorn, *Travels With Myself and Another: A Memoir* (New York: Penguin Putnam Inc., 2001), p. 9.

18. Janice R. MacKinnon and Stephen R. MacKinnon, *Agnes Smedley: The Life and Times of an American Radical*. (London: Virago Press Ltd., 1988), p. 229.

19. William White, ed. *By-Line: Hemingway* (New York: Charles Scribner's Sons, 1967), p. 269 ff.

CHAPTER 6

1. Cable from George Hatem, cited in *LIFE* magazine, March 12, 1951.

2. Peter Rand, *China Hands: The Adventures and Ordeals of the American Journalists Who Joined Forces With the Great Chinese Revolution* (New York: Simon & Schuster, 1995), p. 217.

CHAPTER 7

1. Tuchman, *Stilwell and the American Experience in China, 1911-45*, p. 229 ff.

2. Ibid., p. 240.

3. Ibid., p. 246.

4. Ibid., p. 267

5. Jack Belden. *Retreat With Stilwell* (New York: Alfred A. Knopf, 1943), p. 33

6. *Time*, April 20, 1942.

7. Belden, *Retreat With Stilwell*, p. 38.

8. Alan K. Lathrop, "Dateline: Burma," *Dartmouth Medicine*, http://dart-med.dartmouth.edu/spring04/html/dateline_burma.shtml.

9. Belden, *Retreat With Stilwell*, p. 42.

10. Ibid., p. 50.

11. Ibid., p. 52.

12. Frank Dorn, *Walkout With Stilwell in Burma* (New York: Thomas Y. Crowell Co., 1971), p. 56.

13. Belden, *Retreat With Stilwell*, p. 61.

14. Ibid., p. 64.

15. Ibid.

16. Ibid., p. 65.

17. Ibid., p. 88.

18. *LIFE*, June 22, 1942

19. Belden, *Retreat With Stilwell*, p. 92.

20. Ibid., p. 109.

21. Ibid., p. 152.

22. Ibid., p. 156.

23. Ibid., p. 164.

CHAPTER 8

1. Dorn, *Walkout With Stilwell in Burma*, p. 91.

2. Belden, *Retreat With Stilwell*, p. 176.

3. Ibid., p. 195.

4. Dorn, *Walkout With Stilwell in Burma*, p. 92.

5. Belden, *Retreat With Stilwell*, p. 199.

6. Ibid., p. 207.

7. Ibid., p. 209.

8. Ibid., p. 214.

9. Ibid., p. 215.

10. Ibid., p. 225.

11. Ibid., p. 228.

12. Ibid., p. 229.

13. Dorn, *Walkout With Stilwell in Burma*, p. 98.

14. Edgar Snow, *Journey to the Beginning: A Personal View of Contemporary History* (New York: Random House, 1958), p. 383.

15. *Time*, July 21, 1958.

16. Peter Arnett, *Live From the Battlefield* (New York: Simon & Schuster, 1994), p. 37.

CHAPTER 9

1. Tuchman, *Stilwell and the American Experience in China, 1911-45*, p. 292.

2. Robert Lee Scott, Jr. *Flying Tiger: Chennault of China* (New York: Doubleday, 1959), p. 205.

3. Belden, *Retreat With Stilwell*, p. 243.

4. *Time*, May 11, 1942.

5. Belden, *Retreat With Stilwell*, p. 244.

6. Ibid., p. 233.

7. Dorn, *Walkout With Stilwell in Burma*, p. 104.

8. Belden, *Retreat With Stilwell*, p 265.

9. Ibid., p. 267.

10. Ibid., p. 273.

11. Ibid., p. 277.

12. Joseph W. Stilwell (ed. Theodore H. White). *The Stilwell Papers.* (New York: Sloane Associates, 1948), p. 98.

13. Belden, *Retreat With Stilwell,* p 274.

14. Ibid., p. 289.

15. Stilwell, *The Stilwell Papers,* p. 99.

16. Belden, *Retreat With Stilwell,* p 294.

17. Ibid., p. 295; see also, Dorn, *Walkout With Stilwell in Burma,* p. 152.

18. Tuchman, *Stilwell and the American Experience in China, 1911-45,* p. 296.

19. Belden, *Retreat With Stilwell,* p. 296.

20. Tuchman, *Stilwell and the American Experience in China, 1911-45,* p. 295.

13. Belden, *Retreat With Stilwell,* p. 303.

14. Ibid., p. 301.

15. Ibid., p. 311.

16. Ibid., p. 315.

17. Stilwell, *The Stilwell Papers,* p. 100.

18. Martin Davies, Exit From Burma: A Conscientious Objector's Story, http://www.bbc.co.uk/ww2peopleswar/stories/71/a6913271.shtml (November 2005).

19. Stilwell, *The Stilwell Papers,* p. 101.

20. Belden, *Retreat With Stilwell,* p. 344.

21. Ibid., p. 345.

22. Ibid., p. 346.

23. Ibid., p. 350.

24. Ibid., p. 352.

25. Stilwell, *The Stilwell Papers,* p. 102.

26. Belden, *Retreat With Stilwell,* p. 364.

27. Ibid., p. 364.

28. Alan K. Lathrop, "Dateline: Burma," *Dartmouth Medicine,* http://dartmed.dartmouth.edu/spring04/html/dateline_burma.shtml.

29. Stilwell, *The Stilwell Papers,* p. 104.

30. Ibid., p. 105.

31. Tuchman, *Stilwell and the American Experience in China, 1911-45,* p. 300.

CHAPTER 10

1. Belden, *Retreat With Stilwell*, p. 307.
2. Donovan Webster. *The Burma Road: The Epic Story of the China-Burma-India Theater in World War II* (New York: Farrar, Straus and Giroux, 2003), p. 66 ff.
3. Duane P. Schultz, *The Maverick War: Chennault and the Flying Tigers* (New York: St. Martin's Press, 1987), p. 281.
4. *Time*, August 24, 1942.
5. Weber, "Sequel to the Razz-Berry of Jack Belden, Foreign Correspondent (1910-1989)."
6. Belden, *Still Time to Die*, p. 184.
7. Ibid., p. 198.
8. *LIFE*, December 21, 1942.
9. *Time*, December 28, 1942.

CHAPTER 11

1. Rick Atkinson, *An Army at Dawn: The War in North Africa, 1942-1943* (New York: Henry Holt and Co., 2002), p. 164.
2. *Time*, January 11, 1943.
3. Belden, *Still Time to Die*, p. 206.
4. Rick Atkinson, *An Army at Dawn: The War in North Africa, 1942-1943*, p. 398.
5. John B. Romeiser, (ed.), *Combat Reporter: Don Whitehead's World War II Diary and Memoirs* (New York: Fordham University Press, 2006) p. ix.
6. Don Whitehead, *Beachhead Don: Reporting the War from the European Theater, 1942-1945* (John B. Romeiser, ed.) (New York: Fordham University Press, 2004) p. xxvi.
7. Tennessee Newspaper Hall of Fame. "Don Whitehead, 1908-1981." http://www.cci.utk.edu/~jem/TNHF/Whitehead.html.

8. Ibid. See also, Romeiser (ed.), *Combat Reporter: Don Whitehead's World War II Diary and Memoirs*, p. 1.

9. Romeiser (ed.), *Combat Reporter: Don Whitehead's World War II Diary and Memoirs*, p. 31.

10. Ibid., p. 39.

11. Ibid., p. 108.

12. Ibid., p. 114.

13. Malcolm Moore, *Second World War 70th Anniversary: The Scoop.*,http://www.telegraph.co.uk/comment/6111610/Second-World-War-70th-anniversary-The-Scoop.html.

14. Romeiser, (ed.), *Combat Reporter: Don Whitehead's World War II Diary and Memoirs,* p. 119.

15. Belden, *Still Time to Die*, p. 208.

16. Ibid., p. 209.

17. Atkinson, *An Army at Dawn: The War in North Africa, 1942-1943*, p. 40 ff.

18. Romeiser (ed.), *Combat Reporter: Don Whitehead's World War II Diary and Memoirs,* p. 137.

19. Atkinson, *An Army at Dawn: The War in North Africa, 1942-1943*, p. 425.

20. Belden, *Still Time to Die*, p. 222.

21. Ibid., p. 232.

22. Ibid., p. 233.

23. Atkinson, *An Army at Dawn: The War in North Africa, 1942-1943*, p. 429.

24. *Time*, April 19, 1943.

25. Atkinson, *An Army at Dawn: The War in North Africa, 1942-1943*, p. 443.

26. Ibid., p. 465.

27. *Time*, April 19, 1943.

28. Atkinson, *An Army at Dawn: The War in North Africa, 1942-1943*, p. 477.

CHAPTER 12

1. Belden, *Still Time to Die*, p. 237.
2. *Time*, July 26, 1943.
3. Harry C. Butcher, *My Three Years With Eisenhower* (New York: Simon and Schuster, Inc., 1946), p. 333.
4. Dwight D. Eisenhower, *Crusade in Europe* (Doubleday & Co., 1948), p. 169.
5. Ibid., p. 170.
6. Romeiser (ed.), *Combat Reporter: Don Whitehead's World War II Diary and Memoirs,* p. 157.
7. Omar N. Bradley, *A Soldier's Story* (New York: Henry Holt and Company, Inc., 1951), p. 118.
8. *Time*, July 26, 1943.
9. Belden, *Still Time to Die*, p. 241.
10. Atkinson, *An Army at Dawn: The War in North Africa, 1942-1943,* p. 503.
11. Belden, *Still Time to Die*, p. 241.
12. Romeiser (ed.), *Combat Reporter: Don Whitehead's World War II Diary and Memoirs,* p. 160.
13. Ibid., p. 161.
14. Atkinson, *The Day of Battle: The War in Sicily and Italy, 1943-1944* (New York: Henry Holt and Co., 2007), p. 63.
15. Ibid., p. 70
16. Belden, *Still Time to Die*, p. 254.
17. *Time*, July 26, 1943.
18. Belden, *Still Time to Die*, p. 256.
19. Ibid., p. 259.
20. Romeiser (ed.), *Combat Reporter: Don Whitehead's World War II Diary and Memoirs,* p. 162.
21. Belden, *Still Time to Die*, p. 266.
22. Ibid., p. 265.

23. Romeiser (ed.), *Combat Reporter: Don Whitehead's World War II Diary and Memoirs,* p. 164.

24. Ibid., p. 168.

25. Atkinson, *The Day of Battle: The War in Sicily and Italy, 1943-1944,* p. 110.

26. *Time,* July 26, 1943.

27. Romeiser (ed.), *Combat Reporter: Don Whitehead's World War II Diary and Memoirs,* p. 169.

28. *LIFE,* August 9, 1943.

29. Romeiser (ed.), *Combat Reporter: Don Whitehead's World War II Diary and Memoirs,* p. 174.

CHAPTER 13

1. *Time,* July 26, 1943.

2. Atkinson, *The Day of Battle: The War in Sicily and Italy, 1943-1944,* p. 130.

3. Carlo D'Este, *Bitter Victory: The Battle for Sicily, 1943* (New York: E.P. Dutton, 1988), p. 413.

4. Audie Murphy, *To Hell and Back* (New York: Henry Holt and Co., 1949) p. 7.

5. Ibid., p. 8.

6. Ibid., p. 1.

7. *LIFE,* August 9, 1943.

8. Robert Capa, *Slightly Out of Focus* (New York: Henry Holt and Co., 1947), p. 71.

9. Romeiser (ed.), *Combat Reporter: Don Whitehead's World War II Diary and Memoirs,* p. 178.

10. Capa, *Slightly Out of Focus,* p. 78.

11. D'Este, *Bitter Victory: The Battle for Sicily, 1943,* p. 464.

12. Whitehead, *Beachhead Don: Reporting the War from the European Theater, 1942-1945,* p. 20.

13. *Time*, August 23, 1943.

14. Romeiser (ed.), *Combat Reporter: Don Whitehead's World War II Diary and Memoirs*, p. 188.

15. Murphy, *To Hell and Back*, p. 13.

16. Bradley, *A Soldier's Story*, p. 157.

17. Ibid., p. 158.

18. Belden, *Still Time to Die*, p. 276.

19. Ibid., p. 282.

20. Ibid., p. 283.

21. Romeiser (ed.), *Combat Reporter: Don Whitehead's World War II Diary and Memoirs*, p. 202.

22. Atkinson, *The Day of Battle: The War in Sicily and Italy, 1943-1944*, p. 164.

23. Romeiser (ed.), *Combat Reporter: Don Whitehead's World War II Diary and Memoirs*, p. 203.

24. Belden, *Still Time to Die*, p. 285.

25. Romeiser (ed.), *Combat Reporter: Don Whitehead's World War II Diary and Memoirs*, p. 203.

26. Belden, *Still Time to Die*, p. 286.

27. Atkinson, *The Day of Battle: The War in Sicily and Italy, 1943-1944*, p. 164.

28. Romeiser (ed.), *Combat Reporter: Don Whitehead's World War II Diary and Memoirs*, p. 205.

29. Lucian K. Truscott, *Command Missions: A Personal Story* (New York: E.P. Dutton and Co., 1954)

30. Romeiser (ed.), *Combat Reporter: Don Whitehead's World War II Diary and Memoirs*, p. 206.

CHAPTER 14

1. Richard Tregaskis, *Invasion Diary* (New York: Random House, 1944), p. 89.

2. George S. Patton Jr., *War as I Knew It* (Boston: Houghton Mifflin Co., 1947), p. 64

3. Martin Blumenson, *The Patton Papers, 1940-1945* (New York: De Capo, 1996), p. 333.

4. D'Este, *Bitter Victory: The Battle for Sicily, 1943*, p. 485.

5. Butcher, *My Three Years With Eisenhower*, p. 393.

6. Ibid.

7. Eisenhower, *Crusade in Europe*, p. 200.

8. Quentin Reynolds, *By Quentin Reynolds* (New York: McGraw-Hill Book Co., Inc., 1963), p. 296.

9. D'Este, *Bitter Victory: The Battle for Sicily, 1943*, p. 493.

10. Butcher, *My Three Years With Eisenhower*, p. 399.

11. Capa, *Slightly Out of Focus*, p. 85.

12. Reynolds, *By Quentin Reynolds*, p. 297.

13. Ibid., p. 299.

14. John Steinbeck, *Once There Was a War* (New York: The Viking Press, Inc.), p. 191).

15. Capa, *Slightly Out of Focus*, p. 85.

16. Richard Whelan, *Robert Capa: A Biography* (New York: Alfred A. Knopf, 1985), p. 199.

17. Capa, *Slightly Out of Focus*, p. 87.

18. Butcher, *My Three Years With Eisenhower*, p. 407; Atkinson, *The Day of Battle: The War in Sicily and Italy, 1943-1944*, p. 182.

19. Steinbeck, *Once There Was a War*, p. 151.

20. *Time*, September 27, 1943.

21. Belden, *Still Time to Die*, p. 291.

22. *Time*, September 27, 1943.

23. Barbara Brooks Tomblin, *With Utmost Spirit: Allied Naval Operations in the Mediterranean, 1942-1945* (Lexington, Kentucky: The University of Kentucky Press, 1996), p. 245.

24. *Time*, September 27, 1943.

25. Belden, *Still Time to Die*, p. 294.

26. Ibid., pl. 295.

27. Ibid.

28. Ibid., p. 298.

29. Ibid., p. 301.

30. Ibid., p. 302.

31. Whitehead, *Beachhead Don: Reporting the War from the European Theater, 1942-1945,* p. 42.

CHAPTER 15

1. Personal letter to author.

2. Barbara Brooks Tomblin, *G.I. Nightingales: The Army Nurse Corps in World War II* (Lexington, Kentucky: The University of Kentucky Press, 1996), p. 97.

3. A.J. Liebling, *The Road Back to Paris* (New York: The Modern Library, 1997), p. 341.

4. Undated personal note by Belden, obtained by author.

5. *LIFE*, March 20, 1944.

6. Belden, *Still Time to Die*, p. 319.

7. Personal letter from Belden to Edwin Hunt, undated.

8. Belden, *Still Time to Die*, p. 319.

9. Ibid., p. 320.

10. Ibid., p. 321.

11. Ibid., p. 322.

CHAPTER 16

1. Weber, "Sequel to the Razz-Berry of Jack Belden, Foreign Correspondent (1910-1989)."

2. Diary of John Shaw Billings (March 21, 1944), "The Time-Life-Fortune Papers of John Shaw Billings," University of South Carolina, Columbia, South Carolina.

3. *Time*, May 8, 1944.

4. Belden, *Still Time to Die*, p. 307.

5. Letter from Belden to his mother from Belgium, dated September 18, 1944.

6. Letter quoted in Peter Rand, *China Hands: The Adventures and Ordeals of the American Journalists Who Joined Forces with the Great Chinese Revolution* (New York: Simon & Schuster, 1995), p. 199.

7. Eisenhower, *Crusade in Europe*, p. 270.

8. Whitehead, *Beachhead Don: Reporting the War from the European Theater, 1942-1945*, p. 183.

9. Ibid., p. 187.

10. Liebling, *Mollie & Other War Pieces* (New York: Schocken Books Inc., 1964), p. 161.

11. Belden, *Still Time to Die*, p. 241.

12. Liebling, *Mollie & Other War Pieces*, p. 160.

13. Eisenhower, *Crusade in Europe*, p. 272.

14. Carlos Baker (ed.), *Ernest Hemingway: Selected Letters* (New York: Charles Scribner's Sons, 1981), p. 558 ff.

15. Michael Reynolds, *Hemingway: The Final Years* (New York: W. W. Norton & Co., 1999), p. 98.

16. Carlos Baker, *Ernest Hemingway: A Life Story* (New York: Charles Scribner's Sons, 1969), p. 400.

17. Eisenhower, *Crusade in Europe*, p. 275.

18. Ibid., p. 279.

19. Antony Beevor, *D-Day: The Battle for Normandy* (New York: Viking Penguin, 2009), p. 455.

20. Whitehead, *Beachhead Don: Reporting the War from the European Theater, 1942-1945*, p. 203.

CHAPTER 17

1. Liebling, *Mollie & Other War Pieces*, p. 171.

2. Whitehead, *Beachhead Don: Reporting the War from the European Theater, 1942-1945*, p. 209.

3. Ernie Pyle, *Brave Men* (New York: Henry Holt and Company LLC, 1944), p. 458.

4. Beevor, *D-Day: The Battle for Normandy*, p. 513.

5. Forrest C. Pogue, *Pogue's War: Diaries of a WWII Historian* (Lexington, Kentucky: The University of Kentucky Press, 2001), p. 229.

6. Simone de Beauvoir, *Force of Circumstance* (New York: G.P. Putnam's Sons, 1964), p. 19.

7. Whelan, *Robert Capa: A Biography*, p. 225.

8. Pyle, *Brave Men*, p. 461.

9. Whelan, *Robert Capa: A Biography*, p. 225.

10. Pogue, *Pogue's War: Diaries of a WWII Historian*, p. 201.

11. Capa, *Slightly Out of Focus*, p. 189.

12. Belden, *Still Time to Die*, p. 3.

13. Pyle, *Brave Men*, p. 463.

14. Eisenhower, *Crusade in Europe*, p. 294.

15. See Report on the Communist 'Peace' Offensive - A Campaign to Disarm and Defeat the United States, Committee on Un-American Activities, U.S. House of Representatives, 82nd Congress, House report No. 378, April 1, 1951; Review of the Scientific and Cultural Conference for World Peace, arranged by the National Council of the Arts, Sciences, and Professions, and held in New York City, March 25, 26, and 27, 1949 (Washington, D.C.: Committee on Un-American Activities, U.S. House of Representatives, 1950 (originally released, April 19, 1949).

16. *LIFE*, October 2, 1944.

17. Stephen E. Ambrose, *Citizen Soldiers: The U.S. Army From the Normany Beaches to the Bulge to the Surrender of Germany* (New York: Simon & Schuster, 1997), p. 153.

18. Pyle's last column from Europe, dated September 5, 1944, as quoted in *LIFE*, October 2, 1944.

19. Whitehead, *Beachhead Don: Reporting the War from the European Theater, 1942-1945*, p 271.

20. Ibid., p. 277.

21. Ibid., p. 279.
22. Ibid., p. 282.
23. Ibid., p. 283.

CHAPTER 18

1. Diary of John Shaw Billings (December 29, 1944; January 5, 1945), "The Time-Life-Fortune Papers of John Shaw Billings," University of South Carolina, Columbia, South Carolina.
2. Belden, *Still Time to Die*, p. 321.
3. Letter from Belden to his mother, courtesy of Weber.
4. Kenneth R. Timmerman, "At Least a Fool," *Paris Voices*, 1979.
5. Eisenhower, *Crusade in Europe*, p. 391.
6. Eric Sevareid, *Not So Wild a Dream* (New York: Atheneum, 1976), p. 502.
7. Eisenhower, *Crusade in Europe*, p. 389.
8. Sevareid, *Not So Wild a Dream*, p. 503.
9. Eisenhower, *Crusade in Europe*, p. 391.
10. Ibid., p. 390.
11. Snow, *Journey to the Beginning: A Personal View of Contemporary History*, p. 356.
12. MacKinnon and MacKinnon, *Agnes Smedley: The Life and Times of an American Radical*, p. 294.
13. Epstein, *My China Eye: Memoirs of a Jew and a Journalist*, p. 228.
14. MacKinnon and MacKinnon, *Agnes Smedley: The Life and Times of an American Radical*, p. 262.
15. Ibid., p. 315.
16. Belden, *China Shakes the World*, p. 6.
17. Ibid., p. 9.
18. Ibid., p. 10.

CHAPTER 19

1. MacKinnon and MacKinnon, *Agnes Smedley: The Life and Times of an American Radical*, p. 316.
2. Ibid.
3. Belden, *China Shakes the World*, p. 11.
4. Ibid., p. 13.
5. Ibid., p. 23.
6. MacKinnon and Friesen, *China Reporting*, p. 102.
7. Rand, *China Hands: The Adventures and Ordeals of the American Journalists Who Joined Forces with the Great Chinese Revolution*, p. 291.
8. John F. Melby, *The Mandate of Heaven: Record of a Civil War, China, 1945-49* (Toronto: University of Toronto Press, 1968), p. 242 ff.
9. Belden, *China Shakes the World*, p. 365.
10. *LIFE*, October 13, 1947.
11. Belden, *China Shakes the World*, p. 373.
12. Ibid., p. 371.
13. Ibid., p. 320.
14. Snow, *Journey to the Beginning: A Personal View of Contemporary History*, p. 258.
15. John T. Flynn, *While You Slept: Our Tragedy in Asia and Who Made It* (New York: The Devin-Adair Co., 1951), p. 66.
16. MacKinnon and MacKinnon, *Agnes Smedley: The Life and Times of an American Radical*, p. 317.
17. Belden, *China Shakes the World*, p. 368.
18. Lois Wheeler Snow, *A Death With Dignity: When the Chinese Came* (New York: Random House, 1975), p. 21.
19. Ibid.
20. Ibid., p. 109.
21. Personal letter from Lois Wheeler Snow to author.
22. Weber, "Sequel to the Razz-Berry of Jack Belden, Foreign Correspondent (1910-1989)."

23. New York Post, March 16 and 19, 1949; MacKinnon and MacKinnon, *Agnes Smedley: The Life and Times of an American Radical*, p. 334.

24. Ibid., pp. 301, 338, 340.

25. Ibid., p. 345.

CHAPTER 20

1. Arthur Miller, *Timebends: A Life* (London: Methuen London Ltd.), p. 310.

2. John G. Morris, *Get the Picture: A Personal History of Photojournalism* (New York: Random House Inc., 1998), p. 131.

3. Miller, *Timebends: A Life*, p. 311.

4. Freda Utley, *The China Story* (Chicago: H. Regnery Co., 1951), p. 142.

5. Letter from Belden to Stephen MacKinnon, November 1982, courtesy of Charles W. Hayford.

6. Internal FBI memo dated November 16, 1971, obtained from the U.S. Department of Justice under the Freedom of Information Act.

7. Ibid., memo dated June 12, 1951.

8. Ibid., memo dated July 2, 1951,

9. *CI Reader: An American Revolution Into the New Millenium, Volume One* (Office of National Counterintelligence), p. 178.

10. Ibid., p. 181.

11. Ibid., *Volume Two*, p. 77.

12. Internal FBI memo dated January 10, 1952, obtained from the Department of Justice under the Freedom of Information Act.

13. Ibid., February 7, 1952.

14. Ibid., February 29, 1952.

15. MacKinnon and MacKinnon, *Agnes Smedley: The Life and Times of an American Radical*, p. 274 ff.

16. Internal FBI memo dated June 26, 1952, obtained from the Department of Justice under the Freedom of Information Act.

17. Ibid.
18. John M. Hamilton, *Journalism's Roving Eye: A History of American Foreign Reporting* (Baton Rouge: Louisiana State University Press, 2009), p. 328.
19. Belden letter to Canfield dated July 23, 1950.
20. Hamilton, *Journalism's Roving Eye: A History of American Foreign Reporting*, p. 328.
21. Internal FBI memo dated November 16, 1971, obtained from the Department of Justice under the Freedom of Information Act.
22. Weber, "Sequel to the Razz-Berry of Jack Belden, Foreign Correspondent (1910-1989)."
23. John M. Hamilton, *Edgar Snow: A Biography* (Bloomington and Indianapolis: Indiana University Press), p. 226.
24. Snow, *A Death With Dignity: When the Chinese Came*, p. 25.
25. Letter from David Belden to author and FBI files obtained under the Freedom of Information Act.
26. Timmerman, "At Least a Fool," *Paris Voices*, 1979.
27. Hamilton, *Journalism's Roving Eye: A History of American Foreign Reporting*, p. 329.
28. Rand, *China Hands: The Adventures and Ordeals of the American Journalists Who Joined Forces with the Great Chinese Revolution*, p. 314.

CHAPTER 21

1. Belden, *China Shakes the World* (1970 edition, published by Monthly Review Press), p. ix.
2. Letter from Belden to Stephen MacKinnon, November 1982, courtesy of Charles W. Hayford.
3. Weber, "Sequel to the Razz-Berry of Jack Belden, Foreign Correspondent (1910-1989)."

4. Internal FBI memo dated November 16, 1971, obtained from the Department of Justice under the Freedom of Information Act.

5. Harrison E. Salisbury, *A Time of Change: A Reporter's Tale of Our Time* (New York: Harper & Row, Publishers, 1988), p. 240.

6. FBI telex dated September 23, 1971, obtained from the Department of Justice under the Freedom of Information Act.

7. Internal FBI memo dated October 28, 1971, obtained from the Department of Justice under the Freedom of Information Act.

8. Unpublished note by Belden, dated September 23, 1971.

9. Rand, *China Hands: The Adventures and Ordeals of the American Journalists Who Joined Forces with the Great Chinese Revolution*, p. 314.

10. Sam Tanenhaus, *Whittaker Chambers* (New York: Random House , Inc., 1997), p. 466.

11. Letter from Belden to Lois Wheeler Snow, dated only 1972, courtesy of Snow.

12. Hamilton, *Journalism's Roving Eye: A History of American Foreign Reporting*, p. 329.

13. Letter from Belden to Lois Wheeler Snow, dated only 1972, courtesy of Snow.

14. Interview with author.

15. Letter from Belden to Lois Wheeler Snow, dated October 8, 1978, courtesy of Snow.

16. Letter from Belden to Lois Wheeler Snow, dated January 10, 1979, courtesy of Snow.

17. Kenneth R. Timmerman, "At Least a Fool," *Paris Voices*, 1979.

18. Letter from Belden to "Mrs. Armbuster" dated May 7, 1979.

19. Letter from Belden to Lois Wheeler Snow dated December 5, 1976, courtesy of Snow.

20. Hamilton, *Journalism's Roving Eye: A History of American Foreign Reporting*, p. 329.

21. Letter from Belden to Lois Wheeler Snow dated July 19-20, 1978, courtesy of Snow.

CHAPTER 22

1. Letter from Belden to Lois Wheeler Snow dated October 8, 1988, courtesy of Snow.
2. Letter from Robert McCabe to Durbin.
3. Letter from Belden to Lois Wheeler Snow, courtesy of Snow.
4. Letter from McCabe to Durbin.
5. Durdin letter to McCabe dated February 3, 1989.
6. Durdin letter to McCabe dated March 16, 1989.
7. Durdin letter to Belden dated April 24, 1989, courtesy of Weber.
8. Personal letter from Weber to author.
9. Ibid.

BIBLIOGRAPHY

Ambrose, Stephen E. *Citizen Soldiers: The U.S. Army From the Normandy Beaches to the Bulge to the Surrender of Germany.* New York: Simon & Schuster, 1997.

Arnett, Peter. *Live From the Battlefield.* New York: Simon & Schuster, 1994.

Atkinson, Rick. *An Army at Dawn: The War in North Africa, 1942-1943.* New York: Henry Holt and Co.,2002.

– *The Day of Battle: The War in Sicily and Italy, 1943-1944.* New York: Henry Holt and Co., 2007

Baker, Carlos. *Ernest Hemingway: A Life Story.* New York: Charles Scribner's Sons, 1969.

Baker, Carlos (Ed). *Ernest Hemingway: Selected Letters.* New York: Charles Scribner's Sons, 1981.

Beevor, Antony. *D-Day: The Battle for Normandy.* New York: Viking Penguin, 2009.

Belden, Jack. *Retreat With Stilwell.* New York: Alfred A. Knopf, 1943.

– *Still Time to Die.* Philadelphia: The Blakiston Co., 1944.

– *China Shakes the World.* New York: Harper and Brothers, 1949.

Blumenson, Martin. *The Patton Papers, 1940-1945.* New York: Da Capo, 1996.

Bradley, Omar N. *A Soldier's Story.* New York: Henry Holt and Company, Inc., 1951.

Brinkley, Alan. *The Publisher: Henry Luce and His American Century.* New York: Alfred A. Knopf, 2010.

Burchett, Wilfred. *At the Barricades: Forty Years on the Cutting Edge of History.* New York: Times Books, 1981.

Butcher, Harry C. *My Three Years With Eisenhower.* New York: Simon and Schuster, Inc., 1946.

Capa, Robert. *Slightly Out of Focus.* New York: Henry Holt and Co., 1947.

Chang, Jung, and Halliday, Jon. *Mao: The Unknown Story.* New York: Alfred A. Knopf, 2005.

Collier, Richard. *Fighting Words: The Correspondents of World War II.* New York: St. Martin's Press, 1989.

Cuthbertson, Ken. *Nobody Said Not to Go: The Life, Loves, and Adventures of Emily Hahn.* New York: Faber and Faber Inc., 1998.

Davies, John Patton Jr. *Dragon by the Tail.* New York: W.W. Norton & Co. Inc., 1972.

De Beauvoir, Simone. *Force of Circumstance.* New York: G.P. Putnam's Sons, 1964.

D'Este, Carlo. *Bitter Victory: The Battle for Sicily, 1943.* New York: E.P. Dutton, 1988.

Dorn, Frank. *The Sino-Japanese War, 1937-1941: From Marco Polo Bridge to Pearl Harbor.* New York: MacMillan Publishing Co., 1974.

– *Walkout: With Stilwell in Burma.* New York: Crowell Publishing Co., 1971.

Eisenhower, Dwight D. *Crusade in Europe.* Doubleday & Co., Inc., 1948.

Epstein, Israel. *My China Eye: Memoirs of a Jew and a Journalist.* San Francisco: Long River Press, 2005.

Esherick, Joseph W. (Ed.). *Lost Chance in China: The World War II Dispatches of John S. Service.* New York: Random House, 1974.

Farnsworth, Robert M. *From Vagabond to Journalist: Edgar Snow in Asia 1928-1941.* Columbia: University of Missouri Press, 1996.

Flynn, John T. *While You Slept: Our Tragedy in Asia and Who Made It.* New York: The Devin-Adair Co., 1951.

Gellhorn, Martha. *Travels With Myself and Another: A Memoir.* New York: Penguin Putnam Inc., 2001.

Hahn, Emily. *China to Me.* Philadelphia: The Blakiston Co., 1944.

Hamilton, John Maxwell. *Journalism's Roving Eye: A History of American Foreign Reporting.* Baton Rouge: Louisiana State University Press, 2009.

– *Edgar Snow: A Biography.* Bloomington and Indianapolis: Indiana University Press, 1988.

Hemingway, Mary. *How It Was.* New York: Alfred A. Knopf, Inc., 1976.

Herzstein, Robert E. *Henry R. Luce: A Political Portrait of the Man Who Created the American Century.* New York: Charles Scribner's Sons, 1994.

Hickey, Des, and Smith, Gus. *Operation Avalanche: The Salerno Landings, 1943.* New York: McGraw-Hill Book Co., 1984.

Hotz, Robert B. *With General Chennault: The Story of the Flying Tigers.* New York: Coward-McCann, Inc., 1943.

Larrabee, Eric. *Commander in Chief: Franklin Delano Roosevelt, His Lieutenants, and Their War.* New York: Harper & Row, Publishers, 1987.

Liebling, A.J. *The Road Back to Paris.* New York: The Modern Library, 1997.

– *Mollie & Other War Pieces.* New York: Schocken Books Inc., 1964.

MacKinnon, Janice R., and MacKinnon, Stephen R. *Agnes Smedley: The Life and Times of an American Radical.* London: Virago Press Ltd., 1988.

Mansoor, Peter R. *The GI Offensive in Europe: The Triumph of American Infantry Divisions, 1941-1945.* Lawrence, Kansas: University Press of Kansas, 1999.

Melby, John F. *The Mandate of Heaven: Record of a Civil War; China 1945-49.* Toronto: University of Toronto Press, 1968.

Mellow, James R. *Hemingway: A Life Without Consequences.* Boston: Houghton Mifflin Co., 1992.

Miller, Arthur. *Timebends: A Life*. London: Methuen London Ltd., 1988, p. 310.

Monahan, Evelyn M., and Neidel-Greenlee, Rosemary. *And If I Perish: Frontline U.S. Army Nurses in World War II*. New York: Alfred A. Knopf, 2003.

Morison, Samuel Eliot. *History of United States Naval Operations in World War II. Vol 9, Sicily-Salerno-Anzio, January 1943-June 1944*. Boston: Little, Brown and Company, Inc., 1954.

Morris, John G. *Get the Picture: A Personal History of Photojournalism*. New York: Random House Inc., 1998.

Murphy, Audie. *To Hell and Back*. New York: Henry Holt and Company LLC, 1949.

Patton, George S., Jr. *War as I Knew It*. Boston: Houghton Mifflin Co., 1947.

Peck, Graham. *Two Kinds of Time*. Second Edition, Revised and Abridged. Boston: Houghton Mifflin Co., 1967.

Pogue, Forrest C. *Pogue's War: Diaries of a WWII Historian*. Lexington, Kentucky: The University of Kentucky Press, 2001.

Price, Ruth. *The Lives of Agnes Smedley*. New York: Oxford University Press, 2005.

Pyle, Ernie. *Brave Men*. New York: Henry Holt and Company LLC, 1944.

Rand, Peter. *China Hands: The Adventures and Ordeals of the American Journalists Who Joined Forces With the Great Chinese Revolution*. New York: Simon & Schuster, 1995.

Reynolds, Michael. *Hemingway: The Final Years*. New York: W.W. Norton & Co., 1999.

Reynolds, Quentin. *By Quentin Reynolds*. New York: McGraw-Hill Book Co., Inc., 1963.

Romeiser, John B. (ed.). *Combat Reporter: Don Whitehead's World War II Diary and Memoirs*. New York: Fordham University Press, 2006.

Salisbury, Harrison E. *A Time of Change: A Reporter's Tale of Our Time*. New York: Harper & Row, Publishers, 1988.

– *A Journey For Our Times: A Memoir.* New York: Harper & Row, Publishers, 1983.

Schultz, Duane P. *The Maverick War: Chennault and the Flying Tigers.* New York: St. Martin's Press, 1987.

Scott, Robert Lee, Jr. *Flying Tiger: Chennault of China.* New York: Doubleday, 1959.

Sevareid, Eric. *Not So Wild a Dream.* New York: Atheneum, 1976.

Sheean, Vincent. *Between the Thunder and the Sun.* New York: Random House, 1943.

Snow, Edgar. *Red Star Over China.* New York: Random House, Inc., 1938.

– *The Battle for Asia.* New York: Random House, Inc., 1941.

– *Journey to the Beginning: A Personal View of Contemporary History.* New York: Random House, 1958.

Snow, Helen Foster. *My China Years: A Memoir By Helen Foster Snow.* New York: William Morrow and Company, Inc. 1984.

Snow, Lois Wheeler. *Edgar Snow's China: A Personal Account of the Chinese Revolution Compiled from the Writings of Edgar Snow.* New York: Random House, 1981.

– *A Death With Dignity: When the Chinese Came.* New York: Random House, 1975.

Sorel, Nancy Caldwell. *The Women Who Wrote the War.* New York: Arcade Publishing, Inc., 1999.

Steinbeck, John. *Once There Was a War.* New York: The Viking Press, Inc., 1958.

Stilwell, Joseph W. (ed. Theodore H. White). *The Stilwell Papers.* New York: Sloane Associates, 1948.

Tanenhaus, Sam. *Whittaker Chambers.* New York: Random House, Inc., 1997.

Tomblin, Barbara Brooks. *G.I. Nightingales: The Army Nurse Corps in World War II.* Lexington, Kentucky: The University of Kentucky Press, 1996.

– *With Utmost Spirit: Allied Naval Operations in the Mediterranean, 1942-1945.* Lexington, Kentucky: The University of Kentucky Press, 2004.

Treanor, Tom. *One Damn Thing After Another: The Adventures of an Innocent Man Trapped Between Public Relations and the Axis.* Garden City, New York: Doubleday, Doran & Co., Inc., 1944.

Truscott, Lucian K. *Command Missions: A Personal Story.* New York: E.P. Dutton and Co., 1954.

Tregaskis, Richard. *Invasion Diary.* New York: Random House, 1944.

Tuchman, Barbara W. *Stilwell and the American Experience in China, 1911-45.* New York: Grove Press, 1970.

Utley, Freda. *Odyssey of a Liberal: Memoirs.* Washington, D.C.: Washington National Press Inc., 1970

– The China Story. Chicago, Illinois: H. Regnery Co., 1951.

Webster, Donovan. *The Burma Road: The Epic Story of the China-Burma-India Theater in World War II.* New York: Farrar, Straus and Giroux, 2003.

Weintraub, Sidney. *11 Days in December: Christmas at the Bulge, 1944.* New York: Free Press, 2006.

Whelan, Richard. *Robert Capa: A Biography.* New York: Alfred A. Knopf, 1985.

White, William. *By-Line: Hemingway.* New York: Charles Scribner's Sons, 1967.

White, Theodore H. *In Search of History: A Personal Adventure.* New York: Harper & Row, Publishers, 1978.

White, Theodore H., and Annalee Jacoby. *Thunder Out of China.* New York: William Sloane Associates Inc., 1946.

Whitehead, Don. *Beachhead Don: Reporting the War from the European Theater, 1942-1945* (John B. Romeiser, ed.). New York: Fordham University Press, 2004.

ACKNOWLEDGEMENTS

This book could never have been written without the encouragement and support of many, many good people who saw a need for it and offered to help.

Often throughout the process I was asked why I would want to write a book about someone who was not well-known and that promised little hope of fame or fortune for me or anyone else. I was never able to come up with a satisfactory answer to that question (even to my myself) – other than that I felt that somebody had to do it. Yet many of those who asked the question and others who did not pitched in eagerly and graciously to help when asked. I hope that I have already thanked adequately but would like to offer a special word of thanks to a few of them now.

It was former fellow foreign correspondent, John M. Hamilton, for instance, who early on generously shared what he knew about Belden from his own research on foreign war reporting, which became part of his award-winning book, *Journalism's Roving Eye: A History of American Foreign Reporting,* published in 2009.

Over the years, Hamilton continued to provide much-needed encouragement to me as I worked on the "Belden project" even as his responsibilities at Louisiana State University, where he is currently executive vice chancellor and provost, widened, taking more and more of his free time, and I want to thank him for it.

It was Hamilton, in fact, who first pointed me to Beatrice Weber, the nurse who cared for Belden at an American hospital in North Africa during World War II. It didn't take long, of course, before I jumped on his tip and traveled to Wisconsin to meet an initially and understandably suspicious Weber on "neutral ground" at Ripon College, near her home, and we subsequently became friends. She soon shared generously with me her memories of Belden from North Africa and the weeks she spent with him in Paris as he was battled cancer, as well as the years in between – although she obviously had nothing to gain from doing so. She once told me that their relationship was not one of love between a man and a woman but only one based on compassion and mutual respect, and I believed her. This book – and my life – would not have been as rich had it not been for her.

Hamilton, meanwhile, had also written a book about Belden's friend and fellow journalist Edgar Snow (*Edgar Snow: A Biography*), and Snow's widow Lois Wheeler Snow, who knew Belden well and provided moral and other support to him later in life, was enormously helpful to me as I sought to understand what Belden was like beyond what could be gleaned from his own writing.

Providing extensive support and guidance as well over the years has been Charles W. Hayford, of Northwestern University, whose unshaken affection for Belden and his work led him to call him "hands down the grittiest of the classic wartime China journalists."

Hayford is the editor of the *Journal of American-East Asian Relations*, and he and I met on a cold morning in Chicago seven or eight years ago when I was first thinking of pursuing the project. Then, and ever since, he told me to just get on with it, which was good advice, and I thank him for his unwavering support over the years.

From France, where he lives, Belden's son David also helped, particularly as I sought to sort out his father's early years in the United States before he set out to cover the world's wars in his early 20s. I thank him for helping make that task much easier than it could have been.

Also residing in France, Robert K. McCabe, who retired there after working for the *International Herald Tribune* in Paris from 1977 to 1996 in various editorial capacities, including deputy editor and managing editor, was perhaps Belden's most cherished friend and comforter in Paris as he struggled with the indignities of disease and old age.

"Without you," Belden wrote to McCabe several months before he died in Paris in June 1989, "I would have had an insupportable existence."

I can also report that, without McCabe's assistance, this book would also suffered an insupportable existence. He was always available and willing to answer even the most trivial of questions e-mailed across the Atlantic in the middle of the night, and I am indebted to him for it.

Also extremely helpful were Richard Sousa, director of Stanford University's Hoover Institution Library and Archives, which houses Belden's papers, and his staff, notably Carol Leadenham, as well as Henry G. Fulmer, curator of manuscripts, and his staff at the South Caroliniana Library at the University of South Carolina.

Many others, of course, have also provided assistance and support as I have worked on the book over the past few years, and although unnamed here, I offer them my heartfelt thanks.

INDEX

Made in the USA
Charleston, SC
29 September 2011